Aspects of genre in late Medieval French drama

Aspects of genre
in late
Medieval French drama

ALAN E. KNIGHT

MANCHESTER
UNIVERSITY PRESS

Published by
Manchester University Press
Oxford Road, Manchester M13 9PL, UK
and
51 Washington Street, Dover, N.H. 03820, USA

British Library cataloguing in publication data

Knight, Alan E.
   Aspects of genre in late medieval French drama.
   1. French drama – to 1500 – History and criticism
   2. French drama – 16th century – History and
   criticism
   I. Title
   842'.2   PQ501

   ISBN 0-7190-0862-X

Library of Congress cataloguing in publication data
applied for

Library of Congress catalog card number
82-62255

Photoset in Plantin by
Northern Phototypesetting Co., Bolton
Printed in Great Britain by
Butler & Tanner Ltd, Frome and London

Contents

Introduction

The question of genres is of fundamental importance for understanding all forms of literary and dramatic expression, because the concept of genre connotes, among other things, the set of expectations with which we approach a given work and through which we interpret the work. If, for example, one should read *Aucassin et Nicolette* expecting a typical medieval romance, one would be disconcerted by the upside-down world of the *chantefable* and would, as a consequence, miss the delightful parody of contemporary medieval genres. Or if some personal circumstance or social trend were to cause one to interpret *George Dandin* as a dark comedy of human depravity, then one would hardly suspect that Molière took the light-hearted conjugal farce as his model for that play. But the question of genres is especially important for understanding the late medieval French drama, because the set of critical expectations – elaborated since the romantic rediscovery of the Middle Ages – with which we traditionally approach medieval plays may now be seen as alien to the culture in which the plays were written.

In the present study I have tried to address myself to a few of the problems articulated by Hans Robert Jauss in his richly suggestive essay, 'Littérature médiévale et théorie des genres',[1] particularly the problem of imposing classical concepts of genre on medieval works. This practice has given rise to numerous misinterpretations of medieval plays, especially morality plays, and it may also be responsible for the low esteem in which this genre is universally held. Indeed, the morality play, precisely because it does not fit the classical concept of pure genres, has been the stumbling block of all previous attempts to establish a generic classification of late medieval French drama. In order to avoid the error of seeing medieval plays through classical lenses, I have tried to understand the late medieval drama in terms that were meaningful to the society that gave it birth. As a result, I propose here a basic generic distinction between the plays that represent the world as it was perceived historically and the plays that represent an imagined or fictional universe. Among the latter plays I propose a further generic distinction between the fictive world of the morality play and that of the farce. The former is an ordered world ruled by reason, while the latter is a chaotic world ruled by folly.

Genres, however, are never stable. Their history may be seen as a 'processus temporel de l'établissement et de la modification continus d'un horizon d'attente'.[2] The paradigm of late medieval dramatic genres that I propose here represents a synchronic segment of roughly 85 years (1475–1560). Yet even within this period hybrids appear and must be accounted for historically and culturally. I see the hybrid plays as resulting from certain influences on dramatic expression, one of the most pervasive of which was the procession. Because so much that was theatrical in the late Middle Ages was performed in a processional context, it is often difficult to draw a clear line of demarcation between literal act and dramatic representation.

The final chapter narrows somewhat in focus to deal with the question of how one of the dramatic genres functioned in late medieval society. Specifically, the conjugal farce is examined from the point of view of each of the three principal characters – wife, husband, and lover – and a parallel is drawn with medieval social myths relating to them. This corroborates from a different perspective the characteristics of the farce world that were previously used to distinguish between the farce and morality genres.

I undertook this study fully aware of the great number and complexity of the problems involved. Halina Lewicka has detailed many of these problems as they pertain to the farce in her penetrating essay, 'La Farce et les genres dramatiques du Moyen Age'.[3] Though the present study was begun before that essay appeared, it has turned out to be a response to some of the more difficult problems articulated there. But since no response in scholarly matters is final, I do not claim to have provided the final answer to the question of genres in late medieval French drama. Instead, I offer the following pages as a contribution to the continuing dialogue of medieval scholarship, with the hope that in some small way they will help us better to understand the late medieval manifestations of the eternal theatrical impulse.

Quotations from dramatic texts were taken from original

manuscripts or printed editions in all cases in which they were accessible. References, however, are to modern editions where these exist. A list of the plays quoted, together with indications of both original and modern editions, will be found in the bibliography. In all quotations I have modernized both the punctuation and the capitalization. I have also distinguished between *i* and *j, u* and *v.* Otherwise I have tried scrupulously to reproduce the text in each case exactly as it is found in the original.

I wish to acknowledge my indebtedness to the American Philosophical Society for a research grant in the summer of 1971, which enabled me to gather from the Bibliothèque Nationale and the British Museum much of the material needed for this study. I am also indebted to the Institute for the Arts and Humanistic Studies of the Pennsylvania State University for research fellowships in 1973 and 1977, which enabled me to complete the collection of original sources. I wish to thank Norris J. Lacy, editor of *A Medieval French Miscellany*, for permission to reprint 'The farce wife: myth, parody, and caricature', which appeared in that collection.[4] The article, which forms Part 1 of Chapter VII, has been altered somewhat to achieve a consistency of terminology. I am likewise grateful to John D. Erickson, editor of *L'Esprit Créateur*, for permission to reprint 'The farce lover: serpent in a false Eden', which was published in the spring 1976 issue of that journal. It appears here as Part 3 of Chapter VII in virtually unaltered form.

Notes

[1]Hans Robert Jauss, 'Littérature médiévale et théorie des genres', *Poétique*, 1 (1970), 79–101.

[2]*Ibid.*, p. 91.

[3]Halina Lewicka, *Etudes sur l'ancienne farce française* (Paris: Klincksieck, 1974), pp. 9–17.

[4]Norris J. Lacy, ed., *A Medieval French Miscellany* (Lawrence: University of Kansas Press, 1972), pp. 15–25.

CHAPTER I

The problem of genre

One of the most difficult problems that medievalists must deal with is the recovery of original meaning from verbal texts of a now distant past. The concept of meaning as applied to drama necessarily embraces both the author's meaning and the meanings a play had for its audience. We know that a playwright may address the same text to different levels of audience understanding, thus creating multiple meanings in a single dramatic performance. One reason that so many possible meanings do not lead to a breakdown in communication is that they are organized at a higher conceptual level into larger units of meaning, or genres. A genre is thus a conceptual frame that limits and orders the possible meanings of a text. In this light it becomes apparent that the question of genres and generic distinctions is of crucial importance for a proper understanding of late medieval French drama.

Virtually all medieval plays have, at one point or another in our modern critical tradition, been grossly misunderstood by their interpreters, and many have been condemned as naive, dull, obscene, or worse. The source of this unconscionable lack of sympathy with the plays under study lies in the unexamined assumption that post-romantic models of dramatic structure provide appropriate generic categories for interpreting the dramatic forms of the late Middle Ages. This in turn has led to an almost universal judgment that medieval playwrights paid scant attention to the distinction of genres and that our confusion in the matter derives from a lack of conceptual rigour at the point of origin. This opinion persists today in spite of our knowledge that popular literary and dramatic forms are the most consistently conventional generic types to be found. Medieval drama, as a body of popular and semi-popular plays, should be no exception.

The importance of accurate distinctions in the understanding of verbal texts must not be underestimated. If we posit the hermeneutic axiom that 'all understanding of verbal meaning is necessarily genre-bound', then it follows that 'an interpreter's preliminary generic conception of a text is constitutive of everything that he subsequently understands'.[1] We know from experience, however, that our first generic conception of a text is not always the right one, and we have all found it necessary occasionally to revise a preliminary conception. When dealing with texts as temporally and culturally remote as those of medieval drama, we quickly see how difficult it is to form generic conceptions of the texts that produce what we suppose to be the meanings perceived by medieval playwrights and audiences. It is not surprising, therefore, that earlier critics, faced with such difficulties, chose to interpret the plays by the only standards they knew. In spite of the general lack of success in classifying medieval plays according to genre, it is not the effort expended, but only the results thus far that have been wrong. In any case, it is time to revise our generic conceptions of medieval dramatic texts. We can no longer attribute our present confusion in the matter to the carelessness or naiveté of the playwrights; we must attribute it to our own failure so far to find the proper generic model. Such a model must account for all dramatic genres and their relationships to one another with the fewest possible anomalies. We should note in passing, however, that no referential classificatory system, even in the natural sciences, is without anomalies. Only in purely logical structures such as mathematics is that possible.

The generic model of late medieval French drama that I shall present in the following chapters is one that accounts more fully for the similarities and differences among the plays than any model previously proposed. I have attempted to derive the model from what we know of medieval dramatic theory and practice, rather than impose on the plays our modern notions of the nature and function of drama. The model, or paradigm, is necessarily synchronic, representing dramatic practice in France during an 85-year period from about 1475 to around 1560. This is not to deny that there were generic changes within this period – indeed, late medieval drama as a whole was a veritable laboratory of generic experimentation. I believe, however, that in the present state of our studies we can better understand the diachronic changes by first establishing a synchronic model from which to work. It should be understood that the model does not include the early tragedies and comedies of classical inspiration, which coexisted with the popular and tenacious medieval genres toward the middle of the sixteenth century. Before developing the new model, however, we shall review the earlier generic models and the vague conceptualizations of medieval dramatic structure that form our critical and interpretive heritage.

As early as the sixteenth century a certain amount of confusion in generic concepts resulted from the clash of two very different dramatic traditions: the native medieval drama and the imported but increasingly influential drama of antiquity. Sebillet was aware of the incompatibility of the two traditions, but tried, nevertheless, to make comparisons and equivalents between them.[2] Du Bellay, of course, contemptuously cast out all medieval dramatic genres as usurpers of the place and dignity of the ancient drama.[3] While theorists of the later sixteenth century, such as Laudun d'Aigaliers, still referred to the farce and the morality play, they devoted the major part of their dramatic theorizing to comedy and tragedy. The mystery plays, having been banned in Paris in 1548, were not treated in theoretical writings after the middle of the century. Thus the collective memory of medieval drama was gradually distorted by the normal processes of change and renewal to the point that, a century later, Boileau could write in his *Art poétique*:

Chez nos devots Ayeux le Theatre abhorré
Fut long-temps dans la France un plaisir ignoré.
De Pelerins, dit on, une Troupe grossiere
En public à Paris y monta la premiere,
Et sottement zelée en sa simplicité
Joüa les Saints, la Vierge et Dieu, par pieté. (Chant III)

Boileau knew nothing of medieval dramatic genres, but he had heard of one of the companies that produced the plays, the 'Troupe grossiere', whose name was the Confrérie de la Passion.

Some fifty years later, when the brothers Parfaict undertook their multi-volume *Histoire du théâtre françois*, it was on the basis of the organizations producing the plays that they constructed their model of medieval dramatic genres. To the Confrères de la Passion, of course, they assigned the passion plays, the other biblical plays, and the dramatized lives of the saints. They considered all these plays to be a single generic category, which they labled *mystères*.[4] To the Clercs de la Basoche they assigned not only the production but also the invention of the farce and the morality play.[5] Likewise the *sottie* was

the invention and the dramatic domain of the Enfants Sans Souci.[6]
For the Parfaict brothers these four genres – mystery, morality, farce,
and *sottie* – were distinct because each association exercised a
monopolistic control over its particular type of play. According to this
theory, therefore, any other organization desiring to present plays
would be forced to invent a new genre. While they noted resemblances
between certain types of plays,[7] the authors perceived the four genres
as being essentially separate and equal, feeling that the judicious
reader would have no difficulty in distinguishing one from another.[8]
This classification of medieval dramatic genres has the merit of logical
consistency, but, because it is based on certain historical inaccuracies,
it obscures many of the more fundamental problems involved. Though
they viewed the medieval drama as a somewhat tedious prelude to the
classical drama of France, it is to the credit of the Parfaict brothers
that they did not attempt to explain the former in the categories of the
latter.

Turning to our more immediate critical predecessors, those whose
influence is still felt today, we find a fundamentally different way of
classifying medieval plays according to genre. The rediscovery of the
Middle Ages by the European romantics had led to a radical revision in
the understanding of medieval culture. Moreover, the nineteenth-
century historians of the theatre, particularly those who wrote the
many local and regional histories, had demonstrated that the medieval
genres were not solely in the control of confraternities and Basoche
groups, thereby undercutting the generic classification of the Parfaict
brothers and creating the need for a new synthesis in the study of
medieval drama. Since, however, one's understanding of the medieval
theatre is necessarily influenced by one's conception of the theatre in
general, we should note two dramatic conventions that were deeply
rooted in nineteenth-century French consciousness and that militated
against judging medieval drama by its own criteria. Despite the efforts
of romantic playwrights to the contrary, there was still a tendency
among historians of the theatre to view the tragic and the comic as
wholly separate domains and to equate the former with seriousness
and the latter with frivolity. In addition, the longstanding proscription
of religious plays in public theatres led to a certain uneasiness in
dealing with the medieval biblical and moral plays, particularly when
they were mixed with the frivolity of the comic domain. One can well
imagine that the attempt to classify medieval plays according to
dramatic conventions that the Middle Ages had never heard of gave

rise to grave methodological problems.

The most serious of these problems arose from the probably unconscious tendency to see all drama in terms of the traditional categories of tragedy and comedy. Since the medieval stage knew neither genre in the classical sense, one sought, again perhaps unconsciously, analogous categories in which to classify medieval plays. The first such classification, and one that has become traditional, was the division between religious and comic theatre. But because there are some plays that are neither comic nor religious, some critics prefered to draw the line between the comic and the serious drama. More recently there has been a tendency to move away from these two dichotomies, since many of the religious plays have comic scenes, and to classify the plays as either religious or profane. This too has its problems, as we shall see. It should be said that the post-romantic critics and historians were not insensitive to the problems involved in their classificatory systems, yet they persisted in conceptualizing medieval drama in terms of an alien dichotomy. We may surmise that they assigned a higher priority to interpreting the medieval theatre for their age than in trying to understand what it meant to its own age. This is not to say, however, that they were completely indifferent to the latter concern.

Louis Petit de Julleville published in the 1880s what remains even today the most extensive study of medieval French drama ever to come to fruition. It consists of five volumes, two of which are detailed catalogues of every play and dramatic production known to him.[9] Around the same time Emile Picot was working on a similar history and *répertoire* of medieval drama, which was never completed. His voluminous notes for the study, however, are preserved in the manuscript collection of the Bibliothèque Nationale. The basis of Petit de Julleville's classification of medieval plays is immediately evident in the titles of the catalogues. The second volume of *Les Mystères* contains a description of all the mystery plays divided into three cycles: plays drawn from the Old Testament, those based on the New Testament, and those representing lives of the saints. Though he refers to the 'théâtre sérieux', he conceives of this part of medieval drama as a religious theatre because of its sacerdotal origins and its almost unique preoccupation with ecclesiastical history.[10]

The other catalogue is entitled *Répertoire du théâtre comique*. It is here that we encounter the most serious problems in genre classification. No one can dispute the comic nature of the farces and *sotties*, but most of the morality plays must be classed among the least comic of all medieval dramatic works. While the mystery plays are frequently punctuated with scenes of comic relief, morality plays, apart from a few purely comic moralities, have virtually no such scenes. Petit de Julleville excludes them from the serious theatre, however, because they do not represent religious history. He sees the essence of the morality genre in the intention to moralize, and distinguishes three types of morality plays: moral, religious, and satirical.[11] This classification creates the unsettling paradox of conceptualizing – and therefore interpreting – a significant body of serious and religious drama as comic theatre. Moreover, it led Petit de Julleville by reverse logic into the anomalous position of viewing the comic scenes in the mystery plays as a dramatic abuse characteristic of an ill and decadent genre.[12] Such inconsistencies are inevitable, he believes, because generic distinctions were vague and inexact in the Middle Ages[13] and because such factitious notions as a clear separation of genres belong only to periods of 'littérature polie et savante'.[14] In the remainder of the *Répertoire* he lists the farces and *sotties* together in a single category. Though they might in theory be separate genres, he finds it difficult in practice to distinguish between them.[15] Elsewhere Petit de Julleville speaks of the religious–comic dichotomy in other terms. He sees two theatres in the Middle Ages: one whose function was to edify the spectators while amusing them; the other whose function was to amuse without trying to edify.[16] Again the morality plays are incongruously placed in the latter category.

One of the major weaknesses of a generic model of medieval plays based on an opposition between religious and comic categories or between didacticism and entertainment is that it becomes impossible to deal adequately with the function of the comic in medieval drama. The truth was often spoken in jest in the Middle Ages, and the comic element cut across all dramatic genres to function as a cohesive force among the spectators. Comic plays and scenes served in some cases to release collective tensions, in other cases to reinforce communal values, and in still others to express serious metaphysical truths. In the light of what we know now about the social and psychological functions of laughter, Petit de Julleville's judgment of the nature of the farce – 'son seul objet est de faire rire'[17] – seems shallow indeed. Yet the influence of his work has been so pervasive that this idea is repeated even today.

Ultimately, the most serious problem engendered by Petit de

Julleville's generic model is that it distorts our interpretation of the plays. The religious–comic dichotomy is an analogue, not only of the poetic distinction between tragedy and comedy, but also of the rhetorical distinction between levels of style. For Petit de Julleville the grave or high style was the only possible vehicle for a religious or serious content, while the humble or low style could convey only matter of no significance. This, however, was not the practice in the Middle Ages, where we find the style matched to the speaker rather than to the content. Thus, in conformity with the Christian vision of the world, medieval writers could place serious truths in the mouths of the low and the humble, and playwrights could exemplify such truths in comic scenes. If, therefore, we try to separate the comic plays from the religious, thereby placing them all in an alien conceptual context, we run the risk of considerable distortion and loss of meaning.

To illustrate this point, let us examine Petit de Julleville's interpretation of the *Moralité de l'Aveugle et du Boiteux*, written by André de La Vigne to follow the three-day production of his *Vie de Saint Martin* in 1496. It is an unusual morality in that its characters are farce types rather than allegorical abstractions, and its action involves a number of sight gags equally suggestive of the farce. The blind man, who has just been abandoned in the street by his guide, finds himself near a cripple, who cannot move without help. They decide to form an alliance in which the blind man will carry the cripple on his shoulders, while the latter will act as navigator. Meanwhile, some of the characters of the mystery play, who are still in their places in the theatre, begin to carry the body of St Martin in procession to the church. The two beggars hear that the saint was a miracle-worker and that, should they come close to the procession, they might possibly be cured. The blind man at first wants to be healed, but his partner convinces him that, without their infirmities as excuses for begging, they would be forced to work. There follows a highly comic scene in which the grotesque pair try to run away from the procession, but in their confusion collide with it instead and are instantly healed. The blind man, profoundly moved by the vision of a world he has never seen, thanks God for the miraculous gift of sight. The cripple, however, sees only the loss of his livelihood and curses the saint for the miracle. The story was taken from the legend of St Martin and was also dramatized in another *Vie de Saint Martin*.[18] In the other versions, however, both beggars are thankful for their miraculous cures.

Petit de Julleville finds the generic designation, *moralité*, to be unjustified in the case of this farce-like play.[19] But the paradox is obvious: having classified all morality plays as comic theatre, he is disturbed by the genuinely comic nature of this morality. As a result, he misses completely the serious import of the play. He fears that it was designed to ridicule the miracles of St Martin[20] and wonders if there is not some degree of irreverence towards religion.[21] Though ultimately he thinks not, because medieval religion was too deeply rooted in the people, he is still at a loss to explain why André de La Vigne should make one of the beggars curse the miracle: 'Le poète a-t-il voulu indiquer assez finement qu'il vaut mieux perdre ses jambes que ses yeux?'[22] Yet it is precisely this change that transforms a legendary incident in the life of St Martin into a moral allegory of the human condition. Upon reflection, we grasp the playwright's allusion to the two thieves flanking Jesus on the cross – one of whom accepted God's grace and one of whom refused it. We then become aware that the author has condensed into 250 lines the central structure of the morality form – that is, the presentation of Everyman as a creature torn apart by good and bad impulses. The central figure of the morality play is usually presented as one character, as in *L'Homme Pecheur*, who is good and bad in sequence. In some plays, however, he is divided into two characters, as in *Bien Advisé et Mal Advisé* or in *L'Homme Juste et l'Homme Mondain*, each of whom represents one side of Everyman's moral dilemma. Thus the allegory becomes clear. The blind man is the human soul untouched by grace, yet having a natural inclination toward the light. The cripple is the physical body unwashed of its sins, with its natural tendency to avoid spiritual things. Together, in the wasteland of a world without grace, they form a grotesque and farcical pair pursuing their own selfish ends. When the grace of God strikes, like the lightning on the road to Damascus, the soul welcomes it with joy, but the body resents the loss of its sinful pleasures. Readers familiar with the *Second Shepherds' Play* of the Wakefield cycle will recognize a similar use of farce techniques in this play to represent the fallen world of man without grace.

Comic drama in the Middle Ages was not opaque to the transmission of serious doctrine; it was a clear medium through which the community could see and experience its values. This is not to say that every comic play was a religious allegory – far from it. It does mean, however, that we should read all comic plays, including the non-didactic, in the light of the whole system of late medieval drama and its underlying communal values. We can no longer afford to study the farce or the comic theatre in isolation, viewing it as an escapist diversion having little to do with the serious concerns of the spectators. It also means that we must take special care not to slant our reading of the texts with *a priori* conceptual categories that had no significance when the texts were written. To make generic distinctions based on the separation of comic and religious elements in the medieval drama constitutes a methodological error of serious proportions.

A variation of Petit de Julleville's generic model is found in the work of Eugène Lintilhac, who wrote in the first decade of the twentieth century. He devoted the first two volumes of his *Histoire générale du théâtre en France* to the medieval drama. To be sure, Lintilhac was not a specialist in the medieval period, but his work has had a certain influence on subsequent scholars. Not content simply to imitate his predecessors, he made his own synthesis of medieval dramatic history and his own generic classifications based on a not altogether sympathetic reading of the texts. For the most part he found the plays disappointing and 'pénibles à lire'.[23] This in itself would be sufficient to distort one's interpretation, but there are other factors involved that are more directly related to our concern with genre. The 'chaos' that Lintilhac found in the pre-classical theatre presented many obstacles to a rigorous classification of the plays: 'Les espèces s'y confondent au point d'exclure les groupements par genres tranchés, et les titres témoignent eux-mêmes de cette confusion dans l'esprit des auteurs.'[24] Nevertheless, he was able, by attending to the dominant accents of the plays, to group them into two broad categories: the serious theatre and the comic theatre. There are three sub-categories of the serious theatre: biblical plays, hagiographical plays, and profane plays. The comic theatre, on the other hand, is divided into four sub-categories: comic moralities, dramatic monologues, *sotties*, and farces. The advantage over Petit de Julleville's generic model is that, by viewing the first category as serious rather than religious drama, he is able to include plays, such as *La Destruction de Troye*, that are neither religious nor comic. Petit de Julleville had to treat these as exceptions.

It is not difficult to see analogues to tragedy and comedy in the two categories of serious plays and comic satires, but the major stumbling block in all such classifications is the morality play. Lintilhac sees no generic trait common to the morality plays and for that reason feels no constraint to treat them as a single genre. Some he classifies as miracle plays, which he places in the hagiographic category along with the

Miracles de Nostre Dame. He so classifies *Les Blasphemateurs* and *L'Enfant ingrat*, for example, despite the fact that neither is even remotely related to hagiography. Other moralities he classifies as profane plays of the serious theatre, and the remainder he terms comic moralities. Lintilhac justifies this distribution of the morality plays among other generic categories by citing Thomas Sebillet: 'Nos Moralités tiennent lieu entre nous de Tragédies et Comédies indifféremment'.[25] Sebillet, however, did not mean that the morality play had no identity as a separate genre, but that it was the only genre comparable in magnitude and decorum to ancient tragedy and comedy: 'nos Farces sont vrayement ce que lés Latins ont appellé Mimes ou Priapées'.[26] Moreover, Sebillet treated the morality play as a genre that was uniquely French – not Greek or Latin – and he was very much aware of the tenuousness of his comparison.

One can readily see that Lintilhac's generic model presents as many problems as that of Petit de Julleville. To illustrate how his *a priori* conceptual dichotomy between serious and comic drama led to flagrant misreadings of the plays, let us look briefly at two texts. *L'Enfant prodigue* is a dramatization of the biblical parable of the prodigal son. After the opening scenes, which establish the character and motives of the prodigal, the Acteur reads a section of the biblical parable, which is then acted out. The play thus alternates between reading and dramatization to the end. In spite of the close relationship to the biblical text, Lintilhac finds the play to be among the most profane because 'la plus grande partie de l'action se passe . . . au mauvais lieu, où l'enfant prodigue fait bombance et pis'.[27] Actually, less than half the action takes place in the brothel, but Lintilhac's generic (and moral) preconceptions do not allow such scenes to have a religious significance. Apparently the length of the brothel scenes is sufficient to render the whole play profane.

If we approach the play with the knowledge that the Middle Ages did not exclude such scenes from a religious context, then the action takes on a rather different character. Though nowhere in the text is the play designated a morality, the author has appended an unspoken epilogue in which he explains its allegorical significance: 'Morallement celuy Pere est Dieu et ses deux enfans sont deux manieres de gens au monde: les ungs bons, les autre pecheurs. . . . Et le pays loingtain de Dieu auquel habite le prodigue est l'estat de peché' (D.iii.r). The entire play is thus equated with the moral condition of man or Everyman and his relationship with God. Moreover, the representation of mankind as two characters, one good and one bad, is typical of a number of morality plays. At one point the father addresses the prodigal as 'povre enfant mal adverty' (B.iii.r), which clearly suggests a parallel between the prodigal and the sinful protagonist of *Bien Advisé et Mal Advisé*. The prodigal's older brother, who remains in his father's house, is therefore analogous to Bien Advisé.

If we turn our attention for a moment to *Bien Advisé et Mal Advisé* with its dual representation of Everyman, we find a play in which Bien Advisé, aided by Raison, follows the right path from Foy through the sacraments and the virtues to Bonne Fin. Mal Advisé, on the other hand, is lured by Folie into a life of sin and sensuality, which is represented by tavern scenes no less worldly than those of *L'Enfant prodigue*. Ultimately, after encountering both Honte and Desesperance, he ends at Malle Fin. In terms of basic structure and moral allegory the two plays are virtually identical. Aside from the greater elaboration of *Bien Advisé et Mal Advisé* the major difference in the plots is that the prodigal repents at the end. There is also a difference in types of allegory. The characters in *Bien Advisé et Mal Advisé* are personified abstractions whose relationships represent the moral structure of the world. This is personification allegory, in which the dramatic plot has no significance apart from the meaning of the abstractions. By contrast, the characters of *L'Enfant prodigue* are concrete individuals in plausible human situations. The plot of this play is a meaningful story in its own right, but we are told that the individuals symbolize character types. This is symbol allegory, which requires an additional interpretive step before the pattern of abstract moral relationships becomes evident.[28] Once this step is taken, however, the structural similarity of the two plays may easily be seen.

Despite the strong resemblance between the plays, Lintilhac classifies *L'Enfant prodigue* as a profane 'moralité pathétique' and *Bien Advisé et Mal Advisé* as a 'moralité comique'. We note once again how generic confusion results from the error of conceptualizing medieval drama in terms of the classical distinction between comedy and tragedy. This time, however, the methodological error is compounded by historical value judgments. Because Lintilhac's dramatic history is not limited to the Middle Ages, he views the drama of that period primarily as a prelude to what he considers to be the much greater drama of the seventeenth century: 'Les moralités purement moralisantes, . . . dont le type est *Bien Advisé et Mal Advisé*, ne doivent pas être séparées de l'histoire du genre comique en France

... car elles y annoncent la future comédie de caractère ou de moeurs.'[29] There is thus a teleological bias in all of Lintilhac's study of medieval drama and, what is worse, his generic model is based on the traits that he saw as important in a later historical period. By reading the plays in the context of neo-classical dramatic conventions, he was led to classify as comic moralities those plays in which 'on discerne le germe de la future comédie de moeurs et même de caractère.'[30] It is this same bias that prevents his understanding a morality like *L'Aveugle et le Boiteux*, which he deprecates as a 'farce grossière'. Though granting a certain cleverness in the initial situation, he finds it poorly treated, presumably because he discerns in its action and characters no embryonic comedy of manners.[31] This teleological fallacy, which is not uncommon even today, constitutes another methodological error that distorts our understanding of medieval drama.

There is one other major generic model of medieval drama to be considered, one that has a certain currency among present-day critics. More conscious of the fact that one cannot separate comic and religious elements in the medieval theatre, critics now tend to make a distinction between religious and profane theatre. Jean Frappier has most clearly articulated the reasons for adopting this generic division:

> Le théâtre médiéval ne se caractérise nullement par une distinction nette entre le tragique et le comique. S'il faut établir une ligne de démarcation, elle passe entre le théâtre religieux, issu de la liturgie et des représentations paraliturgiques, naturellement enclin au pathétique et à la gravité, puisqu'il met sur la scène des thèmes et des sujets qui se rapportent à la destinée de l'homme, sans exclure pourtant des incidents comiques et des rôles bouffons, et le théâtre non-religieux, autrement dit profane. Celui-ci, qui se tient plus près de la vie courante, quotidienne, qui peint non sans intentions satiriques la société et les moeurs, admet aussi un drame touchant comme l'*Estoire de Griseldis* et un genre sérieux comme la moralité (bien que certaines moralités soient à classer plutôt dans le théâtre religieux).[32]

This is an advance over previous generic models in that this one eliminates many of the logical contradictions that marred earlier classifications. Nevertheless, some of the problems remain. It is immediately evident in Frappier's description that the morality play continues to be a stumbling block. Though released from the straitjacket of the comic category, it still suffers a schizophrenic split between the religious and the profane categories. And while Frappier avoids Lintilhac's error of deriving medieval genres from seventeenth-century dramatic traits, he is still under the spell of the classical

French style. As a consequence, he finds the morality play to be a cold genre because of its personified abstractions – a quality that is belied by the long popularity of the genre – and he regrets the lack of realistic portrayals of manners.[33] In this he echoes the judgment of Gustave Cohen,[34] whose rather superficial history of medieval French drama also classifies the plays as either religious or profane. Such judgments are tantamount to wishing that the morality play had simply been some other genre.

There is still a tendency, moreover, to view comic scenes as profane drama even when they occur within religious plays. The fact that comic and even grotesque elements can serve a religious purpose in both sacred ritual and drama has been a difficult notion to grasp (or to admit) in our enlightened Western culture. Yet most other cultures, including that of the Middle Ages, have traditionally blended the comic and the religious without any sense of incongruity. Nineteenth-century critics saw an unbridgeable chasm between the two elements and viewed the medieval practice of playing comic scenes in religious plays as abusive. Cohen carries this dichotomy to the ludicrous extent of dividing his discussion of Jean Bodel's *Jeu de Saint Nicolas* between the two volumes of his history.[35] Frappier, at least, has a sense of the conceptual and dramatic unity of this play, yet he too perceives it as a mixture of comic and religious elements.[36] There is something ultimately distorting about the notion of 'mixture' or 'mélange' here, because it suggests an artificial combination of elements that are not normally found together. Yet if there is one constant in medieval drama, it is the association of comic and religious elements in plays depicting the collective memory of the past. So much so, that playwrights and audiences cannot have perceived it as an artificial mixture of incongruous elements, but rather as an association rendered dramatically necessary by the nature of the world.

The view that all comic scenes are to be equated with profane drama is carried even further in a recent work of Jean-Claude Aubailly. In regard to the *Jeu de Saint Nicolas*, he understands that the notion of a 'mixture' of religious and comic elements weakens the case for the unity of the play. He argues, therefore, that because of a lack of interaction between the human and supernatural planes, the work is entirely profane.[37] To be sure, his arguments are based on a careful reading of the text and are quite persuasive as long as one assumes that there is a religious–profane dichotomy in medieval drama. Nevertheless, we are left in the anomalous position of having to classify

the dramatization of a well-known miracle of Saint Nicolas as a
profane play. Aubailly also classifies *Courtois d'Arras*, the parable of
the Prodigal Son, as a profane play because of the playwright's
concern for 'realism' and his sense of the comic in the tavern scenes.[38]
But if we think of the play as exclusively profane, we are apt to miss the
didactic concern of the playwright in the symbolic equation of urban
and pastoral settings with inner states of sin and grace, thereby losing
an important dimension of the meaning of the work. We know that in
medieval dramaturgy the effort to recreate the 'reality' of the past,
including scenes of a purely comic nature, was not incompatible with
the religious purposes of the mystery plays. I do not mean to imply that
early thirteenth-century dramaturgy is comparable in all respects to
that of the late medieval period, but in neither period did people make
the same distinction between religious and profane that we make
today.[39] Therefore the attempt to classify medieval plays in terms of
religious and profane genres forces them into the structural categories
of an alien mentality, distorting their meaning in the process. As was
the case with the religious–comic and the serious–comic
classifications, the religious–profane dichotomy constitutes a
methodological error. We must therefore abandon the categories of
religious, serious, comic, and profane as generic classifications of
medieval plays. This is not to say that we must necessarily stop using
these words as descriptive terms – they are, after all, part of our mental
world – but as terms for classifying plays according to genre, they are
not meaningful.

The difficulties that historians and critics have encountered in
describing relationships among medieval plays constitute what we may
call the problem of genre, a problem that by its nature admits of no
easy or immediate solution. Like all questions of genre and
understanding – and these two things are inextricably bound together,
as we noted in the beginning – this question too must follow the
circular hermeneutic path. The better we understand the plays, the
more we can refine our concepts of their genres; and the more
accurately we define their genres, the clearer will our understanding of
the plays become. It is in the spirit of furthering our progress along this
path that I shall propose in the following chapters a generic paradigm
for classifying the plays of the late medieval French theatre. Though
not radically new, the paradigm is based on a shift in perspective that
will enable it to account for more of the known facts about the plays
than do previous classifications. It also has the advantage of resolving

some of the anomalies that we have noted in this brief survey of past attempts to define late medieval dramatic genres.

Notes

[1]E. D. Hirsch, *Validity in Interpretation* (New Haven: Yale University Press, 1967), pp. 74, 76.

[2]Thomas Sebillet, *Art poetique françoys*, ed. Félix Gaiffe (Paris: Droz, 1932). See Chap. VIII.

[3]Joachim Du Bellay, *La Deffense et illustration de la langue françoyse*, ed. Henri Chamard (Paris: M. Didier, 1948), pp. 125–26.

[4]François and Claude Parfaict, *Histoire du théâtre françois*, 15 vols. (1735–49; rpt. Geneva: Slatkine Reprints, 1967), I, 33–43.

[5]Parfaict, II, 86.

[6]Parfaict, II, 178.

[7]Parfaict, III, 201.

[8]Parfaict, III, 83.

[9]Louis Petit de Julleville, *Les Mystères*, 2 vols. (Paris: Hachette, 1880); *Les Comédiens en France au Moyen Age* (Paris: Cerf, 1885); *La Comédie et les moeurs en France au Moyen Age* (Paris: Cerf, 1886); *Répertoire du théâtre comique en France au Moyen Age* (Paris: Cerf, 1886).

[10]Petit de Julleville, *Les Mystères*, 201–2.

[11]Petit de Julleville, *La Comédie*, pp. 45–49.

[12]Petit de Julleville, *Les Mystères*, I, 5, 440.

[13]Petit de Julleville, *Les Mystères*, II, 36, 93.

[14]Petit de Julleville, *La Comédie*, p. 46.

[15]Petit de Julleville, *Répertoire*, p. 104.

[16]Petit de Julleville, *Les Mystères*, I, 1.

[17]Petit de Julleville, *La Comédie*, p. 11.

[18]Petit de Julleville, *Les Mystères*, II, 535–38.

[19]Petit de Julleville, *Répertoire*, p. 39.

[20]Petit de Julleville, *Les Mystères*, II, 73.

[21]Petit de Julleville, *La Comédie*, p. 103.

[22]Petit de Julleville, *La Comédie*, p. 102.

[23]Eugène Lintilhac, *Histoire générale du théâtre en France*, 5 vols. (Paris: Flammarion, 1904–11), I, 56.

[24]Lintilhac, I, 57.

[25]Lintilhac, II, 111.

[26]Sebillet, p. 165.

[27]Lintilhac, I, 313.

[28]Robert Worth Frank, Jr, 'The art of reading medieval personification allegory', *English Literary History*, 20 (1953), 240.

[29]Lintilhac, I, 303–4.

[30]Lintilhac, II, 111.

[31]Lintilhac, II, 127.

[32]Jean Frappier, *Le Théâtre profane en France au Moyen Age* (Paris: Centre de Documentation Universitaire, 1960), p. 1.

[33]Frappier, p. 17.

[34]Gustave Cohen, *Le Théâtre en France au Moyen Age*, 2 vols. (Paris: Rieder, 1928–31), p. 72.

[35]Cohen, I, 34; II, 14.

[36]Frappier, pp. 45–46.

[37]Jean-Claude Aubailly, *Le Théâtre médiéval profane et comique* (Paris: Larousse, 1975), p. 24.

[38]Aubailly, *Le Théâtre profane*, p. 28.

[39]Alan E. Knight, 'From the sacred to the profane', *Tréteaux*, 1 (1978), 41–49.

CHAPTER II

History and fiction

Augustine, in his early treatise, *De Ordine*, asserts that philosophy has two objects: the study of God, whereby man comes to know his origin, and the study of the soul, whereby man comes to know himself (II, 18). God, for Augustine, was not directly knowable, but his providence was clearly discernable in the history of the world. Augustine eventually elaborated a scheme of universal history that provided the Middle Ages with a conceptual framework for explaining the origin and destiny of man. The soul, however, was held to be directly knowable and Augustine would have each person undertake a programme of searching self-examination in order to grow in virtue and moral probity. To do otherwise would be out of harmony with the order of the universe.

Since Augustine's philosophy helped shape the thinking of the Middle Ages and provided some of the basic mental categories of the next thousand years, it is perhaps not far-fetched to see in his conception of philosophy's goals a parallel to the twofold concern of late medieval drama. On the one hand there were plays concerned with the ways of God among men, and with his historical manifestation in the Bible and the lives of the saints. In actual production these plays were addressed to God in a para-liturgical act of praise, petition, or thanksgiving. On the other hand there were plays concerned with the ways of men among themselves, and with the moral nature of individual and collective human acts. These plays were addressed to mankind, teaching lessons with symbol and allegory and giving examples of behaviour to be imitated or to be avoided. If occasionally they were rooted in historical circumstances, they did not re-enact historical events, but rather interpreted them symbolically, allegorically, or sometimes evasively to avoid reprisals. These are categories of the most general kind, based on medieval notions of the radical distinction between the nature of God and the nature of man. This distinction was so fundamental and pervasive in medieval thought that similar binary patterns may be found in other contexts, where they frequently form the basis of generic distinctions.

The church provides an obvious example of a binary structure that is pertinent to our inquiry because of its close relationship to the drama. In the medieval church, the liturgy, particularly the mass, was the central collective act in which God was made manifest to his worshippers and in which his sacrifice was commemorated. This memorial act of worship was interpreted allegorically as the history of Christ's life and passion, in which context the liturgy, with its constant tendency toward spectacle, often became a highly dramatic representation of those historical events. The sermon, on the other hand, was the principal public teaching device of the church. It served as a moral guide both for the flock and for the individual soul, relying mainly on the techniques of biblical exegesis and hypothetical example to convey the lessons of Christian conduct. Whether solemn, threatening, or entertaining, the sermon and its *exempla* were addressed to the people rather than to God. These two functions of the medieval church – commemoration of the past and moral guidance – may be qualified as memorial and exemplary functions. These terms may also be applied to the texts on which the ritual acts are based. The liturgical text is relatively stable, presenting anew in its yearly cycle the events of an unchangeable past, while homiletic texts constantly change as they bring new examples to bear on the moral questions of the moment.

Medieval vernacular literature also functioned in ways that may be qualified as either memorial or exemplary. The epic, for example, though not an act of worship, was an analogous ritual celebration of heroes of the past. It functioned as the collective memory of the community, and the singing of an epic was a collective act of self affirmation and identification. While history and cosmology were largely undifferentiated in this genre, we may say that the epic was history to the extent that its linear model of time had displaced the cyclical model of time in myth and ritual, and to the extent that its heroes were derived from the real world. The courtly romance, on the other hand, was a narrative form in which the collective recalling of an immanent past was replaced by the gradual unfolding of an unfamiliar plot. Its function was to reveal the unknown, to teach and to justify the new. Its truth was to be found, not in the *sensus literalis* of narrated historical facts, but in a second meaning or *sensus moralis* to be interpreted by its audience,[1] and through which the romance exemplified a value structure and code of conduct in harmony with the second feudal age.

Medieval historiographical writings shared certain characteristics with the romances – a justification of the new, for example – but the chief distinction between the two types of narrative lay in the former's systematic reference to the external world as opposed to the closed, self-referential system of the latter.[2] Another opposition of the memorial-exemplary type may be seen in the distinction between historiographical writings and moral treatises, the latter tending to include fictional *exempla* illustrating behaviour to be imitated or avoided. Even when *exempla* are based on the lives of real people, they assume a pre-established narrative pattern or fictional shape. The enormous variety of medieval *exempla* suggests still another opposition between certain short narrative forms. Hagiographic texts, while not always historical in our sense, are at least externally referential in contrast to the closed texts of the fable, parable, *conte*, *fabliau*, and *nouvelle*, which incline toward either didactic moralizing or satiric criticism. The opposition between history and fiction is less clear-cut in this case because of the strong affinity of saints' lives for the narrative shape of the folktale and because of the understandable desire to make them didactic and exemplary.

Medieval drama exhibited the same tendency to organize itself along the memorial-exemplary axis. The mystery plays, taken as a whole corpus, dramatized universal history from creation to doomsday, providing the whole community with a vivid picture of man's origin and destiny. Here too history and cosmology were largely undifferentiated, but the mystery plays were historical in the sense that they were externally referential and that their linear model of time had displaced the cyclical model of time in the liturgy. They were the collective memory of late medieval Christendom, and the dramatic representation of the familiar stories served a function analogous to the singing of epics in an earlier age. It is highly significant in this regard that the author of the *Instructif de la seconde rethoricque*, published in the *Jardin de plaisance* (1501), groups mystery plays with historical narratives and romances in his instructions for composing such works. The last section of the *Instructif* is entitled: 'Pro misteriis compilandis, cronicis, romanicis et hystoriis'.[3] All other plays were

unfamiliar stories, so to speak. They were the fictions invented for a
special purpose – to teach, to criticize, to entertain, or, for a special
occasion, to honour a lord. Like the short narrative fictions mentioned
above, they tended to be either didactic allegories, such as the morality
plays, or satiric criticism, such as the farces and *sotties*. The morality
plays taught the individual to know himself, as opposed to his
collective identity, and the farces and *sotties* ridiculed his foolish and
ethically deviant behaviour in society.

These notions concerning the drama are not radically new. The
possibility of classifying all late medieval plays as either historical or
fictional was noted by both Petit de Julleville[4] and Lintilhac,[5] but
neither historian perceived the generic implications of the
history–fiction distinction. Consequently neither used the distinction
as the basis for a classification of genres. I believe, however, that if we
probe more deeply into this distinction, we will see that it constitutes
not only a conceptual opposition in terms of the role it plays in shaping
collective mental categories, but also a structural opposition in terms
of its influence in shaping dramatic forms.

There is precedent for this broad generic distinction in the late
medieval usage of the words *histoire* and *fiction*, despite the fact that
the same words were also used to designate certain limited concepts
that we may exclude here. *Histoire*, for example, could refer in a
limited sense to a painting, statue, or storied tapestry. It was also used
as a technical dramatic term, as in *jeu d'histoire* or *histoire par
personnages*, referring to the mimed or still tableaux that often lined
the route of a procession. Though these are narrow usages of the word,
they nevertheless assume that the events or personages represented
were historical. The term *fiction* was often used to mean a lie or
deception. It too had a technical theatrical meaning, which we find in
Jean Foulquart's account of the coronation of Louis XII in Reims in
1498. He and Coquillart went to 'visiter les lieux pour faire les fictions
a l'entree du roy'.[6] Here *fiction* refers to the physical staging or stage
settings of processional tableaux, which were probably allegorical in
nature. From the fourteenth century on, however, the word is
encountered with the meanings 'invention fabuleuse; fait imaginé à
plaisir'.[7] This is the meaning we find contrasted with *histoire* in the
Avision (1405) of Christine de Pisan. After the death of her husband,
Christine studied both history and the works of the poets, taking
particular pleasure in the poets' 'belles matieres mucees soubz fictions
delictables et morales'.[8] The term *fiction* meaning 'poetic invention' is

found in a dramatic context in an account of the entrance of Charles VIII into Rouen in 1485. Among other events marking the occasion was a comic play described as 'une matiere faicte sur pastoureries et estoit une finction traictee sur bucoliques'.[9]

There did exist, therefore, in the late Middle Ages, a distinction between works referring to historical, or reputedly historical, events and works invented by the poet for instruction or pleasure. We see that Christine used both historical and fictional works for instruction. Later in the passage cited above she refers to poetry as the 'science de poesie'. This parallels the function shared by history and romance of revealing or teaching what is unknown to the reader. In the drama, however, the history plays were comprised of a series of events centering on the passion, its antecedents, and its consequences – stories of fundamental cultural importance already known to the medieval audience from other sources. Obviously the stories could not be changed, only repeated. Though historical in content, the passion plays are related to the epic in their social function, which was the ritual repetition and reinforcement of the immanent collective memory of the community. The fictional plays, on the other hand, not only could be changed, but had to be constantly changed to give force to their teaching function – the desire to know what happens next and the pleasure of surprise being powerful mnemonic devices. Hence the steady formulation of new plots and new dramatic situations for these plays. In one sense the history plays too were continually renewed. Since they could not change their plots, surprise was achieved by an ever more complex stage machinery and an ever more elaborate spectacle.

One distinguishing characteristic of each type of play is found in its relationship to truth. The criterion of truth for the history plays is their degree of conformity to past events in the real world, or, to be precise, their degree of conformity to the community's concept of past events. The history plays are not themselves the truth, but only a representation of true events by means of material images. Jehan Bouchet, referring to the 1536 production of the *Actes des apostres* at Bourges, wrote in his *Epistres familieres*:

Dieu le donnant, verrons un jour en gloire
Par verité ce qu'on veoit par hystoire.[10]

Fictional plays, on the other hand, are not constrained to represent an external reality, but are required to represent a moral truth. Their criterion of truth is the degree of conformity to a general moral principle as represented in a particular, hypothetical example. Truth is an abstract meaning in such plays; it has a potential application to events in the real world, but is not a representation of them. The essential distinction between the history play and the fictional play in its relationship to truth may be seen in the *Moralité, mystere et figure de la passion* of Jean d'Abundance. The history play versions of the passion of Christ include the characters and events of the biblical narrative. Here, however, we have a presentation of the passion that includes allegorical characters such as Devotion and Nature Humaine, and in which the historical events are not represented. Instead, there is a debate between La Dame Debonnaire and two Old Testament figures, Noé and Moyse, about the necessity for the death of her son, L'Innocent, who is ultimately crucified by Envie Judaicque and Gentil Trucidateur. Throughout the play, the concern is obviously not with historical facts, but with the meaning of the passion. Devotion concludes the play with a plea to the audience:

Icy ferons fin de ceste figure;
Contemplez la avecques devotion,
Pensant tousjours et mettant soing et cure
Au mystere de la vraye passion. (2353–56)

This morality play is therefore an allegorical figure (*figura*) of the passion, which dramatizes the meaning instead of the events of the passion. Its purpose was to increase devotion rather than historical consciousness on the part of the spectators.

Gréban makes the same distinction between historical and moral truth in his *Mystère de la passion*, where the Prologue, sketching the action of the first day, says:

Illec vouldrons laisser l'istoire
par moyen d'interlocutoire
et moraliser ung petit. (1667–69)

He then introduces five allegorical characters, including Misericorde and Justice, who will take part in the debate concerning the salvation of mankind. The Prologue of the second day refers to the same scene as a 'procés moral' (9950). The debate between Mercy and Justice is not therefore a historical scene, but an allegorized (that is, fictionalized) representation of a theological truth. In this regard, Guillaume Des Autels, who defends the morality play against the 'morally pernicious' genres of comedy and tragedy, concedes that 'on trouve estrange en nostre Moralité la fiction des personnes inanimees: pource (paravanture) qu'il est difficile d'observer le decore à les introduire parlantes'.[11] Here *fiction* refers to the invention, in the rhetorical sense, of non-living, abstract characters who are used to dramatize a moral truth. Des Autels prefers the morality play to comedy and tragedy precisely because of this relationship to truth.

The historical plays of the Middle Ages were what Northrop Frye calls 'myth plays' because they re-enacted the stories of central concern to medieval society.[12] Like myths, they were concerned with origins. They illustrated for the medieval community the creation of the world, the fall of man from original justice, and especially the redemption of mankind from its state of sin. Myths that explain a society's origins are called etiological myths. By the same token, the mythical dimension of the historical plays may be termed etiological in that the plays explained the origin, nature, and condition of humankind. By contrast, the fictional plays addressed themselves to the pragmatics of moral choices in everyday life. They might therefore be called 'ethic plays' because they directed medieval spectators to think and act in ways that would lead them ultimately to salvation. Thus the fictional plays were concerned with goals instead of origins. They looked, as it were, in the opposite direction. Because the morality plays were oriented toward specific ethical goals, they may be characterized as teleological plays. We may ascribe a similar teleological character to the farces and *sotties* in that they pointed humorously to the consequences of allowing certain weaknesses in the social fabric to remain uncorrected. These two major genres, then, functioned in opposite ways in medieval society: the historical plays oriented the members of the community toward their origins, while the fictional plays oriented them toward their goals.

The historical plays never lost their traditional relationship to the liturgy. Early plays, such as the *Passion du Palatinus* and the *Passion d'Autun*, retained formal textual vestiges of the liturgical drama in their narrative passages, analogous to the chanted Latin narrative of the *Jeu d'Adam*.[13] These gradually disappeared as the passion plays were transformed from stylized ritual dramas to more realistic historical plays. Many other liturgical characteristics and functions were preserved, however. Rey-Flaud points out a number of these: the presence of ecclesiastics in the drama and in places of honour in the theatre, the wearing of liturgical vestments on the stage, the religious nature of opening and closing ceremonies including sometimes the

celebration of mass in the playing area, and the production of a play as
an act of thanksgiving or petition. In general, he considers the mystery
plays to have been an authentic religious phenomenon.[14] The morality
plays, on the other hand, were more closely related to the homiletic
tradition of teaching, persuading, and converting. A morality play
might occasionally be the dramatization of an actual sermon, as was
the *Moralité, mystere et figure de la passion* of Jean d'Abundance
mentioned above.[15] More important, however, for questions of genre
are the analogous functions of the sermon and the morality play. Both
aimed to instruct the community in matters of Christian doctrine,
religious polemics, or even secular ethics. Both also stressed the
importance of personal choice, particularly in questions of conduct
leading to eternal reward or punishment. Thus the medieval liturgy
and mystery plays were theocentric acts by which the participants
acknowledged God's presence in the community, while sermons and
morality plays were homocentric acts by which the individual was
taught the necessity for personal choice in determining his eternal
destiny.

The distinction between the historical and fictional genres of late
medieval drama can be further refined if we draw a parallel with the
philosophical distinction between the categorical and the hypothetical.
Whereas today the term 'historical' may carry with it a connotation of
critical historical consciousness, 'categorical' suggests the absolute
character of mythical history in which past events take place only *in
illo tempore* and in which all the past is equally past and bears equally
on the present. And whereas 'fictional' may now be associated with
modern prose genres, 'hypothetical' connotes both invention
(*inventio*) in the rhetorical sense and example (*exemplum*) in the moral
sense. Plays of this type use invented plots to exemplify an abstract
moral truth. The distinction, therefore, rests on the difference between
a categorical past and a hypothetical situation.

The categorical or historical genres are temporal and chronological
in conception, and in production they functioned so as to represent a
distant but significant past to the audience. Even a past so mythical
and absolute as the story of creation was made palpably present to the
spectators. The hypothetical or fictional genres are atemporal and
psychological in conception, and for the medieval audience they made
the invisible inner world of man visible on the stage. By 'atemporal' I
do not mean that the plays' actions lack temporal sequence (though
sometimes they do), but that time does not serve to bring the action to

completion as it does in the historical genres. In the morality plays the fact of central importance is the inner disposition of the main character as he moves among the timeless allegories, while in some of the *sotties* time itself is personified, and therefore stopped and distanced in order to be examined.

Generally speaking, drama is a mirror in which we see ourselves as an integral part of the world, recognizing at the same time that we are separate and distinct from the world. One of the principal functions of drama, therefore, is to help us establish boundaries between the self and the various worlds of which the self is a part. In this sense the mystery plays were a kind of *speculum historialis*, defining the boundaries between the present, with all its tentativeness and uncertainty, and an absolute, categorical past. We should note also that in the plays of the last judgment, the distant future assumes the same kind of mythical, categorical character. The fictional plays from this perspective were a kind of *speculum moralis*, defining the boundaries between the world of everyday experience and a hypothetical world in which allegorical abstractions and human types acted out the various moral and ethical choices available to the audience of those days. Medieval playwrights, sensitive to the requirements of each genre, often made the boundaries between audience and play world explicit in the prologues to the plays.

In a history play, the Prologue – the word designates an actor's role as well as a text – who presented the story, characters, and staging to the audience, would generally establish a sense of temporal distance from the events to be re-enacted. Sometimes this temporal boundary was fixed by the mythical *in illo tempore* as we find in the *Mystère du roy Advenir*, where the Prologue narrates:

En Ynde, en ce tempor illa,
Y avoit ung roy qu'on nomma
Avenir de son propre nom. (25–27)

The Prologue of the *Mystère de la passion* of the Sainte Geneviève manuscript expresses the same notion in French as he describes the days before Christ's sacrifice:

Ou temps de lors, cil qui mouroient
En enfer tout droit avalloient. (41–42)

Usually, however, the required temporal distance is established by the narration in the past tense of the historical events worthy of remembrance that will presently be dramatized. As the Prologue of

Jean Michel's *Passion* states:

Par quoy present est nostre entente
faire demonstrance evidente
de ses fais dignes de memoire. (10–12)

The Prologue then narrates, in the form of a sermon on the
incarnation, the important events of universal history that preceded
the passion. More commonly, the Prologue would narrate the
historical events that the audience was about to see represented on the
stage. Gréban, for example, provides a Prologue for each of the four
days of his *Mystère de la passion*, in which only the historical events to
be represented on each day are narrated.

  Just as it was necessary to create in the spectators' minds a sense of
temporal distance from the historical events, it was also important to
connect the stage and the actors with those events. Many Prologues
identify the characters and the stage settings by telling the audience, in
the future tense, what the characters are about to do. The Prologue of
the *Vie et hystoire de madame saincte Barbe* presents the setting of the
saint's life in the following way:

Monstrer vous veuil tous les estages
Et l'ordonnance de nostre jeu
Selon l'estat des personnages,
Lesquelz ont prins chacun son lieu.
Premier, voila Dieu et ses Anges;
Cest eschafaut c'est Paradis,
Environné des sainctz Arcanges
Que Dieu a formé des jadis.
Et apres, voicy l'Empereur,
Qui est appelé Marcien,
Persecutant par son erreur
Tout le povre peuple chrestien.
Voila ses gens et son bernage,
Qui a tout mal l'assisteront.
Et en la fin mourra de rage
Et les diables l'emporteront.[16]

Occasionally the historical narrative and the designation of stage
settings are mixed, with the result that the tense of the discourse
alternates between past and future. The Prologue of the *Passion de
Semur* tells the audience that Noah and his family were the only
survivors of the flood:

En l'arche Dieu les preserva,
Sy comme vous le verrés ja

Par similitude jouer;
Le lieu pourrés cy adviser. (162–65)

In either case the action of the play was firmly linked to a series of past events and a temporal boundary was established between those events and the present.

Among the fictional genres it was the morality plays, particularly the longer ones, that were likely to be preceded by a Prologue in which the characters and the staging were introduced to the public. Here, however, the boundary to be established was between the everyday world as commonly perceived by the spectators and a hypothetical model of the world in all its moral dimensions. As we know, any representation of a moral world must include, either explicitly or implicitly, the entity with power to enforce the moral laws. In the late medieval world vision, that power was obviously the Christian God, who asserted his authority over the lawlessness of a lesser power, Lucifer. Some of the earlier and lengthier morality plays represented the whole moral order, including heaven and hell and their respective emissaries, whose function it was to help or harm mankind. Since these plays were not re-enactments of historical events, the stage settings did not represent geographical locations. Instead, the stage presented to the audience a kind of moral topography, not unlike that of artistic representations of the last judgment. One of the functions of the Prologue was to identify the characters, who were allegories of moral attributes, and to explain to the audience the topography of the stage, whose spatial arrangement was an allegorical representation of the relationship between good and evil. One of the clearest of such representations is found in the Prologue to *Bien Advisé et Mal Advisé*:

Veez Paradis en ce hault estre
Ou est Jesus le roy celeste,
Saint Michiel et Saint Gabriel.
Les ames portees y seront
Des bienadvisez qui mourront.
Et veez cy le destre chemin
Par ou on va a Bonne Fin.
C'est des vertus la droitte voye;
Ceulx qui yront auront grant joye. (A.ii.r)

The Prologue then introduces all the virtuous allegories, who are placed at intervals along the ascending road to Paradise. He next calls attention to the other road:

Et veez cy le chemin senestre
Dont Maladvisé sera maistre. (A.ii.v)

He presents to the audience all the vices that will be encountered along
this descending path, at the end of which is Malle Fin and the infernal
pit:

En ceste valee est Enfer
Ou est Demon et Lucifer,
Avec eulx le diable Satan,
Belial et Leviatan,
Qui les ames tourmenteront
Des maladvisez qui mourront. (A.ii.v)

The two protagonists begin the play at a point between the two roads.
With them is Franche Voulenté, a morally neutral character, through
whom each must choose his own way. It is noteworthy that, with the
exception of the reference to Maladvisé quoted above, the Prologue
makes no statement about specific actions of the characters in the play.
All other references to future action concern, not the characters, but
mankind in general and the members of the audience in particular.
This strongly suggests that the morality play was perceived less as a
series of temporal events than as a series of states of mind that together
formed a compelling dramatic image – we might say a hypothetical
model – of the moral order.

　　If the protagonist is an institution or a collectivity rather than an
Everyman type, then the play tends to organize itself around the state
of being of that group. Raison, introducing the morality of *Les Trois
Estatz*, explains:

Et en present vouldrons monstrer
L'estat du monde seurement. (A.i.v)

This, obviously, does not refer to a realistic representation of the
world, but to an allegorical representation of the moral condition of
the three estates. Yet it is the 'true' state of the world that the play
deals with. Here again we note the relationship to truth that we
discussed earlier, a relationship that is explicitly stated by the Preco in
the introduction to *L'Envie des freres*:

Bourgeoys, marchans, dames et damoyselles,
Je vous salue en generalité,
Vous suppliant que prestez voz oreilles
Affin d'ouyr nostre moralité
Que faicte avons, non par mondanité,

Mais pour le vray declarer seulement
Au nom de Dieu. Pourquoy la verité
Vous cognoistrez icy presentement. (p. 87)

The Middle Ages saw nothing incongrous in declaring moral and psychological truths by means of speaking allegories in fictional dramatic genres. As we know, however, this was a way of defining the boundary between the real world and a hypothetical moral world that Renaissance playwrights would eventually reject with scorn.

Late Antiquity saw two major schools of biblical exegesis in competition with each other. There was a figural interpretation of the Bible, practised generally by the Church Fathers, which saw a connection between two historical events or persons: the first signified or pointed to the second, while the second encompassed or fulfilled the first.[17] In opposition to this point of view was the allegorical interpretation practised by Philo and the Alexandrian school. They saw 'in the destinies of Israel . . . an allegory of the movement of the sinful soul in need of salvation, its fall, hope, and ultimate redemption'.[18] These two interpretive points of view persisted throughout the Middle Ages and we see them reappear in the historical and fictional genres of late medieval drama. The passion plays represented the history of the world figurally, with Old Testament episodes such as the flood and the sacrifice of Abraham being included precisely because they were seen as prefigurations of New Testament events. Real events stood for other real events, thus maintaining the historicity of both elements of the figural sign. Morality plays, on the other hand, represented the moral world allegorically. A dramatic fiction stood for the reality of ethical principles, thus preserving the abstract, intellectual nature of the allegorical sign.

Just as events can stand for other events in the figural view, persons (characters in the plays) can stand for other persons. Abel and Isaac, for example, are figures of Christ in the passion plays. By contrast, allegory requires that characters stand for human types (Homme Pecheur), abstractions (Raison), or institutions (Eglise). Medieval playwrights were not concerned with character development in the same way that later playwrights were, and one would not, of course, expect to find in medieval plays the finely shaded psychological portraits that became conventional in plays of the neo-classical and modern periods. It does not follow, however, that medieval character portrayal was simplistic or naive. Nor is it the case that playwrights were ignorant of psychological motivation. One has only to think of

the motivations provided for such acts as the murder of Abel or the
suicide of Judas. This, however, was not the primary goal of medieval
character portrayal. We have seen that the basic function of the
history plays was to make manifest the power and the presence of God
in the world. From the figural perspective, characters in these plays are
instruments of the divine will and vehicles for the manifestation of
God in history. We post-romantics, being more attuned to our own
culture, in which feeling has become the primary source and
justification of social values, tend to be less sensitive to the hieratic and
sacred dimensions of earlier societies. Yet the great value of the history
plays in the late Middle Ages lay not in the portrayal of the inner world
of personal feeling, but in the demonstration of an immutable bond
between the everyday world and the invisible realm of metaphysical
powers. It is this bond that makes the figural interpretation of history
possible.

Characters in the fictional genres were created to function in a
different manner. The allegorical plays are of course filled with
walking abstractions whose 'character' cannot change or develop. But
the human characters of the morality plays, because they must make a
choice, are studies in volition and the use of free will. Even characters
like Homme Juste and Homme Mondain, whose names suggest that
their fate is predetermined, must make a choice at the beginning of the
play. Moreover, their persistence in the choice they make is with the
full consent of their wills. Didactically, this is a warning to the
spectator that habitual sinfulness is not easily abandoned, even when
the end is in sight. Homme Mondain, for example, responds to the
urgings of Congnoissance as follows:

Saulver ou dampner ne t'esmoy,
Car pour toy je n'en feray,
Mais mon vouloir je parferay
Puis qu'ay jusq'icy prosperé. (A.v.v)

Paradoxically, it is these allegories of mankind (Chascun) or of a
segment of mankind (Le Blasphemateur) that come closest to our
modern notions of character development. Morality plays do not deal
with individuals, but they do deal with the inner, volitional life of the
person.

Farce characters are, in many ways, at the opposite pole from
morality characters. True, they tend to be types representing segments
of humanity, but they are not free to make the same kind of choice.

Their actions, consisting usually of tricks and deceptions, are responses to similar provocations rather than free choices touching significant parts of their lives. The farces are, in fact, images of moral bondage in which the characters are slaves to their own humours. The aspect of character brought most into relief in the farces, therefore, is the humorous rather than the volitional aspect.

When we look at the structure of late medieval plays, we notice that all genres tend to be linear or processional in form as opposed to the 'crisis' shape of tragedy and comedy. We find a parallel to this type of structure in the Old Comedy of Aristophanes, where, as Frye points out: 'the distinguishing feature is the *agon* or contest. This feature makes for a processional or sequential form, in which characters may appear without introduction and disappear without explanation'.[19] This is in sharp contrast to New Comedy structure, which requires that all characters be an integral part of the plot, the goal of which is usually to bring a young couple together. There is, of course, no such New Comedy structure in medieval drama; nor is there any dramatic form that parallels the tragic structure. Instead, medieval plays imitate the sequential structures of history and episodic biography, where characters are not functions of a plot. The *agon* of medieval drama is found in the contest between the forces of good and the forces of evil. In the history plays this is the struggle between God and Lucifer for the souls of men, while in the morality plays it is the battle between the virtues and the vices for the moral allegiance of the individual. Even the farces, which are the least obviously linear in form, are not the closed structures that New Comedy plays are. One could imagine the author of *Pathelin*, for example, adding another episode in which the shepherd is cheated in his turn, whereas Molière could have added nothing to *L'Ecole des femmes* because the fundamental premises of the comic world are changed with the marriage of Horace and Agnès.

There are two basic relationships of these linear forms to their contents, which correspond to the historical and fictional genres. The history plays are chronological representations of the past, in which the sequence of events is of primary importance. The morality plays are psychological representations of states of mind, in which a conventional plot represents the timeless struggle between good and evil. Of primary importance here is the fact that different characters appear in a fixed set of conventional roles. Thus the history plays are structured by sequential or syntagmatic relationships that 'bear on the possibility of combination', while the morality plays are structured by set or paradigmatic relationships that 'determine the possibility of substitution'.[20] In the former, historical events are combined in a diachronic sequence in order to re-present the past as it was lived. The result is a kind of horizontal sequence, suggestive of the flow of time. In the latter, a pre-existing linear plot structure with fixed roles allows the substitution of different characters from a vertical or synchronic set of possibilities. This permits different human protagonists to play the Everyman role in different moralities, while various virtues and vices may be selected by the playwright to vie for his allegiance. This paradigmatic structure enhances the didactic function of the morality plays by encouraging the spectators to imagine themselves in the role of the human character, whether he be Chascun, Genre Humain, or Homme Pecheur.

At the same time each genre also participates to some degree in the opposing structure. Because history was understood figurally in the Middle Ages, the history plays comprised a diachronic genre that was also to some extent perceived synchronically. That is, the full significance of the linear sequence of events could only be perceived vertically, so to speak, by relating all the events to a divine plan. Similarly, because the largely atemporal allegory of moral struggle and decision could be represented only in time, the morality plays comprised a synchronic genre that was also perceived diachronically. From this point of view time becomes an important factor in the definition of the morality play, as we shall see in the next chapter. Thus plays of both genres revealed their full meaning only when seen as simultaneous expressions of both dimensions.

In this light the question of which is the 'primary' metaphor of the morality play, the psychomachia (or battle of virtues and vices) or the pilgrimage, assumes a totally different character. Bernard Spivack approaches the morality play from the structural perspective of the psychomachia, seeing the spiritual journey as a variation of that structure.[21] Thus the 'basic metaphor of the morality play', which is the 'conflict between Good and Evil in the human soul', becomes a twofold metaphor of moral conflict and moral sequence.[22] Edgar Schell, on the contrary, argues that the allegorical journey 'is really the primary metaphor' of the morality play.[23] Taking a cue from Spivack, he attempts to demonstrate a structural relationship between *The Castle of Perseverance* and the narrative *Pèlerinage de la vie humaine* of Guillaume de Digulleville (or Deguilleville). Both Spivack and Schell are seemingly unaware of the fact that a French morality play, *L'Homme Juste et l'Homme Mondain,* is an adaptation for the stage of both *Le Pèlerinage de la vie humaine* and its sequel, *Le Pèlerinage de l'âme.* Obviously the French playwright thought of his morality play as having the form of a pilgrimage, yet it is in this play that the scenes of battle between virtues and vices are the most elaborately developed. Judging from this rather striking example, it would seem that the expansion of one element requires an equal expansion of the other in order to keep psychomachia and pilgrimage in balance. If this is true, then the question of which structure is the primary metaphor of the morality play turns out to be a false problem.

From the figural–allegorical point of view, both elements are equally necessary. In the historical plays the sequence of past events represents the pilgrimage of mankind to its ultimate destiny, but the meaning of the pilgrimage is derived only from the figural association of those events with the still and timeless world of eternal truth. In the morality plays the eternal opposition between good and evil is made visible by means of allegorical representation, but its relevance to the individual becomes apparent only when it is expressed in terms of a temporal example. Where the salvation of the 'hero' depends on making the right choice (between good and evil) at the right time (in order to die in a state of grace), then conflict and sequence, as expressed in psychomachia and pilgrimage, must be viewed as being of equal importance. The element of moral choice, while implicit in each of the two forms considered singly, assumes a crucial importance when both are combined in the morality play. We should note in this regard that the images of conflict and sequence that provide the necessary components for moral choice in the morality play have their source in different domains. The image of conflict derives its particular shape from the *Psychomachia* of Prudentius where we see a struggle between the virtues and the vices taking place in the human soul. The soul itself, however, is not an agent in this struggle, only a locus. The conflict, therefore, is not in response to particular situations in the sequence of a human life, but is a paradigmatic struggle exemplifying the nature of the virtues and vices. The image of sequence in the morality play derives from the real life pilgrimage, where there is a human agent who progresses toward a geographical goal. Obviously, there are no allegorized virtues or vices to be encountered along the way. Written accounts of such pilgrimages often interpreted the progress figurally as, for example, an imitation of the Via Dolorosa. In addition, the temporal progress toward an earthly site that had a

spiritual significance provided a general metaphor of the progress of
human life toward its eternal reward. In the morality play the images
of conflict and sequence come together in the human protagonist who
must make choices between virtue and vice along the pilgrimage route
of life. The element of moral choice, therefore, lies at the crux of the
paradigmatic axis of conflict and the syntagmatic axis of sequence, and
for that reason may be designated the central action of the morality
play.

Up to this point we have been trying to make a broad generic
distinction between two large bodies of late medieval drama, the one
historical because it dramatized past events, the other fictional because
its plots were invented. In doing so we have examined this distinction
from different points of view including the liturgical and homiletic
traditions, categorical and hypothetical representations of truth,
figural and allegorical modes of expression, and syntagmatic and
paradigmatic structures. We all know, however, that the real world is
never so neatly compartmentalized as theoretical paradigms and
taxonomic tables suggest. The function of such paradigms, after all, is
not to represent the world in all its prolific variety, but to impose on the
world's variety a pattern that guides our thinking along certain lines or
that enables us to know and understand things from particular
perspectives. In this ordering of medieval dramatic genres, as in all
paradigms, there are areas where distinctions blur. Likewise, there are
characteristics that refuse to stay neatly in their assigned slots or that
seem to fit in more than one slot. But this fact alone is not sufficient to
mark the failure of the paradigm. Indeed, one might expect the
successful paradigm to account in some way for the blurring and
overlapping.

There are at least two kinds of overlapping between the historical
and fictional genres. First there is a semantic overlap in certain history
plays where we find a *sensus moralis* in addition to the *sensus literalis*.
This may be exemplified by several cases that Petit de Julleville
records. In 1470 a 'moralité' of *Sainte Suzanne* was played in
Chambéry; in 1474 a group of actors played a 'moralitatem sancti
Adriani' in Forcalquier; finally, in 1512 a 'moralité de la vie de sainte
Suzanne' was produced in Montélimar.[24] Petit de Julleville considers
the Susannah play to be the one found in the *Mistere du Viel
Testament*. He is probably right, since we know that the play was
published separately. Yet the designation of a mystery play as a
morality made no sense to Petit de Julleville and he was quick to

attribute his own confusion to the Middle Ages: 'on sait que le moyen âge ne se piqua jamais d'aucune exactitude dans la qualification des divers genres littéraires'.[25] The confusion derives from the fact that the medieval usage of the term 'moralité' was much broader than the simple designation of a dramatic genre. It was used to mean, among other things, 'sens moral qu'un auteur ou son lecteur tire d'une oeuvre littéraire'.[26] The historical events of a mystery play might be understood as representing only themselves (*sensus literalis*), but they might also be seen as figures of other events or as allegories of ideal modes of behaviour (*sensus moralis*). If a playwright wanted to stress the figural meaning of a historical play, he could do so by adding the word 'moralité' to the title. This is apparently one of the reasons for the title of the *Moralité de la vendition de Joseph*, a play extracted from the *Mistere du Viel Testament* and published separately by Pierre Sergent. The descriptive title concludes with the statement: 'Et est ledict Joseph figure de la vendition de nostre saulveur Jesucrist'.[27] The term 'moralité' might also be added to the title of a history play because of the presence of allegorical characters in the play. This is the case with the *Moralité nouvelle du sacrifice de Abraham*, the first play in the *Recueil Trepperel*, in which the characters Justice and Misericorde debate before the throne of God. Note also that Arnoul Gréban at the end of his *Mystère de la passion* designates this type of allegorical 'Procès de Paradis' as a 'moralité' (33,941 ff.). In the *Moralité de la vendition de Joseph* we find, not only the allegorical 'Procès de Paradis' scenes, but also a scene in which Envye turns the sons of Jacob against their brother Joseph.[28] Thus the allegorical mode of presentation and interpretation normally associated with the morality plays could be suggested for a history play by the addition of the word 'moralité' to the title.

The second kind of overlapping in this broad generic division involves the memorial and exemplary categories of late medieval drama. We earlier used these terms to characterize the social functions of the historical and fictional genres respectively. If we return for a moment to that point of view, we will begin to see the extent to which these two broad genres overlap in their functional relationship to the medieval audience. Basically the historical genres commemorate a sacred past by reaffirming for the community whatever is 'digne de mémoire', while the fictional genres teach lessons in human ethics by presenting examples of conduct both good and bad. It is well known, however, that medieval preachers used *exempla* as memory images so that the congregation could remember the lessons of the sermon.[29] It follows that the morality plays, which are in essence dramatized *exempla*, also functioned as memory systems stimulating the audience to remember what was required for salvation. In this light it is quite evident that the memorial function, which was most closely associated with the history plays, belonged in part to the morality plays as well.

By the same token, the exemplary function, which was most closely associated with the morality plays, may also be attributed in some measure to the history plays. The *exemplum*, which is a narrative device for relating the theoretical world to the practical world, was developed to a high art by medieval preachers and writers. It consists of three elements: a situation requiring a decision, the decision itself, and a new situation showing the inevitable consequences of the decision.[30] These elements were always incorporated in morality plays and indeed medieval playwrights consistently thought of the morality play as a dramatic *exemplum*. In the prologue of the early (1427 N.S.) *Moralité du jour saint Antoine*, the Docteur quotes St Gregory as saying, 'Magis movent exempla quam verba'. He then explains:

Pour ce voulons par personnages,
Par exemples et par figure
Monstrer Pechié par quoy les sages,
Se Dieu plaist, en auront moins cure. (65–68)

A century later the association of morality play and *exemplum* was still strongly felt. Three plays from three different sources – *L'Homme Pecheur, Le Lymon et la Terre*, and *L'Envie des freres* – all refer in their final lines to the preceding action as an 'example'. On the other hand, as Aristotle pointed out, *exempla* can be true or historical as well as fictional.[31] Plays based on the lives of the saints, though historical in content, often assumed the function of *exempla*. Saints were people who had made right decisions in difficult situations and were therefore to be emulated by the members of the audience. The association between saint's life and *exemplum* was likewise expressed in the prologues to some of the plays. The Prologue to the *Cycle de mystères des premiers martyrs* tells the audience that the saints have shown them good works 'par exemplaires convenables' (32). Similarly, the Prologue of *La Pacience de Job* refers to the play as 'cct hystoire et examplaire' (14). Because of this close association between plays dramatizing saints' lives and the concept of moral *exemplum*, such plays could have been called moralities. This may, in fact, have been

the case in the three performances noted by Petit de Julleville that were
mentioned above. One exception to this seems to have been the life of
Christ. For the Middle Ages there was no more perfect example of
human life, but apparently because his life was so deeply embedded in
the broader context of universal history, the passion plays were not
thought of as *exempla*.

This type of overlapping in terms of social function did not blur the
boundaries of generic distinctions at the textual level. *La Pacience de
Job*, judged by the text alone, was still a history play of the Old
Testament cycle. There were, however, certain generic consequences
of this functional overlapping of the memorial and exemplary genres.
At its core, the saint's play is the story of an individual who acts as an
instrument of God's will in the world. The saint makes personal moral
decisions, but they are presented in the context of universal history. At
the core of the morality play, on the other hand, is the inner or
psychological landscape of moral choice in the person of a
universalized human type. Thus what distinguishes these two genres
from each other is not so much content as point of view and context. As
ideas about the drama changed in the sixteenth century, the heroes of
the two genres began to move toward one another in conception. The
saint figure was detached from the workings of Providence and placed
under the influence of a fate emanating from his character, while the
Everyman figure became an individual whose inner conflicts were
outwardly dramatized. The result was a dramatic character much
closer to the tragic hero, as we find, for example, in Jan Bretog's
Tragedie de l'amour d'un serviteur envers sa maistresse (1571). Petit
de Julleville considers this play to be a pure morality,[32] but the
allegories (Vénus and Chasteté) are analogous to the goddesses in
Greek tragedy and, more important, the point of view is completely
different in that we sympathize with the hero in his fall and pity him in
his death.

Long before the appearance of tragedy in Renaissance France, the
morality play and the saint's play had shown an affinity for each other.
In the beginning, however, when the two genres were mixed, the result
was a kind of hybrid genre in which each form maintained the outline
of its generic structure. One of the most striking of these early hybrids
is the *Moralité d'ung empereur qui tua son nepveu*. The dramatic
action of this play may be seen as a fusion of two stories, that of the
emperor and that of the nephew. When we analyse them separately,
the different generic structures become quite clear. The story of the

nephew is a morality play: he is given instruction in how to do good; when he becomes emperor, he forgets his instruction and falls into evil; he is punished as he had been warned he would be. The story of the emperor is an incident from a saint's life: he is a saintly man who, because of old age, turns over the crown to his nephew; he sees the nephew abuse his new-gained power and punishes him by death; at his own death the chaplain witholds communion because he refuses to confess the 'murder'; the sacred host comes of itself to the emperor, signalling that he has been an instrument of God's will. Both stories deal with moral choices, but the nephew's story is clearly a morality structure (which will become more evident in the next chapter), while the emperor's story concerns the accomplishment of divine will through a human agent. The hybrid nature of the play is reflected in the Trepperel edition where the title page calls it a *moralité* and the first page of text calls it a *mistere*. A similar generic hybrid is indicated by the title of another play: *Moralité ou histoire rommaine d'une femme qui avoit voulu trahir la cité de Romme.*

I would like to close this chapter on the distinction between the historical and the fictional genres with a quotation from the Epilogue of Théodore de Bèze's *Abraham sacrifiant* (1550), a play considered to have been something of a novelty in its day:

Je vous supply', quand sortirez d'icy,
Que de vos coeurs ne sorte la memoire
De ceste digne et veritable histoire.
Ce ne sont point des farces mensongeres,
Ce ne sont point quelques fables legeres:
Mais c'est un faict, un faict tresveritable,
D'un serf de Dieu, de Dieu tresredoutable.
Parquoy seigneurs, dames, maistres, maistresses,
Povres, puissans, joyeux, pleins de destresses,
Grans et petits, en ce tant bel exemple
Chacun de vous se mire et se contemple.

Here we see clearly the distinction between history and fiction. Bèze, the religious polemicist, equates fiction with lies. We likewise see clearly the memorial and exemplary functions of drama. In spite of the fact that the social and political contexts had changed greatly from the fifteenth century, the medieval generic categories persisted in the minds of the new playwrights.

Notes

[1]Paul Zumthor, *Langue, texte, énigme* (Paris: Seuil, 1975), pp. 246–48.

[2]Zumthor, *Langue*, pp. 245, 248.

[3]Eugénie Droz and A. Piaget, eds., *Le Jardin de plaisance et fleur de rhétorique*, vol. I, Reproduction en fac-similé (Paris: Firmin Didot, 1910), fol. c.ii.r.

[4]Petit de Julleville, *Les Mystères*, I, 1; *La Comédie*, p. 45.

[5]Lintilhac, II, 110.

[6]Guillaume Coquillart, *Oeuvres*, ed. Michael J. Freeman (Geneva: Droz, 1975), p. xxxi.

[7]Walter von Wartburg, *Französisches Etymologisches Wörterbuch* (Tübingen: Mohr; Basel: Zbinden, 1948–), s.v. *fictio*.

[8]Christine de Pisan, *Lavison-Christine*, ed. Sr Mary Louis Towner (Washington: The Catholic University of America, 1932), p. 163.

[9]Petit de Julleville, *Répertoire*, p. 346.

[10]Jehan Bouchet, *Epistres morales et familières du Traverseur* (1545; rpt New York: Johnson Reprint Corp., 1969), Ep. 101.

[11]Guillaume Des Autels, *Replique de Guillaume Des Autelz aux furieuses defenses de Louis Meigret* (Lyon: Jean de Tournes, 1551), p. 64.

[12]Northrop Frye, *Anatomy of Criticism* (Princeton: Princeton University Press, 1957), p. 282.

[13]Willem Noomen, 'Passages narratifs dans les drames médiévaux français', *Revue Belge de Philologie et d'Histoire*, 36 (1958), 776.

[14]Henri Rey-Flaud, *Le Cercle magique* (Paris: Gallimard, 1973), p. 279.

[15]Emile Roy, *Le Mystère de la passion en France du XIVe au XVIe siècle* (1903; rpt. Geneva: Slatkine Reprints, 1974), pp. 445 ff.

[16]Quoted from David H. Carnahan, *The Prologue in the Old French and Provençal Mystery* (New Haven: Tuttle, Morehouse, & Taylor, 1905) p. 173.

[17]Erich Auerbach, 'Figura', in *Scenes from the Drama of European Literature* (New York: Meridian Books, 1959), p. 53.

[18]Auerbach, p. 55.

[19]Northrop Frye, 'Old and New Comedy', *Shakespeare Survey*, 22 (1969), p. 3.

[20]Jonathan Culler, *Structuralist Poetics* (Ithaca, Cornell University Press, 1975), p. 13.

[21]Bernard Spivack, *Shakespeare and the Allegory of Evil* (New York: Columbia University Press, 1958) p. 83.

[22]Spivack, pp. 100–01.

[23]Edgar T. Schell, 'On the imitation of life's pilgrimage in *The Castle of Perseverance*', *Journal of English and German Philology*, 67 (1968), 236.

[24]Petit de Julleville, *Les Mystères*, II, 33, 36, 103.

[25]Petit de Julleville, *Les Mystères*, II, 36.

[26]Wartburg, *FEW*, s.v. *moralis*.

[27]Quoted from James de Rothschild, ed., *Le Mistere du Viel Testament*, 6 vols., SATF (Paris: Firmin Didot, 1878–91), I, xxxi.

[28]*Le Mistere du Viel Testament*, II, 343–56.

[29]Frances A. Yates, *The Art of Memory* (Chicago: University of Chicago

Press, 1966), p. 85.

[30]Karlheinz Stierle, 'L'Histoire comme exemple l'exemple comme histoire', *Poétique*, 3 (1972), 183.

[31]See Aristotle, *Rhetoric*, II, 20.

[32]Petit de Julleville, *Répertoire*, p. 34.

CHAPTER III

Farce and morality play

The distinction made in the previous chapter between historical and fictional genres is a distinction of a somewhat general and theoretical nature. Setting aside the historical genres as being less problematical (at least in the present state of dramatic criticism), we shall turn our attention now to the problems that have traditionally been raised by the fictional genres. These include the broad distinction between the morality play and the farce, as well as more specific distinctions within each of these two broad categories. The latter includes the thorny problem of the difference between the farce and the *sottie*. Our discussion will proceed, then, in the next two chapters, from the general distinctions previously made toward gradually more specific distinctions as we move to more detailed levels of generic classification.

At the end of the well-known farce, *Le Cuvier*, Jaquinot, who has just tricked his wife into recognizing his authority as master of the house, turns to the audience and says:

Car retenez, a motz couvers,
Que par indicible follye
J'avoys le sens mis a l'envers.
Mais mesdisans sont recouvers
Quant ma femme si est raillee
Qui a voulu en fantasie
Me mettre en subjection.
Adieu, c'est pour conclusion. (I, 49)

In a recent article on *Le Cuvier*, Jean-Charles Payen interprets the line 'Car retenez, a motz couvers', as implying the possibility of an allegorical reading of the farce.[1] Indeed, as he points out, the notions of folly and the world turned upside down are strongly stressed, and these themes are reinforced by a well-developed system of demonic and scatalogical imagery. The turning point of the play occurs when the domineering wife, who has fallen into the washtub and cannot get out by herself, is forced to submit to her husband's authority as the price of being extricated from her misery. This incident, as Payen suggests, might be read allegorically as an immersion in the cleansing waters of redemption, after which reason is restored and the world is righted anew. Payen's conclusion falls just short of calling *Le Cuvier* a morality play: 'On pourrait presque dire que le *Cuvier* est une sorte de "moralité", si le genre de la moralité ne supposait d'autres types de personnages. . . . Mais il n'en reste pas moins que la pièce n'est pas seulement l'histoire d'une crise domestique. Elle a un *sens*, c'est-à-dire une signification seconde'.[2] Clearly the play *can* be read allegorically, but one is left with a nagging uncertainty as to whether it *should* be read in that way. We know that virtually any story or sequence of events can be interpreted as an allegory. It only requires that one superimpose another story or mental structure on the first and say that one stands for the other. We know also that allegory as an interpretive mode was widespread in the Middle Ages, but even then there was no universal agreement as to when a text should be read allegorically. Some medieval readers imposed allegorical readings on all texts, while others did not. The question here is not whether the twentieth-century critic can find an allegorical meaning in *Le Cuvier* – of course he can – but whether the medieval audience perceived the farce as a morality play.

The answer to this question depends on the answer to a prior question. Were the farce and the morality play perceived as clearly distinct genres in the late Middle Ages? This has been a vexed question for over a century now. At their extreme limits the two types of plays are obviously different, but there seems also to be a significant area of overlap. Where, for example, does one classify the *farce moralisée*? The confusion on this issue, however, derives, not from a lack of clear generic categories in the late Middle Ages, but from a modern misunderstanding of those categories. There is ample evidence from both internal and external sources that the farce and the morality play were perceived as completely distinct genres that could not be mixed or blended in any way. Moreover, they were thought of as representing opposing views of the moral world. The evidence for the opposing moral worlds is, of course, intrinsic to the fictions represented by the two genres, while the evidence for the late medieval perception of the genres as distinct comes from areas extrinsic to the fictions: titles, historical documents, and theoretical writings. Let us examine the external evidence first.

Ideally one should have to look no further than the titles of the plays to determine their genres, since almost every play has a title that includes a generic designation: for instance, *La Farce du cuvier, La Moralité de Charité*, etc. The titles, however, have long been a source of confusion because the genre designations found in them seem to be inconsistent among themselves. A play like *Les Trois nouveaulx martirs*, whose characters (Mariage, Proces, Mesnaige) are pure allegories, is called a farce. *Les Vigilles Triboullet* is called 'farce ou sotie' in the title, while *Estourdi et Coquillart* is called 'sotie et farce'. There are numerous other examples of such confusing genre designations.[3] Because of this confusion, historians and critics of drama have traditionally considered both playwrights and public to have had little interest in notions of genre as far as drama is concerned. Yet this seems strangely at odds with what we know of the medieval mania for classifying and categorizing. There is another possible explanation for the eccentric genre designations in the titles, which is that the confusion is on our part and not theirs. It is quite possible that the titles seem inconsistent to us because they do not fit our preconceived notions of dramatic genres. The genre designations of the titles are, I believe, in virtually every case consistent with medieval concepts of dramatic genres, but this will become clear only in the light of other types of evidence and of our discussion of the sub-genres. We shall therefore set the question of titles aside for the moment and return to it in a subsequent chapter.

The second type of external evidence is comprised of contemporary references to medieval productions of plays. I have collected more than 650 references by genre to plays performed in the course of the fifteenth and sixteenth centuries (1380 to 1600). The references were made for the most part by chroniclers, municipal accountants, and other types of record-keepers. They were gleaned from secondary sources, mainly nineteenth- and early twentieth-century historical and archeological studies of French cities and regions, as well as historical studies of medieval drama. All references, however, are direct quotations, or purportedly so, from the original documents. Though there is a certain desirable randomness, there is no large degree of scientific rigour in the sampling. As a consequence, conclusions drawn from it are valid only to the extent that they are supported by other evidence.

The most frequently used terms before 1450 were the general designations *jeu* and *jeu de personnages*. These, however, tell us nothing about genre. The most frequently used generic designation in the same period was *mystère de la passion*. The two longer terms disappear by the middle of the sixteenth century: *jeu de personnages* because it falls out of usage in favour of more specific genre designations; *mystère de la passion* because the plays themselves were condemned and suppressed. In the course of the fifteenth century new terms appear, some ephemeral, such as *jeu de rimes* and *jeu de partures*, and others more durable, such as *farce, moralité*, and *histoire*. What is significant, however, in these references is not the mention of a dramatic genre in isolation, but the combinations of genre designations by which the writers attempted to cover a large segment of the dramatic spectrum. Before 1475 the distinctions among types of plays are rather vague. In Ypres in 1422 a troupe from Lille played 'jeux d'istores et de partures'.[4] In Amiens in 1449 some actors played 'jeux de personnages et par signes'.[5] The distinction made in these and similar cases was possibly between silent tableaux (*histoires, par signes*) and spoken plays. This is not entirely certain, however, because the term *histoire* could also be applied to a spoken play. In Lyon in 1457 'aulcuns des clers de la chancellerie du Roy nostre Sire avoient fect et joué farces et jeuz en public'.[6] Here one of the terms is more specific, but we have no way of knowing what kind of *jeux* were distinguished from the farces.

After 1475 a clear pattern begins to emerge. In Poitiers in 1476 the choirmaster of St Hilaire le Grand was forbidden to take part in 'ludis seu jocis, vulgariter et galice nuncupatis *farces, moralités* et hujuscemodi', while two years later all members of the chapter were likewise forbidden to have anything to do with playing 'moralitates, farsias, joca et hujusmodi'.[7] From this time on the generic terms *farce* and *moralité* are more and more frequently linked in order to designate the whole body of non-historical or fictional drama. One still finds vague references such as 'farces et jeux' or 'moralités et jeux'. One also finds references to programmes of individual plays, such as the 'moult belle moralité, sottie et farce' played for the Cardinal de Bourbon in Paris in 1482.[8] But the general and inclusive reference to the fictional genres came ultimately to be 'farces et moralités'. A few examples will suffice. In Paris in 1492 the Gallans Sans Soucy played several 'moralitéz, farces et esbatemens' for the queen, Anne de Bretagne.[9] The *esbatemens* were not necessarily plays, but were more likely dances, games, or other entertainments. In any case, there is no evidence that they were *sotties* as Nelson claims.[10] Paris, preparing for the royal entry of the new queen, Eléonore d'Autriche, summoned 'maistre Jehan du Pont Alaix et maistre André, Italien, . . . ausquels mondit sieur le gouverneur a enjoint faire et composer farces et moralitez les plus exquises et le plus brief que faire se pourra pour resjouyr le Roy et la Reyne'.[11] From 1530 to about 1560, the period in which most of the extant plays were printed or copied, the terms *moralité* and *farce* are frequently encountered in combination. After 1560, with the increasing use of the new terms, *tragédie* and *comédie*, the old pair of genre designations is no longer inclusive. A striking example of the interference of the old and new terms is found in the municipal register of Amiens for the year 1555. I quote *in extenso* because of the light it sheds on early professional troupes:

Sur la requeste presentee audit echevinage par Anthoine Soene, enfant de Ronain en Dauphiné, et ses compagnons joueurs d'histoires, tragedies morales et farces, adfin qu'il leur fust permis de jouer en ceste ville lesdites moralités et farces . . . il leur a esté permis de jouer en chambres moralités honnestes et non sentant aucun point d'heresie, l'espace de six jours seullement a la charge qu'ils ne joueront pendant le service divin; aussi que par avant jouer aucunes moralités ni farces ils seront tenus nous les exhiber et apporter pour les veoir et visiter; memes qu'ils ne poulront sonner le tambourin, mais bien poulront attacher affixes es carfours et a l'huis de la porte ou ils joueront lesdites moralités et farces.[12]

Apparently the comedians presented themselves as a modern troupe playing the newest types of plays, such as *tragedies morales*, but the clerk who recorded the aldermen's deliberations – perhaps even the aldermen themselves – thought only in the old terms of *moralités* and *farces*.

Descriptions of acting groups, such as the one above, provide us with further insight into early sixteenth-century conceptions of dramatic genres. From Béthune in 1511 comes a reference to a group of 'jueurs de moralitez et farces'.[13] In 1538 in the town of Villers-Cotterêts near Soissons a group of six 'joueurs de farces et moralitez' played 'nouvelles farces et comedies de matieres joyeuses' for the king, François I.[14] Here a troupe that billed themselves as players of the traditional genres is described, perhaps by a court clerk who was aware of the new interest in comedy, as players of *comedies*. In the same year in Paris, Pierre de la Oultre is described as a 'maistre compositeur et joueur de farces et moralitez'.[15] Until about 1560 troupes that played non-historical genres were usually described as 'joueurs de moralités et farces'. After that date one still finds references to the two traditional genres, but they are often combined with references to tragedies and comedies.

We may draw several conclusions from this survey of contemporary references to dramatic genres. They must, however, as noted above, be considered tentative until corroborated by evidence from other areas. First, for a period of roughly 85 years (1475–1560) the terms for designating the major dramatic genres were widely and generally agreed upon. Second, the two major fictional genres, the farce and the morality play, were perceived as two distinct and separate genres. In the total census of 654 items there were only seven references to *sotties* and five references to *farces moralisées*. By comparison there were 140 references to farces and 72 references to morality plays. We may judge from these numbers that the *sottie* and the *farce moralisée* were either extremely minor genres that were rarely played, or else they were subgenres that were understood to be included in the set, 'farce et moralité'.

The third type of external evidence is found in the theoretical writings of contemporary poets and rhetoricians. Christine de Pisan, though not writing on the theatre, provides us with a valuable insight into the medieval concept of the structure of knowledge. In her autobiographical work, *L'Avision*, written in 1405, she describes her education and her formation as a writer, which began with a thorough study of history and poetry. She later studied other *sciences* such as philosophy and theology, but her emphasis on the propaedeutic nature of history and poetry is striking:

> Comme l'enfant que au premier on met a l'a.b.c.d, me pris aux hystoires ancienes des le commencement du monde, les hystoires des Hebrieux, . . . des Francois, des Bretons et autres plusieurs hystoriagrafes. . . . Puis me pris aux livres des pouetes . . . me delittant en leurs soubtilles couvertures et belles matieres mucees soubz fictions delictables et morales et le bel stile de leurs metres et proses deduittes par bel et polie rethorique.[16]

Here, on the threshhold of the great fifteenth-century flourishing of popular drama, we find the two broad generic categories of history and fiction formulated as categories of elementary instruction. The context is different, to be sure, but not so different as may at first appear, since medieval drama was, among other things, a collective teaching instrument. We have already seen how group identity was reinforced by the history plays and how behavioural norms were inculcated by the rhetoric of moral fictions. Like the study of history and poetry for Christine, the drama served a propaedeutic function for a largely uneducated audience. The resemblance, however, does not end there. According to Christine, poetic fictions, unlike historical events, were made to be 'delictables et morales'. The description is no doubt a medieval rephrasing of the Horatian 'dulce et utile', but at the same time it points to the fundamental generic distinction that was later made between farces (*delictables*) and morality plays (*morales*).

If these two genres were perceived as distinct in terms of their relationship to the audience, they were also seen as differing in their prosodic natures. Toward the end of the fifteenth century, the two types of plays are mentioned briefly in the *Art de rhetorique*, attributed variously to Jean Molinet and to Henry de Croy.[17] Speaking of the common *rime plate*, which he calls *rime doublette*, the author says: 'plusieurs histoires et farses en sont plaines'. By contrast, certain stanzaic forms, when they appear in drama, are found in morality plays: for example, 'vers sizains se font en moralitez et jeux de personnages'.[18] While this is generally true, the exceptions are sufficient to lead to confusion if one were to base genre distinctions on this type of criterion alone. The point I wish to make is that the author of the *Art de rhetorique* perceived the farce and morality play as being the two major categories of poetic drama. Other types of plays were apparently covered by the vague term, *jeux de personnages*.

By 1501, the date of publication of the *Jardin de plaisance et fleur de rethoricque*, the generic categories that contained all of medieval drama were clearly set at three. The *Instructif de la seconde rethoricque*, published in the above work, devotes its final chapter to explaining:

... comme l'on doit composer
Moralitez, farces, misteres
Et d'autres romans disposer
Selon les diverses matieres. (c.i.v)

The chapter is divided into three sections, each dealing with one of the dramatic forms mentioned. The word *romans* refers to non-dramatic, narrative works. Pierre Fabri, in the *Grant et vray art de pleine rhetorique* (1521), classifies among the expositive genres 'toutes farces, moralitez, histores, mysteres, et aultres introduisans pluralitez de personnages'.[19] Fabri uses four terms to designate the dramatic genres, but they are clearly divisible into historical and non-historical categories. The latter, again, is comprised only of morality plays and farces. Thomas Sebillet, writing in the same year that the *Parlement* banned the mystery plays in Paris (1548), does not mention that genre at all in his *Art poétique françoys*. He confines his discussion of French drama to the two traditional genres of morality play and farce, which he compares to the drama of Antiquity: 'Nos Moralités tiennent lieu entre nous de Tragédies et Comédies indifféremment: et nos Farces sont vrayement ce que les Latins ont appellé Mimes ou Priapées.'[20] Even Du Bellay, that implacable enemy of all medieval genres, maintains the same classification, though not the same equivalences with ancient genres, in his *Deffence et Illustration*: 'Quand aux comedies et tragedies, si les roys et les republiques les vouloient restituer en leur ancienne dignité, qu'ont usurpée les farces et moralitez, je seroy' bien d'opinion que tu t'y employasses.'[21] Whatever differences may have existed in the minds of the poetic theorists concerning the nature of medieval drama, they always saw the farce and the morality play as belonging to clearly distinct domains and as constituting poetic genres incapable of being assimilated one to the other.

The internal evidence for this fundamental generic dichotomy is found in the two opposing types of fictional worlds created by the playwrights. In order to penetrate these worlds without bias, we must first rid ourselves of two commonly held, but misleading, notions about the farce. First there is the notion that farces were played in the Middle Ages for the sole purpose of making people laugh. Implicit in this notion is a radical devaluation of the farce as a dramatic genre. In contrast to the edifying mystery plays and the didactic morality plays, the farces are often viewed as pandering to the crude tastes of the lower classes. First of all, farces were not limited to a single stratum of medieval society. They were played for and appreciated by all social levels, including the royal courts. More importantly, however, this patronizing view of the farce fails to take into account the psychological function of the comic in all societies. It fails also to recognize the fact that a number of widely appreciated popular comic genres, whether dramatic or not, are absolutely essential to the viability of human social groups. Obviously the farces were played to make people laugh, but laughter is possible only in a meaningful cultural context where certain elements are in conflict. In this context the farce creates a comic fictional world in which the conflicting elements of the real world (for instance, sexual desire versus social constraint) are brought into relief to serve as catalysts for the social tensions resulting from such conflicts. In all areas of cultural life where fears and anxieties arise from social repressions or from conflicts among value systems, the comic 'combines a sense of mastery with a feeling of pleasure'.[22] The comic release of tension achieved by such popular genres is often only temporary, but it may also be a permanent mastery of collective anxieties. In the latter case we see 'the value of the humorist's achievement, for he banishes man's greatest fear, the eternal fear, acquired in childhood, of the loss of love'.[23] We must see the medieval farce, then, not as a concession to the uncultivated taste of the masses, but as a human, cultural necessity on the same level in this regard as the mystery and morality plays.

The other misleading notion is that the farce is a realistic genre. For more than a century it has been a critical commonplace to see the farce as being, 'en son réalisme intrépide, un miroir du temps aussi fidèle qu'expressif'.[24] The desire to find a mirror that would reflect life in the Middle Ages is understandable, but it is unfortunate that the farce, even allowing for comic exaggeration, has been thought to present such an image. There are, it is true, realistic elements in the farces: characters eat, work, and make love (usually illicit love); they also represent common trades, crafts, and callings. These elements, however, are not put together in the farce in the same way that they exist in the real world. Instead, they are assembled so as to create a quite different world – an abstracted, fictional, farce world that could never exist in reality. There is a parallel in this regard with the work of Hieronymus Bosch. A close inspection of his paintings reveals that they are made up for the most part of highly realistic details. Yet Bosch, who was also involved in dramatic productions, has put these details together in such a way as to create a world totally estranged from everyday reality, a private world of moral landscapes and cosmological visions. In a similar way the farce playwrights have created an equally fantastic world of symbolic actions, incredible behaviour, and impossible coincidences.

Dramatic fiction is a verbal and gestural discourse that creates imaginative worlds in which affect and action are brought closer together, in which desires are fulfilled and anxieties mastered by means of conventional, pre-existing generic structures. By contrast, non-fictional dramatic discourse, such as the medieval history plays, consists of intentionally referential statements about the real world. Non-fictional drama, however, can be seen or read as dramatic fiction,

as we view the history plays today, by removing the referential frame
and replacing it with a fictional frame. We cannot, of course, go back
in time and experience the farces and morality plays as the medieval
audience did. The only way we can enter the separate and distinct
worlds of these two genres is by reading the texts. But if we do so with
special attention to the choice of words, we will perceive first a
recurrence of certain verbal motifs and then a dominance of certain
patterns of images both within and among the plays. This will provide
us with some preliminary notions of the parameters of these two
imaginative worlds.

We have already noted that demonic imagery is prominent in the
language of *Le Cuvier*. This image system extends through virtually
all the farces, not only in words, but also in decor – the devil disguise,
for example, in *Martin de Cambray*, and the burning house in *Resjouy
d'Amours*. This verbal and visual imagery creates a semantic focus for
our interpretation of farce episodes, which consist largely of tricks,
ruses, lies, deceptions, and other demonic practices. In this light we
begin to perceive dramatic action in the farce, not as a series of real-life
practical jokes, but as a comic analogue of demonic activities in the
fallen world. This is quite different from the appearance of demonic
elements in the morality world, where a real hell and real devils may
intrude upon the action of the play. There the tricks, lies, and
deceptions are not just clever means of gaining a petty personal
advantage, they are instruments of eternal damnation in the hands of
demons and vice characters.

If the verbal (*lexis*) and visual (*opsis*) imagery of the farce and
morality play belong to two different worlds, we might ask whether the
other aspects of drama as defined by Aristotle show an equally clear
differentiation. (Obviously, the use of Aristotle's six constituent parts
of drama here is only a schematic convenience and implies no
necessary relationship between Greek and medieval drama.) Music
(*melos*) was an integral part of medieval drama and is an aspect of that
theatre that has been too little studied. It is difficult to say with
certainty that particular musical genres had fixed semantic
relationships with dramatic genres. We do know, however, that
morality plays such as *Bien Advisé et Mal Advisé* and *L'Homme
Pecheur* included only sacred music, while musical farces were
constructed around popular *chansons* of a secular nature. Where
sacred music appears in the farces, it is almost always in the form of a
parody.[25]

The type of plot (*mythos*) that appears in each genre is more clearly distinguished. The plot of a farce is most often comprised of a trick played by one character on another – the word *farce* means 'trick', after all. Sometimes the deceived character plays another trick in return. This tends to give the farce an episodic type of plot, having no permanent change of situation or character at the end. One could imagine, as we have already noted, a continuation of *Maistre Pathelin* in which a still cleverer rogue comes to dupe the shepherd. Farce conflicts, therefore, tend not to be resolved, but only momentarily neutralized for the sake of bringing the play to a close. Morality plays, particularly those that treat the whole life of the Everyman character, tend to be episodic also, but with a significant difference. The main character is always moving toward the ultimate goals of conversion and salvation (or damnation) and every episode is directly related to the final goal. Morality conflicts are therefore fully resolved, and the plot ends with a dramatic action that is complete in the sense that it could not be continued by simply adding another episode.

On examining the character types (*ethos*) in the two genres, we again find a sharp distinction between the characters who live in the farce world and those who live in the morality world. If we ask 'Who does what? and why?', we get very different answers according to the genre. Farce characters act in order to deceive, and often their actions are really reactions to other characters who have deceived them or are in the process of doing so. Their goal is virtually always to gain at another's expense some selfish, personal advantage such as status, power, goods, money, or sex. Their actions change nothing essential. By contrast, characters in the morality plays act out of completely different motives. Here I include only the characters representing human types, since the allegorical abstractions act only in accordance with their particular nature (e.g., Pride) and cannot act in any other way. The human morality characters act always in relation to a future goal, a goal that is imposed on them by an external and supernatural power. They are taught, or they know already, which acts will bring them to their goal and which will lead them away from it. They may choose to be morally good and deny themselves earthy gratifications in order to achieve a heavenly reward; or they may choose to be morally bad and, like farce characters, opt for the immediate gratification of selfish desires. The crucial difference in the worlds of the two genres in this respect is that the morality characters must act on the basis of an external moral standard, while farce characters have no such standard to guide their actions. Morality characters are free to accept or reject the established ethical code, but their choice is significant in that it has meaningful consequences – meaningful, that is, in terms of their ultimate salvation or damnation. The actions of farce characters have no such ultimate consequences. Morality characters are either moral or immoral; farce characters are amoral. Again, if we ask such questions as 'Who is punished (or rewarded)? for what? and by whom?', we find that the answers are different for each genre. Generally speaking, the morality genre is a dramatization of the world of Christian ethics, whether Catholic or Protestant. Thus there is always a divine power – sometimes represented on the stage, sometimes only invoked by the characters – who is ready to reward the good and punish the wicked. In the farce world there is no such power and no ethical standard to which the characters are expected to conform. Cleverness is the only ethical imperative. Farce characters are occasionally punished, as when a wronged husband takes the stick to his unfaithful wife or to her lover; but this is no more than personal revenge, and the wrong itself has no broader ethical status than trespass on personal property.

Let us now look beyond the characters and their actions for the thought (*dianoia*) or meaning of the dramatic discourse itself. Here we should be able to translate patterns of observed action into laws of the morality world or of the farce world. Occasionally such laws are overtly formulated in the plays themselves – 'à trompeur, trompeur et demi', for example, is a pervasive law of the farce world. Usually, however, we must abstract from the second level of dramatic discourse – that between author and audience – the behavioural norms, the ethical standards, the underlying value systems of the two worlds. If we ask 'What are the objects of desire in each case?', the answers will overlap somewhat because, as we have seen, the immoral morality character often wants the same things as a farce character. The only difference is that he does not have to deceive to get them; he only has to yield to temptation. But if we ask the same question in the context of 'What is good and what is evil?', then the vast difference between the two worlds becomes immediately apparent. In the morality plays there is not only a proximate good or evil, which is the object of each moral choice made by the human characters, but also an ultimate good or evil – that is, salvation or damnation – to which the protagonists of the morality world are finally destined. Among the characters of these plays we also find supernatural representatives of the forces of good and evil. Such concepts have no meaning in the farce where one can speak of good and evil only by analogy. Whatever is immediately desirable may be called 'good' and whatever is to be avoided may be called 'evil', but strictly speaking the farce deals only in the immediately desirable or undesirable. There are no ultimate consequences in the farce world. Schoell makes a similar distinction between the immanent world of the comic theatre and the transcendent world of the serious theatre.[26] Thus two very different value systems inhere in the two genres. Because all drama involves conflicts that are ultimately conflicts of values, we should inquire as to which values are in conflict in the distinct and separate worlds of the farce and the morality play.

In both genres virtually all dramatic conflicts are either problems of authority or problems of rationality. There is, however, a sharp distinction between the farce and the morality in how these problems are treated. In the farce world all authority has been debased and disorder reigns. As one curious pilgrim puts it in *Troys Pelerins et Malice*:

Or alons pour voir la desordre
Qui se faict maintenant au monde. (34–35)

Wherever there is power (usually in the ruling institutions) authority is corrupted by every imaginable vice; wherever there is weakness (usually in individuals) rebels move into the power vacuum. Thus, for example, in the conjugal farces, the husband is often weak and impotent, while his wife is domineering and sexually insatiable. Adultery, which is a matter of usurped authority, is made possible by the husband's inability to wield his *bâton*. Similarly, reason has been not only debased, but abandoned in the farce world and folly rules the day. Folly, in fact, is the primary characteristic of the farce world, for corruption of authority was generally viewed as a form of folly. Other kinds of folly found in the farce range from the harmless lunacy of the Badin to the vicious madness of Folle Bobance. Whatever type is involved, however, folly is never eliminated from the farce world. The most that one can expect at the end of a play is a neutralization of foolish conflicts. For this reason the farce world is an ethical jungle in which only the shrewd and the wily are fit for survival. It is a world of retributive justice with no possibility of appeal because there is no higher law or higher power.

This is the crucial difference between the farce world and the morality world. In the latter we meet with many of the same kinds of folly and vice as in the farce, but there is always a higher power to punish the wicked and reward the good. Every human character and every human institution represented in the morality world is faced with a choice between good and evil. The morality character knows, moreover, what the consequences of his choice will be and that they are certain to follow. Homme Mondain, for example, is very much aware that he is on the road to Malle Fin when he says:

Se je fais bien, bien trouveray;
Et se je fais mal, mal j'auray.
Je scay bien qu'a gaing ou a perte
J'auray payement de ma desserte
Et non autre. (A.v.v)

The morality character must choose, and it is reason that enables him to make the right choice. Raison, it should be noted, is a central figure in many of the morality plays. Thus, contrary to the farce, reason is the primary characteristic of the morality world in terms of its constant availability as a sure guide to the good. If one loses the 'voye de Raison', there is always a way back through repentance for the individual and through reform for the institution.

We have examined both external and internal evidence for making a fundamental generic distinction between farce and morality play and have found two quite different fictional worlds depicted in the two genres. Before making further divisions into sub-genres, let us probe more deeply into these two worlds, comparing them from different points of view and searching out the generic implications of their opposing natures. We have seen that the farce world is dominated by folly and the morality world is dominated by reason. Let us make certain at this point that we understand what was meant by reason or *ratio* in the Middle Ages. There were two generally accepted meanings of the word. First, *ratio* was one of the two operations of the rational soul, the other being *intellectus*. Thomas Aquinas considered them to be two aspects of the same power of understanding: 'Intelligere enim est simpliciter veritatem intelligibilem apprehendere. Ratiocinare autem est procedere de uno intellecto ad aliud, ad veritatem intelligibilem cognoscendam'.[27] This is very close to what we mean today by deductive reasoning. The other meaning of *ratio*, however, was quite different and was closer to what we would today call conscience. Its function was to perceive the good and to lead man to choose good over evil:

Nearly all moralists before the eighteenth century regarded Reason as the organ of morality. The moral conflict was depicted as one between Passion and Reason, not between Passion and 'conscience'. . . . The explanation is that nearly all of them believed the fundamental moral maxims were intellectually grasped. If they had been using the strict medieval distinction, they would have made morality an affair not of *ratio* but of *intellectus*. This distinction, however, even in the Middle Ages, was used only by philosophers, and did not affect popular or poetic language. On that level *Reason* means Rational Soul. Moral imperatives therefore were uttered by Reason.[28]

This is the kind of reason symbolized by the character Raison in the morality plays, and it is this reason that pervades the morality world as an ordering principle.

Jean Gerson, in explaining the function of reason in human conduct, imagined reason to be a schoolmistress and the heart and the five senses to be her unruly pupils. In one of his sermons he describes the rational function thus:

Ces VI disciples sont communement en chascune personne entiere et bien ordonnee et doyvent estre reapriz en l'escole de l'ame par le soubz maistre commis du grant maistre Jhesu Crist, lequel je nomme cler soutif Entendement, qui a pour sa compaignie Raison la saige, et leur fille est Conscience la veritable.[29]

Here the two aspects of the rational soul, *ratio* and *intellectus*, are assigned an equal share of the responsibility of disciplining the sensual appetites. They must teach their charges 'vraye doctrine et bonne moeurs' because the heart and senses are by nature 'folz, nices, ignorans, vagues, rebelles et mal endoctrinez a cause du peché originel'. Gerson's allegory is an image of the dramatic inner struggle or psychomachia between the forces of reason and order and the forces of folly and chaos. Indeed, Gerson was not unaware of the dramatic possibilities of the conflict. Around 1380 he wrote a morality play, *Le Coeur et les cinq sens*, based on the same allegory.[30] The dialogue is not called a morality play in the manuscripts – we seem to be at the very beginning of the morality tradition – but it dramatizes the same morality world that will characterize the genre until the appearance of hybrid forms in the sixteenth century.

In Gerson's play, God confers upon Raison the task of teaching good conduct to the six indocile students. She teaches the lesson, but no sooner does she relax her attention than the students rebel and flee to the school of iniquity. They are ultimately called back by Conscience, but not before a foul-smelling pile of sins has accumulated in the schoolroom. The sins can be disposed of only through repentance and confession. The play ends with Conscience accusing each of the shame-faced pupils of the misdeeds for which he is responsible. We should note that for the purposes of the play Gerson excludes the philosophical distinction between *intellectus* and *ratio*, since Entendement does not appear in the play at all. In the sermon, Raison was the spouse of Entendement and Conscience was their daughter. In the play, Raison represents the whole rational soul, including Entendement, and is called the spouse of God. Again, Conscience is the daughter. This, then, is the sense in which reason becomes the dominant characteristic of the morality world.

Let us compare the world of Gerson's morality play with the fictional world of another play based on the same subject: *La Farce des cinq sens de l'Homme*. The characters include L'Homme and his five senses, except that a character named Les Piedz has replaced the sense of smell with the power of locomotion – possibly for dramatic reasons. The final character in the play is Le Cul, who is the source of the dramatic conflict. The play opens in a mood of harmony and tranquility. L'Homme thanks God for having given him his five senses:

J'ay mes cinq sens qui nullement
De moy bien servir ne sont las.
Si vueil continuellement
Avecq eux tous prendre soulas. (p. 300)

He then calls his senses to share the pleasures of a banquet with him. They prepare the feast and proceed to eat, drink, and sing together in idyllic harmony. At this moment Le Cul rouses himself from the shadows to complain of being excluded from the banquet and demands that he be numbered among the senses so he can participate in the festivity. An acrimonious debate ensues between Le Cul and the five senses, in which L'Homme takes virtually no part. Soon the verbal thrusts become physical and Le Cul is struck by Les Mains. He then retreats to his fortress and bars all passage in or out. At this point L'Homme is seized with a violent colic, but can gain no relief because Le Cul has barred the door to the *retraict*. The five senses lay siege to the redoubt, but the siege is repulsed and two of the senses are 'wounded' by being covered with excrement. Ultimately L'Homme makes peace with Le Cul and admits him to the company of the senses.

Les Mains is forced to serve and take care of Le Cul for the rest of his life.

What strikes one immediately about this farce is how closely its plot resembles that of a morality play, particularly those plays such as *L'Homme Juste et l'Homme Mondain* in which the virtues and vices engage in pitched battles. It even contains the topos of the besieged castle common to moral literature and dramatized in the English morality, *The Castle of Perseverance*. Indeed, the play calls itself a *farce moralisée*, but we must be cautious in our interpretation of this term. Petit de Julleville considered all plays so designated to be morality plays 'qui se confondent presque avec les farces et les sotties'.[31] He therefore catalogued and discussed them together with the farces. This is probably the reason he considered the morality to be a comic genre. He preferred, apparently, to see the serious moralities as exceptions within the morality genre than to see the allegorized *farce moralisée* as a type of farce having no generic relation to the morality play. But in fact there is a clear generic distinction between the two kinds of plays. The word *moralité* had been used since the twelfth century to designate a moral teaching or doctrine. Both moral treatises and literary works embodying moral teaching (often through allegory) were called *moralités*. When such teaching came to be dramatized in the late Middle Ages, the plays were quite naturally called *moralités*. The verb *moraliser*, however, in the fourteenth century developed the meaning 'parler par allégorie'. The adjectival form *moralisée* meant 'comportant une explication allégorique; interprété de façon non littérale'.[32] A *farce moralisée*, therefore, is not a morality play, since that genre implies a serious lesson in moral behaviour, but a farce in which the characters are allegories. Specifically, the farce of the *Cinq sens de l'Homme* resembles the morality play, not because it is generically related to that form, but because it is a parody of the morality play. The generic differences between the two plays dealing with the five senses will become clearer as we examine the fictional world of each.

Not only is there no character named Raison in *Les Cinq sens de l'Homme*, but the notion of a morally ordered world is not even implied. There is no superior moral standard for which the characters should aim; there are no supernatural powers able to reward good and punish evil. The only powers in the play reside in the characters themselves. Even the kind of psychological insight that the morality achieves by allegorizing man's inner functions is not possible in this

play because only the external senses are represented. What in the
morality plays is called a psychomachia is here transformed into a
physiomachia as the five senses, the sources of physical pleasure,
struggle against the unwelcome intruder. There is no moral choice to
be made; for the most part characters react automatically rather than
after mature deliberation. There is no metaphysical opposition
between good and evil; there are only the physical polarities of
pleasure and pain, comfort and discomfort.

The husband in the farce of *Jeninot* expresses the general attitude of
farce characters toward pleasure and pain:

> Pourquoy fault il tant de tourment souffrir
> En ce monde pour avoir seulement
> La pauvre vie et a la fin mourir?
> Bref, cela n'est point plaisant. (p. 289)

His desire to make life more comfortable is the prelude to the hiring of
a servant; but, as one would expect in the farce world, it is also the
prelude to disaster. The servant turns out to be a consummate fool. In
Les Cinq sens de l'Homme, which opens with the preparations for a
sumptuous banquet, the senses are doing all they can to make
L'Homme more comfortable. While eating and drinking, they sing a
song that expresses the ideal of pleasure and comfort in the farce
world:

> L'Homme a tant lyesse chere
> Qu'il employe ses cinq sens
> A faire joyeuse chere,
> Car il est de peu contens.
> Il ne vise pas aux despens,
> Ne a amasser grant richesse.
> Fy d'avarice qui ard gens;
> Il n'est tresor que de lyesse.
>   L'HOMME
> Vive soulas! Vive largesse!

Compare this to a speech on the same subject – pleasure – from
L'Homme Juste et l'Homme Mondain. Oultrecuydance is attempting
to lure Homme Mondain into a life of sin by convincing him to
abandon the moral guidance of Raison:

> Se ma doctrine veulx tenir
> Tu vivras en felicité.
> Tout plaisir veult de moy venir
> Sans aucune perplexité. (f.vi.v)

Not only is pleasure – that is, the pleasure of the senses – equated with
sin, but it is also unalterably associated with a doctrine opposed to the
teachings of Raison. Homme Mondain must choose between the two
doctrines. In order to trick him into choosing the pleasure of the senses,
Oultrecuydance inverts the moral values of the two systems, calling
him a fool for listening to Raison:

Es tu fol et mys hors du sens
Comme une povre beste sans
Entendement, qui ne scait riens?
Avec Raison, soucy tu sens. (f.vi.v)

This is obviously a reversal of Raison's argument in which the
functions of the rational soul had been equated with reason and
therefore with good, and the functions of the sensitive soul – the five
external senses – had been equated with folly and evil. By contrast,
pleasure is the norm in the farce world. Farce characters live in a world
governed by sensual desires and unconstrained by the requirements of
reason. Actions within the farce world itself are therefore neither good
nor evil. If, however, we view the farce world from the broader
perspective of the whole moral system, it will be seen as a metaphor of
moral folly, an image of what the real world would be like without the
guiding rudder of reason. It is from this perspective alone that evil may
be imputed to social institutions in the allegorical farces.

The ancient Greeks, with their keen sense of fate, conceived of life as
being either comic or tragic. Greek drama, therefore, represented life
as either comedy or tragedy. The Middle Ages, dominated by the
Christian concepts of sin and free will, conceived of humans as being
either moral or immoral. Medieval drama, therefore, represented man
as either rational or irrational. The Middle Ages also created a third
dramatic genre, the history play, in which order and chaos, reason and
folly, good and evil contended with each other in a cosmic struggle
until the final victory of the forces of good at the end of time. The
ancient Greeks had an analogous view of the world, but it was
expressed in epic song rather than in dramatic representation. It is the
function of fiction, however, to analyse reality and to break cosmic
wholes into their constituent parts. The fictional genres, therefore,
represent the world as being either under the dominion of reason or
under the dominion of folly. This moral paradigm is encountered
again and again in the philosophy, the literature, and the moral
treatises of the Middle Ages.

There is an *exemplum* among the *Contes moralisés* of Nicole Bozon that tells of a wise man and a fool, who were travelling together, when they came to a fork in the road. The wise man suggested they take the road to the right, but the fool insisted they go to the left. The wise man consented and they took the road to the left, whereupon they were captured, beaten, and robbed by thieves. Bozon interprets the moral thus: 'Ces deus compaignons sont cors et alme; le quarfouke de la veie si est frankes arbitrement a prendre bien od mal, ou la alme sovent se assent a mal par atret de la char'.[33] This is a succinct and accurate description of the moral world dramatized in the morality plays. Every human act is a fork in the road requiring a moral choice. Some of the plays represent Franc Arbitre on the stage as a morally neutral allegory ready to assist Everyman in his choice of road. But whether or not Franc Arbitre is present as a dramatic character, free will is always part of the morality world, as well as the fork in the road – that is, the necessity to choose. If, however, we remove the wise man from the paradigm, leaving only the fool and his kind, then the world and the genre both change. We move from the rational order of the morality world to the comic chaos of the farce world.

Another index of the distinction between the two worlds of farce and morality play is the difference in the representation of time in the two genres. As is often the case, however, the topos of time (*argumentum a tempore*) is closely related to the topos of place (*argumentum a loco*). Among the topoi of place that the Middle Ages inherited from Antiquity was that of the *locus amoenus* – the pleasance or garden of delight.[34] This could be either an idealized natural garden, where time brings things to fruition, or a mythical garden of perpetual spring, where time has been suspended. We find the mythical garden in the *Roman de la Rose*, where Guillaume de Lorris calls it 'le lieu plaisant' (117), and in the *Jeu d'Adam*, where the opening stage directions describe the Garden of Eden as an 'amenissemus locus'. In such timeless gardens everything is suspended in the state of greatest desirability: the rose is perpetually in the bud and the fruit is forever at full ripeness. But the unstable link between desire and satisfaction is precisely the weakness that the myth exploits, for the nature of desire is at odds with timelessness. When human desire is introduced into the garden, then the rose must be picked and the fruit must be eaten. The result is a fall from the garden of perpetual delight into the cycle of sowing and labour and harvest, into the wasteland of aging and death; in short, a fall into time.

The farce world is the antithesis of the terrestrial paradise. We have already noted the frequency of infernal imagery in the farce, which relates it to the fallen world, but there is another antithetical relationship between the farce world and the *locus amoenus*. Each in its own way is an enclosed space. The mythical garden is an enclosure from which time is excluded, but where fruition is perpetual. Time cannot be introduced into the garden without disastrous consequences, and taking possession of its fruit is a temporal act. After L'Amant plucks the Rose, he wakes from his dream and the garden vanishes. When Adam and Eve eat the fruit, they taste morality, which is a consequence of time, and are expelled from the garden. The farce world is an enclosure in two senses. Most of the plays, because they deal with domestic themes, take place in the interior of a house. Note, for example, the frequency of the locational referent, *ceans*. In some literary genres the house is a symbol of domestic virtues, but in the farce it is an antithetical transformation of the *locus amoenus*, brought about by the need for protection against the hostile elements in a fallen world. The protection that it affords in this context, however, is illusory, for the farce world is a temporal enclosure where time brings nothing to fruition. We shall examine this from another perspective in the final chapter.

The other sense in which the farce world is an enclosure is that, being an image of the fallen world, it is an endless cycle of desire, deception, and illusory satisfactions. Just as it is difficult to enter the timeless plenitude of the *locus amoenus*, so it is difficult, if not impossible, to escape the closed cycle of fruitless agitation in the farce world. Escape is possible, in fact, only with aid from outside the enclosure, only with the appearance of a saviour–hero who can break the bonds of temporal desire. Where this happens, the whole farce world is liberated and we move into a completely different genre. In this light we can see how natural it must have seemed to medieval playwrights to use the farce world in other genres as a representation of the fallen world of man. *The Second Shepherds' Play* is not a farce, because the saviour–hero appears at the end, bringing God's grace and the hope of salvation to those trapped in the sterility of a world without grace. Yet the first part of the play, considered apart from the whole, is indistinguishable from a farce. We have already seen why *L'Aveugle et le Boiteux* is not a farce; but again we note how easily the farce world becomes a metaphor of man's sinful state before the miraculous coming of grace.

The relationship between the farce world and the *locus amoenus* is further evidenced by a kind of nostalgic memory of a utopian existence. Bon Temps is pictured as belonging to the past, and any expectation of his return is a delusion. There is occasionally a portrait of the ideal wife or a sketch of what marriage must have been like in a golden age. In the farce of *Le Savetier et le Moyne*, for example, the Savetier describes his wife in the following terms:

Elle vous a ung corps tant gent,
Ung nez faictifz, bouche riant,
Et est faicte comme de cire.
Et si ne demande que de rire;
Si je vueil plourer, elle pleure.
Rire et plourer tout a une heure,
Je fais d'elle ce que je veulx. (110–16)

As one would expect in the farce world, however, this turns out to be part of a deception that enables the Savetier to escape an expected beating from his irascible wife. A final example of this nostalgia for a better world is found in the farce of *Resjouy d'Amours*. At his first encounter with Tendrette, Resjouy greets her with an elaborate speech in which he invokes Venus, Pallas, and Juno as tutelaries of the love, wisdom, and riches he finds in her. These three figures were also associated with the *locus amoenus*. In a manuscript of the *Echecs amoureux* there is a miniature depicting a walled garden of earthly delights, at the door of which Nature stands holding the key. Inside we see a nude Venus holding a mirror, symbolizing the amorous life. Beyond her are the figures of Pallas and Juno, who symbolize the active and the contemplative life.[35] Again, in the farce the three goddesses are invoked as part of an amorous deception. Such portraits and allusions in the farces are but wistful reminiscences of a long-lost ideal state. They are half-remembered dreams of paradise in the fallen world of the farce, where time is but an endless cycle of sterile repetitions.

The representation of time in the morality world is quite different. We saw in the previous chapter that the morality play combines the topoi of the psychomachia and the pilgrimage, forming a new genre that is more than the sum of its two components. The added dimension is largely attributable to the way time functions in the morality world. Here, too, time and place are related. The psychomachia is a timeless struggle within the soul of man. The soul is not a place in the same sense as the *locus amoenus*, yet it is metaphorically the site of the

struggle, which we may call by analogy the *locus certaminis*. Time is
excluded in the sense that the contention between good and evil is the
consequence of an eternal opposition. Unlike the thematic antecedents
of the farce world, where we saw a fall from one type of enclosure to
another, the morality world opens up with the addition of the infinitely
extendable linear topos of the pilgrimage. While the psychomachia
lays emphasis on man as the arena of the conflict, the pilgrimage takes
him out of himself and makes him a spectator of the same conflict
between good and evil. Sometimes, like Dante, the pilgrim is witness to
the struggle in others; sometimes, like Guillaume de Digulleville, he
sees himself projected into the struggle in a dream.

In the morality play, however, the two patterns are combined to
form a quite different generic structure. Because the conflict between
good and evil that Everyman is witness to occurs within himself, he is
obliged to take part and to become an actor in the conflict. He must
choose, therefore, between good and evil, and he knows that his choice
has future consequences. The morality play is in a sense a mimesis of
the fallen world, but unlike the farce, it is not a closed world. The
pilgrimage, as an allegory of life, provides an exit and a goal at the end.
As Raison instructs Chascun in the *Moralité du Lymon et de la Terre*:

Tousjours il te convient scavoir
Que la vie n'est q'ung voyaige
Dont le monde est ung passaige. (a.iv.v)

Time in the morality world is not therefore endlessly repetitious, nor
does it encourage one to look back with nostalgia to a lost past. Instead,
it is oriented toward the future, toward a utopia or heaven that has not
yet been attained. Time is productive in the morality world, bringing
the acts of the protagonists to fruition at the end. Bien Advisé stresses
the progress toward a goal: 'Tousjours tendons a nostre fin; /
Tousjours sommes en mouvemens', while Mal Advisé alludes to the
obligation to act: 'Prenons le temps comme il viendra' (a.iii.r). At the
end of the play the latter accepts responsibility for the choices he has
made:

J'ay mis mon temps et ma saison
Sans juste cause et sans raison . . .
J'ay gasté mon temps follement. (h.vi.r)

Meanwhile, Confession commends Bien Advisé for his good actions:

Vous avez vostre temps usé
Tousjours a mener bonne vie. (i.ii.r)

We see, then, that the psychomachia is a conflict of principles abstracted from time and space, while the pilgrimage is a moral progression given a geographic projection. The morality play, in combining the two, minimizes the spatial projection and substitutes a kind of temporal geography – that is, the stages the characters reach in the pilgrimage of life are more significant in their temporal aspect than in their physical location. Time is no mere episodic sequence, but an organic development in which moral choices come inevitably to fruition.

We began this chapter with the question as to whether or not *La Farce du cuvier* should be read allegorically as if it were a kind of morality play. I have attempted to show that the farce and morality genres represent two fictional worlds so far apart that at no point do they coincide. Occasional resemblances in such things as subject matter are superficial and are not generically relevant. I have also attempted to show that all of medieval drama represents a moral universe, reflecting in some way the ethical norms of the society, but that there are decisive differences in the ways that each genre depicts that universe. The moral norm is explicit in the morality play, being directly expressed on both levels of dramatic discourse: Raison teaches Homme Pecheur, for example, the difference between right and wrong within the fiction, while the playwright teaches the audience the same lessons by means of his allegory. By contrast, the moral norm is implicit in the farce, being indirectly expressed on only the second level of dramatic discourse. There are neither moral lessons nor moral sanctions from higher powers in the farce world, but farce playwrights did reinforce certain of society's norms by negative examples. *Le Cuvier* clearly represents an amoral world and it is certainly a negative example of how to run a household, in terms both of Christian morals and social ethics. As such, it falls squarely within the farce genre. It does, however, have an explicit moral statement at the end, for which there are at least two explanations.

Medieval writers had a penchant for adding explicit moral conclusions to works whose moral implications may have been obscured by too much indirectness. It should be remembered that many of the stories used in the farces, *fabliaux, contes,* and *nouvelles* were taken from a constantly circulating body of world folk tales and were not necessarily medieval or even European. Stories carried by travellers from one part of the globe to another would reappear at different times, in different cultural contexts, and in different genres.

When such tales were used in medieval genres, they were embedded in the allegorical–moral traditions of writing prevalent at the time. Thus when there was conscious moral reflection on a story, it would appear, not as an integral part of the plot, as in the morality plays, but as a supplemental moral conclusion. Many fabliaux, for instance, conclude with an explicit statement of the moral to be drawn from the tale. In order for a playwright to draw a similar moral from a farce, he must have the actors step outside the dramatic fiction and address the audience directly. This is precisely what happens at the end of *Le Cuvier*.

The other explanation for the explicit moral at the end of the play has to do with the nature of the hero. One of the functions of the hero in all of literature and drama is to mediate between the social group comprising the audience of the work and a metaphysical entity important to that group: fate, providence, honour, society, and the like. In ironic–satirical genres like the farce, however, there is no hero – no one capable of such mediation. The farce, as we have seen, is a closed world in which the neutralization of conflicts within the plays replaces the mediational function of the heroic genres. There is no hero to create the conditions for the establishment of order; instead, the farce can only neutralize the threat of disorder. Occasionally there are farce husbands who re-establish order and authority in their households, as Jaquinot does at the end of *Le Cuvier*, but these are pseudo-heroes. Jaquinot regains his authority by ruse and trickery, not by the strength and sacrifice required of a real hero. Other husbands sometimes re-establish their authority by physical force, meaning the *bâton*; but this is the pseudo-authority of forced submission rather than the real authority willingly granted to the hero because he has earned it. All such situations, which might at first glance seem to teach moral lessons in a way similar to the morality plays, clearly belong to the irrational world of the farce. 'Ou force a droict, raison n'a lieu', says a character in *Les Quatre Ages* (p. 15). Again, we see that *Le Cuvier* falls squarely within the farce world, and for Jaquinot to make an explicit moral statement at the end, he had to step out of that fiction into the real world of his early sixteenth-century audience.

Notes

[1] Jean-Charles Payen, 'Le "cuvier": farce allégorique?', *Revue d'Histoire du Théâtre*, 25 (1973), 257.

[2]Payen, p. 260.

[3]Lewicka, *Etudes*, p. 9.

[4]Léon Lefebvre, *Histoire du théâtre de Lille de ses origines à nos jours*, I (Lille: Lefebvre-Ducrocq, 1907), 97.

[5]Georges Lecocq, *Histoire du théâtre en Picardie depuis son origine jusqu'à la fin du XVIe siècle* (Paris: H. Menu, 1880), p. 138.

[6]Emile Picot, *Répertoire historique et bibliographique de l'ancien théâtre français*, a manuscript in the Bibliothèque Nationale: Nouv. Acq. Fr. 12633, fol. 444.

[7]Henri Clouzot, *L'Ancien Théâtre en Poitou* (Niort: L. Clouzot, 1901), pp. 325–26.

[8]Petit de Julleville, *Répertoire*, p. 343.

[9]Petit de Julleville, *Répertoire*, p. 349.

[10]Ida Nelson, *La Sottie sans souci* (Paris: H. Champion, 1977), p. 8.

[11]Emile Picot, *Pierre Gringore et les comédiens italiens* (Paris: Morgan et Fatout, 1878), p. 25.

[12]Alexis Dubois, *Récréations de nos pères aux XVe et XVIe siècles* (Amiens: L. Challier, 1860), p. 11.

[13]Petit de Julleville, *Répertoire*, p. 361.

[14]Raymond Lebègue, 'Tableau de la comédie française de la Renaissance', *Bibliothèque d'Humanisme et Renaissance*, 8 (1946), 300.

[15]Petit de Julleville, *Répertoire*, p. 383.

[16]Christine de Pisan, *L'Avision*, p. 163.

[17]Eugénie Droz and A. Piaget, eds., *Le Jardin de plaisance et fleur de rhétorique*, vol. II, Introduction et notes (Paris: E. Champion, 1925), pp. 45–48.

[18]Ernest Langlois, ed., *Recueil d'arts de seconde rhétorique* (Paris: Imprimerie Nationale, 1902), p. 218.

[19]Pierre Fabri, *Le grand et vrai art de pleine rhétorique*, ed. A. Héron, I (Rouen: E. Cagniard, 1889), 37.

[20]Sebillet, p. 165.

[21]Du Bellay, pp. 125–26.

[22]Ernst Kris, *Psychoanalytic Explorations in Art* (New York: International Universities Press, 1952), pp. 212–13.

[23]Kris, p. 216.

[24]Lintilhac, II, 271.

[25]Howard Mayer Brown, *Music in the French Secular Theatre, 1400–1550* (Cambridge, Mass.: Harvard University Press, 1963), pp. 169–80.

[26]Konrad Schoell, *Das komische Theater des französischen Mittelalters* (Munich: Wilhelm Fink, 1975), p. 34.

[27]Thomas Aquinas, *Summa Theologiae*, I, 79, 8.

[28]C. S. Lewis, *The Discarded Image* (Cambridge: Cambridge University Press, 1964), pp. 158–59.

[29]Robert Bossuat, 'Jean Gerson et la moralité "du coeur et des cinq sens." ' *Mélanges de philologie romane et de littérature médiévale offerts à Ernest Hoepffner* (Paris: Les Belles Lettres, 1949), pp. 352–53.

[30]Bossuat, pp. 356–60.

[31]Petit de Julleville, *La Comédie*, p. 50.

[32]Wartburg, *FEW*, s.v. *moralis*.

[33]Nicole Bozon, *Les Contes moralisés de Nicole Bozon*, ed. Lucy Toulmin Smith and Paul Meyer, SATF (Paris: Firmin Didot, 1889), p. 52.

[34]Ernst Robert Curtius, *European Literature and the Latin Middle Ages* (Princeton: Princeton University Press, 1967), pp. 195–200.

[35]Jean Seznec, *The Survival of the Pagan Gods* (New York: Pantheon, 1953), pp. 107–08.

CHAPTER IV

Sub-genres of farce and morality play

Having established the thesis that the fundamental differences between the farce and morality worlds provide the grounds for a valid generic distinction between them, let us move on to the problem of delineating sub-genres within each of the two broad categories. Emile Picot, in an attempt to classify all morality plays according to genre, proposed the following six categories: mystical; polemical; satirical and facetious; concerning women; concerning children; and historical. The major flaw in this classification, which is immediately evident, is that the categories are not mutually exclusive. This, of course, is always the result when subject matter (women and children) and modes of writing (satire) are juxtaposed in the same classificatory paradigm. Picot was not, however, unaware of the problems that his classification entailed: 'Nous ne prétendons pas que nos divisions soient parfaites, ni que telle pièce que nous rangeons parmi les moralités satiriques ne puisse pas être aussi bien placés parmi les moralités historiques'.[1] Picot's trial classification was no doubt helpful as a starting point, but in order to avoid ambiguity, one must identify categories that are mutually exclusive. I propose that we begin our classification by discriminating between morality plays whose protagonists are representations of human beings such as Chascun and morality plays whose protagonists are personifications of non-human entities such as Eglise. We may call the one class personal moralities and the other institutional moralities. Not only do the two classes not overlap in this regard, but there is more than just a difference in types of protagonists, as we shall see.

We have already discussed a number of the personal moralities and their characteristics. They include the plays, such as *L'Homme Pecheur* and *Le Lymon et la Terre*, that trace the career of the human protagonist from birth to death on the pilgrimage of life. We have seen that he must make moral choices at frequent intervals along the way, and that he sometimes chooses good and sometimes evil. A few plays, such as *Bien Advisé et Mal Advisé* and *L'Homme Juste et l'Homme Mondain*, turn this ambivalence into two characters, one who always chooses good and one who always chooses evil. Even so, the characters are not predestined, since a choice must be made at each moral juncture. The plays mentioned so far all dramatize the whole of life's pilgrimage from birth to death, but most personal moralities incorporate only a segment of the journey or only an aspect of man's moral condition. The main character of *Le Gouvert d'Humanité* is a young man and the principal vice is Luxure. There is no attempt to treat other stages of life in this play. *Les Blasphemateurs du nom de Dieu* treats only a segment of adult life, which leads to death for two of the blasphemers; the other two repent and are spared. This play, however, narrows the moral scope to a single, quite specific vice, which is reflected in the names of the characters: for example, Le Blasphemateur, L'Injuriateur.

A group of personal moralities treats the question of childhood or, more specifically, parental responsibilities toward children, since every wayward child in such plays has parents who fail to apply the strict discipline he needs. The parents in *L'Enfant ingrat* ruin themselves financially in order to give their child every advantage. He then refuses to acknowledge them as his parents because they are poor. He is ultimately brought back to reason by an intervention from heaven. The child in *L'Enfant de perdition* murders his parents for their money, but he remains unrepentant to the end. Both plays are really beyond our period of concern, being printed in 1589 and 1608 respectively. Yet both exhibit a well-defined morality play structure in that each protagonist is led into error and then either repents or not, according to the case. An earlier morality that combines both types of children is *Les Enfants de Maintenant*. The two youths, Finet and Malduict, are led astray by Jabien and Luxure. Malduict repents in the end, but Finet despairs and goes to the gibbet. This follows the pattern of those plays that present simultaneous examples of good and bad moral conduct.

In all the above examples of personal morality plays the protagonist is an abstracted or generalized human figure. Even if he has the name Humanité, as in *Gouvert d'Humanité*, the collective concept is allegorized by means of a single individual who lives through a single

lifetime or part of a lifetime. It is possible, however, for the pilgrimage
of life to be broader than a single lifetime, as is the case in the *Moralité
de Genre Humain*. In this play Genre Humain represents the human
race that has been languishing in the prison of Peché 'Puis .v. ou .vi.
mille ans que je fus nés' (a.ii.r). The moral choice that Genre Humain
made is not represented in the play, but it is referred to many times so
that it is always foremost in the spectator's mind. Genre Humain
laments, for example, as he waits in prison:

> Pour le mors d'une seulle pomme
> Ne suis seullement en fumiere,
> Mais je suis qui tout quicte et somme,
> Privé d'eternelle lumiere
> Et condampné en la taniere
> De Mort qui tout fine et consomme.
> De vie ay perdu la lumiere
> Pour le mors d'une seulle pomme. (a.ii.v)

He has long since repented of his sin, but at this point no saviour has
come to free him from prison. It is the advent of a saviour and the
liberation of Genre Humain that constitute the action of the play. The
historical dimensions of the play are readily apparent, but it is in no
sense a history play. Most of the characters are personified
abstractions – Nature, Secret Divin, Joyeulx Espoir – but those who
are not – La Vierge, Le Filz – act out the meaning and implications of
biblical history rather than the events themselves. *Genre Humain* is
still a personal morality play that sets an example of repentance and
turning away from sin.

At the other end of the scale there are morality plays whose scope is
extremely narrow. In the *Moralité de Langue Envenimee*, for example,
the main character exemplifies the single sin of bearing false witness
against one's neighbour. There is necessarily much repetition or
reinforcement of the lesson against malicious gossip in this relatively
long play of about 2800 lines. Yet it has some unusual features that
should be accounted for in our consideration of genre. In the first half
of the play the author has chosen to stress the psychomachia, including
the preparations for the battle and its aftermath. The two camps are
represented by Langue Envenimee and Danger on one side and Doulx
Parler, Franc Cueur, and Feaulté on the other. These three are
accompanied by Bonne Renommee. The object of Langue Envenimee
is to take Bonne Renommee away from them. In this part of the play
the author presents Langue Envenimee as a genuine vice character –

that is, a non-human personification of one of the sins, whose normal abode is with the devils in hell. She introduces herself as responsible for Eve's disobedience and Christ's crucifixion. Her father is Satan and her mother is Envie. She is the sister of Yvresse, and Jalousie was her nurse. She and Danger, together with the denizens of hell, prepare the attack on the three virtuous characters: 'Nous . . . leur feron grant guerre' (B.iv.r). On the other side there is great anxiety before the assault as Franc Cueur reports:

Cuide que Langue Envenimee
Et Danger ont fait leur armee
Pour nous venir tantost assauldre. (C.iii.v)

The weapons in the battle are vicious lies versus protestations of innocence, but the lies prevail over the truth and Bonne Renommee is lost. The virtuous characters then appeal to heaven for aid in their moment of distress. So far the characters have been non-human abstractions engaged in a traditional psychomachia, but at this point the perspective shifts to the pilgrimage aspect of the morality genre and we see the same characters as representations of human beings who have chosen their route in life. The medieval spectators had this perspective in view from the beginning of the play, since two roads were represented in the decor. At one point, as the vices approach, Feaulté cries:

Danger, fuy toy de ceste voye;
Et la faulce Langue Enragee,
Va t'en bien loing de nostre voye. (C.iv.r)

In the second half of the play, God sends his archangel, Michael, to aid the afflicted and punish the wrongdoers. Franc Cueur, in an act of repentance, admits that they erred in not immediately fleeing the scandal brought by Langue Envenimee, as Bonne Renommee had urged them to do. We see them here as human characters who made a moral choice and suffered the consequences of their choice. Much more impressive, however, is the punishment of Langue Envenimee, who is struck dead and condemned to hell by the archangel. She then appears in hell as Anima, suffering the torments of the damned. Here we see a completely human character, who repents too late of having chosen the route to Malle Fin. Satan is no longer her father, but her 'maistre d'escolle/Qui m'aprenoit tant de mal dire' (F.ii.r). Her human father is worthy only of her curses:

Tous mes amis et mes parens
Si soient dampnez en cest enfer,
Et mon pere principalement,
Car il me devoit chastier.
Le feu d'enfer le puisse ardre! (F.iv.r)

By the end of the play the spectators see Langue Envenimee, not as an abstract vice, but as a real person punished for the sin of slander. The play as a whole, then, in spite of some unusual features, belongs to the sub-genre of the personal morality.

In another play of narrow scope, the *Moral joyeulx du Ventre*, the main character is an organ of the body rather than a whole person. Again, this type of representation is only a dramatic device to reduce the scope of moral concern so that the spectators can more easily focus on the single sin of gluttony. Here, too, at the beginning of the play Ventre more resembles an allegorical vice character than he does a human character. His actions, in fact, are reminiscent of the comic posturing of the vice in English morality plays. Eventually his outrageous over-indulgence has the effect of reducing his companions – Jambes, Coeur, and Chef – to a somnolent stupor. Their many prayers to heaven are heard, however, and Ventre, seeing the results of his sin, repents and begs forgiveness. He finally realizes that 'les membres divisés/D'avec le corps sont rendus inutilles' (p. 23). Repentance is, of course, a personal act; and a play in which the main character repents of his sins falls clearly within the sub-genre of the personal morality. There are three traits that all personal morality plays share: 1) there is at least one human protagonist, who is usually represented as a whole person, though occasionally as an organ of the body; 2) the protagonist makes moral choices in the eternal struggle between good and evil, where he may be confronted by the whole array of virtues and vices or tempted merely by a single sin; 3) the moral choices are made in a temporal sequence representing the pilgrimage of life, which may span an entire lifetime or confine itself to a segment such as youth.

The other class or sub-genre of morality plays is the institutional morality. In these plays the protagonists are allegorical representations of institutions such as the three estates or Eglise. Obviously, institutions do not make personal moral choices, which means that these plays will incorporate a different type of dramatic action. Similarly, the metaphor of the pilgrimage of life is no longer applicable, which means that a different image of temporal progression will obtain. Raison may also appear as a character in this type of play, but her function is to guide institutions rather than individuals. Her opening speech in the *Moralité des trois estatz reformez par Rayson* explains a great deal about the nature of the institutional morality:

Je suis Raison par tout nommee,
De tous preudommes destree,
Qui jadis chascun gouvernoit.
Loix et coustumes ordonnoit,
Qui bien ont esté mainteneues,
Et quant a present, sont perdues.
Chascun fait a sa voulenté;
On n'a cure de verité.
Qui prent l'autruy, soit droict ou tort,
Le foible est mengié du fort;
Qui plus en prent, plus est eureulx.
Le Monde est si mal eureux
Qu'il en est pouvre devenus.
Les troys estatz si sont perdus,
Ilz ne se scavent gouverner. (a.i.v)

We are here in the same world that is portrayed in the personal morality: moral standards are in force and there will be an ultimate accounting – 'Dieu les en pugnira', says Clergie of those who pillage the church. But institutions do not act in the same way as individuals. There are no individual sins and there can be no personal repentance for wrongs perpetrated by an institution. Instead, we see in the above speech that institutions (laws, customs) decline or degenerate over a long period of time. The cause is not a single incident, but a gradual accumulation of wrongs by different people at different times until eventually the whole institution has become corrupt. What this type of play deals with, then, is not personal moral choices, but the present debased condition of certain institutions. As institutions decline, Raison is lost and might makes right.

The process of degradation is exemplified in the morality called *Les Quatre Ages*, a dramatization of the ancient myth of the loss of the Golden Age. In the beginning:

Chascun estoyt seigneur et maistre,
Chascun pouvoyt poseder terre,
Tant qu'il vouloyt, sans noysse ou guerre. (p. 5)

But Age d'Argent comes along to give knowledge and experience to the innocent and to construct houses for mankind, who had lived simply and freely in the garden of nature. He is soon displaced by Age d'Arain, who introduces the weapons of war. He in turn is replaced by Age de Fer, who rules the world with deception, fraud, and hypocrisy. At the end of the play, Age d'Or returns to pray for God's vengeance on Age de Fer. At the same time he applies the moral to the members of the audience:

Conclusion, nobles seigneurs,
Sy de bref ne changés vos meurs,
L'ire de Dieu sur vous viendra.
Par quoy je dy en mos expres,
Le jugement de Dieu est pres. (p. 23)

Here lies the key to the lesson taught by the institutional morality. Once an institution is corrupt, it cannot repent as an individual; it can only be reformed. In *Les Tois Estatz*, Le Monde pleads with Raison to reform the three estates:

Je ne scay qui a droit ou tort,
Mais certes, Raison, je suis mort
Se brief remede n'y mectez
Qu'aultrement soyes gouvernez.
Si vous supply, dame Raison,
Que metiez refformacion. (a.iii.v)

In *Envye, Estat et Simplesse* we are given an example of institutional reform when Estat expels Envye from his company.

Dramatic allegory, however, is but symbolic representation. Reform in the real world is a matter of many individuals making moral choices in a collective context. Each member of an institution must change in order for the institution itself to be reformed. This is what Age d'Or meant by 'changés vos meurs'. Moreover, if they refuse to change, then God's wrath will fall on all members of the institution. War, famine, and plague were usually interpreted in the Middle Ages as punishments for institutional and social corruption and as warnings of the need to reform. At the end of Henry du Tour's *Moralité de Paix et de Guerre*, Le Soldat says to the audience: 'Sy Paix desirons recevoir,/Qu'un chascun faice amendement'. The institutional morality dramatized the dynamics of institutional decay and regeneration and, at the same time, presented a moral choice to the audience as a group.

The early adherents of the reform movement in France found this dramatic structure particularly well suited to their efforts to rid the church of corruption. In 1533 Mathieu Malingre wrote a morality entitled *La Maldie de Chrestienté*, which dramatized the illness (i.e., corruption) of Chrestienté, the false cures and deceits of Hypocrisie and Peché, and finally her restoration to health by Le Medecin Celeste. At about the same time appeared a play entitled *La Verité cachee*, which was published in three editions before 1560. In this play the ideas of the reform movement are institutionalized and represented in a character called La Verité, who preaches the truth to Le Ministre, Le Peuple, and Aucun. The new ideas are too radical for Ministre and Peuple, who refuse to give up the comfortable security of the religion to which they are accustomed. Aucun, however, is converted by La Verité and turns away from the errors of a corrupt institution. The actions of the two characters, Aucun and Peuple, one of whom accepts the truth while the other rejects it, strongly suggest the pattern of action in such personal moralities as *Bien Advisé et Mal Advisé*. There is a crucial difference, however. The protagonist of a personal morality represents qualities common to all human beings. Thus every member or potential member of the audience is able to identify with the protagonist as an individual. It is in this sense that Everyman is a truly universal character. Aucun and Peuple, on the other hand, represent groups within human society, separated according to religious beliefs. They are not, therefore, universal characters with which every person can identify, but personifications of institutionalized ways of thinking.

The farce may also be divided into two sub-genres that correspond to the sub-genres of the morality play. We distinguished the latter on the basis of the characters that inhabit the morality world. The same kind of division can be made among the inhabitants of the farce world, where we find types of individual persons on the one hand and personified abstractions on the other. The sub-genre of the farce that corresponds to the personal morality I will call, for want of a better term, the typical farce. This suggests both that the plays so designated belong to the type we commonly think of as farce, and that the characters in such plays are types rather than individuals. In this category we find the conjugal farces (by far the largest group), as well as the school, trade, and courtroom farces. These are the plays in which wives deceive their husbands, in which students are perennially stupid, and in which lawyers smart enough to deceive drapers can in turn be deceived by shepherds.

Names are as meaningful in the typical farce as they are in the allegorical genres, and they provide us with clear indications of character types. The names of characters in these plays fall generally into four categories, of which the first is comprised of proper names. We find a large number of characters with names such as Jehan, Colin, Gaultier, Pierre, Hubert, Jenette, Alison, and Guillemette. Many of these names, especially in their diminutive forms, had secondary, often pejorative, meanings that immediately typified the characters. Jaquet, Mahuet, and Naudet, for example, were types of witless or stupid imbeciles; Huet and Jenin were names for cuckolds.[2] Some farce characters were further typified by the addition of descriptive words to the proper name: for example, Martin Bâton, Robin Mouton, Trubert Chagrinas, and George le Veau.

The second category is comprised of names designating personal relationships, of which the most common are the names identifying a conjugal relationship: Le Mari and La Femme. Sometimes blood relationships are designated: La Mère, Le Fils, La Tante; and sometimes social relationships: Le Voisin, La Commère. Finally, a character who bears a rather special relationship to the married couple is L'Amoureux.

The third category is comprised of names designating a status, profession, or trade. As in the second category, all such names are preceded by the definite article. Here we find, for example: Le Seigneur, Le Capitaine, Le Badin, Le Curé, Le Juge, La Théologienne, Le Savetier, La Laitière, La Chambrière, Le Varlet, and L'Aveugle. Occasionally names of this kind have double meanings, as does Le Ramonneur, and they may also be modified so as to form such names as Le Capitaine Mal en Point.

The fourth category is comprised of names made from descriptive words and phrases. This is one of the devices commonly used in farce to create a character type immediately – a necessity in short, rapid-action plays where character cannot be developed through dialogue. Adjectives are easily turned into proper names, giving us characters such as Cautelleux and Peu Subtille. Adjectives like these with pejorative meanings are usually understood literally, but names based on adjectives with positive meanings are usually understood ironically. Sadinette, which means gracious and gentle, is the name of a woman who tricks both husband and lover. The word also has sexual connotations. Tendrette, which Cotgrave defines as 'tender, young; soone induced',[3] is the name of a young wife who is easily talked into deceiving her husband. L'Avantureulx is the name of a cowardly soldier. Some names are made from adjectival phrases, such as those denoting the perennially impecunious farce characters, Mince de Quaire and Legier d'Argent. Other names are made of participial phrases: Resjouy d'Amours, the golden-tongued gallant, for instance, and Besongnefaicte, the foolish chambermaid. There is a strong tendency in the typical farce to literalize proverbs and common sayings, which occasionally produces unusual names. Lavollee is the bride married in haste in the farce of *Regnault qui se marie a Lavollee*. The two women of *Les Femmes qui font renbourer leur bas* have Espoir and De Mieulx do the work for them because, as one of them explains, 'elles ont espoir de mieulx' (181–82).

A few typical farces have what appear to be allegorical characters in them. In *Les Maraux enchesnez* we encounter a character named Justice, who is apparently supervising the work of the two chained convicts. This, however, makes him more like an officer of justice than a personification of the abstract concept of justice. In *Les Chamberieres* there is a character named Debat, who, like a vice in a morality play, provokes a fight between two chambermaids. The rift is ultimately healed by a Cordelier, and Debat is driven away with blows. Despite the allegorical character, the play clearly belongs to the world of the typical farce, as can be shown by the following comparisons. In *Le Debat de la Nourrisse et de la Chamberiere* the two women are already fighting when the play opens. They are being watched, however, by another servant, Johannes, who takes great delight in the violent altercation, urging them on in asides to the audience. Then, pretending to be a police officer, Johannes tries to arrest the women for disturbing the peace. They recognize him, however, and give him a sound beating. Ultimately they all make amends and end up drinking muscadet from the master's cellar. Though there are some differences, the role of Johannes is remarkably similar to that of Debat. In *Le Raporteur* Le Badin plays the role of the *agent provocateur* and succeeds in involving Le Mari, La Femme, and La Voyesine in a terrible fracas that lasts until they realize who was responsible for the false reports they all heard. Like Debat and Johannes, Le Badin pays for his tricks with a good drubbing. We see then that, while Debat has the appearance of a genuine allegorical character, the role he plays is, at a deeper level, one of the standard roles of the typical farce. One can make a similar case for Barat, who plays the role of farce trickster in *Cautelleux, Barat et le Villain*.[4]

The other sub-genre of the farce, parallelling the institutional morality, is the allegorical farce. In this kind of play the characters are no longer the recognizable human types of the typical farce, but personifications of institutions, social types, or abstract ideas. Such personification allegories cannot be confused with institutional moralities, because the world they portray is unmistakably the farce world of trickery and deception with neither moral sanctions nor an ultimate principle of order. Even though both genres treat some of the same moral problems, the point of view from which the problems are seen is quite different in each case. Institutions and social groups are depicted by both genres in states of moral decline, but the morality play always promises an ultimate accounting, while the allegorical farce can only attack present abuses with satire and ridicule. In the 'brave new world' of the allegorical farce the traditional virtues are rejected by everyone, because it is the only way to survive. The farce of *Bien Mondain* ends on the following chilling note:

Car vous voyez au temps present
Que ung chascun faict comme Cacus
Qui fasoit de vices vertus. (p. 198)

Such plays clearly belong to the farce world instead of the morality world. Furthermore, their allegorical nature provides the basis for a valid generic distinction between them and the typical farces. This is a distinction, moreover, that contemporary writers and printers were aware of, and they frequently differentiated the allegorical farces from the typical farces by entitling the former *farces moralisées* or, less frequently, *sotties*. We will examine shortly the relationship between these two types of allegorical farces.

The characters in the allegorical farces may be divided into three classes of personification. First there is the personification of abstract ideas. In this category we find virtues such as Vertu and Sapience, along with the more numerous vice characters such as Malice, Asnerie, Folle Bobance, and Grosse Despense. There are other abstractions such as Tout, Rien, Bien Mondain, Peu d'Acquest, and Le Temps Qui Court, as well as representations of the various kinds of folly. In the second category we find personifications of institutions, such as Honneur Spirituel and Pouvoir Temporel, and of institutionalized activities, such as Marchandise and Mestier. The third category is made up of what we may loosely call social types. Here we find characters such as Les Gens Nouveaulx, Le Monde, and Chascun. The Chascun of the allegorical farce is different from the Chascun or Everyman character of the personal morality. The farce genre, in effect, requires that he play a different kind of role. Whereas the human protagonist in a morality play is a universalized individual who can and must make personal moral choices, the Chascun of the farce is a collective personification of the kinds of morally corrupt actions that everyone engages in. It is because of this collective or distributive personification that characters in the allegorical farce are frequently divided into groups of two or more: Le Premier Nouveau, Le Second Nouveau, etc.

Perhaps the most striking characteristic of the allegorical farce is the personification of folly. We have already seen that the farce world in general is ruled by folly instead of reason. In the typical farces this means that the characters live by a kind of vulpine ethic, perpetually trying to outwit one another. The allegorical farces, however, are permeated with the concept that all is folly and all men are fools. Not only is folly portrayed in both abstract and concrete representations, but also all the shades of meaning of this complex concept are personified. The world is governed either by pure abstractions such as Folie or Mère Folie, or by foolish activities such as Folle Bobance. Those who are governed, in whatever estate, are fools as well. In *Folle Bobance* three of the characters are: Le Premier Fol, Gentil Homme; Le Second Fol, Marchant; and Le Tiers Fol, Laboureux. Fools run the gamut of possibilities: innocent, simpleminded, brash, mocking, stupid, and vicious.[5] Observers of the world, deceivers and deceived alike, are fools. Folly may be benign or even wise; but frequently institutions, social groups, and the world itself are protrayed as victims of a vicious and malignant kind of folly. In the contentious and often violent times of the late Middle Ages, Folie was seen as 'Mere et nourisse de discors' (*La Folie des Gorriers*, 579). By whatever type of folly people may have been afflicted, it was a certitude in the allegorical farces 'Qu'aujourd'uy Toult le Monde est fol' (*Tout le Monde*, 292).

Following the practice of the late Middle Ages, we may distinguish at least two kinds of allegorical farces: the *farce moralisée* and the *sottie*. At this level of classification it is less certain that unambiguous criteria can be established for a clear generic division between the two kind of plays, but there is a tendency toward differentiation in the plays themselves that must be accounted for. Aubailly groups all the allegorical farces together and calls them *sotties*.[6] Arden draws up a similar list of allegorical farces, likewise calling them all *sotties*.[7] Both are indeed right in grouping such farces together, and one must applaud the effort to distinguish them from the typical farces. I have chosen, however, to call these plays as a class simply allegorical farces in order to make a further distinction between the *farce moralisée* and the *sottie*. Though both sub-genres make use of allegorical and non-referential characters, there is a perceptible difference in their representations of the fictional world – a difference that is signaled by a distinction in the types of fools and folly. The *farce moralisée* represents a world gone wrong; social institutions and people in general are in the grip of a vicious folly from which no one is able to break free. The fools in these plays are vice characters, who are responsible for the degradation of the social and moral order. They are called *fous* or *folles* and their dementia is *folie*. The *sottie*, however, represents a stance apart from the world gone wrong. These plays are often peopled with wise or benign fools, clowns, and acrobats, whose function is to reveal, ridicule, and censure the folly around them. They are called *sots* or *sottes* and their dementia is *sottise*.

In the late Middle Ages and the Renaissance the words *fol* and *sot* both carried a great variety of meanings, including meanings in opposition to one another. Such words can hardly be expected to fit neatly into fixed semantic categories, yet they were not coextensive in meaning. Cotgrave quotes the following proverb (s.v. *fol*): 'Le fol est sot quant et quant, mais tout sot n'est pas fol.' In *Tout le Monde*, when one of the Compaignons sees Tout le Monde approaching in a costume symbolizing the three estates, he tries to decide whether he is a *fol* or a *sot*:

> Ou il est afollé,
> Ou c'est quelque sot avollé
> De nouveau qui vers nous s'adresse. (78–80)

Les Sobres Sots is a dialogue between five Sots and a Badin, in which the Badin attempts to distinguish between *sos*, *fos*, and Badins. He names five kinds of *sos*: 'maleureux'; 'sobres'; 'sos par nature ou par usage'; and 'sieurs d'ais' – the last type being henpecked husbands. A Badin, on the other hand, can be wise; people fear and respect him. The comic bias in favour of Badins is, of course, obvious. He then names seven kinds of *fos*: 'dangereux'; 'joyeux'; 'etourdis'; 'glorieux'; 'subtilz'; 'mutins'; and 'nouveaulx'.[8] The following dialogue illustrates the fact that, even though the distinctions were hard to define, they were perceived as being significant:

> LE .IIe. SOT
> C'est assés des fos disputé,
> Des sos et des badins ausy.
>   LE .IIIe.
> Il est temps de partir d'icy;
> Ce badin nous faict arager.
>   LE BADIN
> Par Dieu, j'oseroys bien gager
> Que la plus part de tous ses gens
> Qui nous sont venus veoir ceans
> Pour escouter nos beaulx propos
> Sont sieurs d'ays ou folz ou sos;
> Prenés lesquelz que vous vouldrés.
>   LE .IIIIe. SOT
> Je croys bien, mais vous nous tiendrés
> Plus sages que badins ou fos,
> Ne ferés pas?
>   LE BADIN
>   Ouy. A propos,
> Je t'ay dict en d'aulcuns pasages
> Que sos ne seroyent estre sages,
> Mais badins le peuent bien estre. (374–89)

In the allegorical farces the characters that are called *fols* tend to be vicious, malignant fools. They personify the great evils of the time: the mad pursuit of money; the insane new policies of the ruling classes. They also personify those who perpetrate such evils to the detriment of Le Monde. Folle Bobance calls an assembly of all fools: 'Je veulx tenir mes troys estas'. Gentil Homme, Marchant, and Laboureux answer her call and these 'meschans folz desservellez', following her counsel, lead a life of wild extravagance. It is not, however, until they reach the state of complete poverty that they see her for the 'diablesse cornue' that she is. In *La Folie des Gorriers*, Folie characterizes herself as:

> Mordent, malicieuse, cuisante,
> Mesdisant, de tous vices plaine,
> Trouble, faulce et inhumaine,
> Triste, ignorante, perverse,
> Rude, cautelleuse, diverse. (571–75)

The characters that are called *sots*, on the other hand, tend to be benign fools. They are clowns, jesters, and acrobats, who observe and ridicule the folly of the world. Their function, like that of the clown, is to peel away the mask of propriety and self-importance in order to reveal the fool beneath. Charles Estienne in his *Paradoxes* (1554) defines *sot* and *sottie* (that is, *sottise*) in the following way:

Le sot ne se sent espoinct de tant d'esguillons de fortune: ne cherche combats à oultrance: n'ha plaid, ne procès, ne querele pour acquerir ou debarre son bien: . . . finablement n'est aucunement subject à personne, et vit en plaine franchise et liberté. . . . La sottie, ainsi que la poésie, est aucunement celeste, et remplist le cerveau de ses supposts d'un esprit de prophetie et fureur divine.[9]

This spirit of prophecy can be found in the plays themselves[10] as the *sots* prepare for the return of Bon Temps and dream of a utopian world where the vices of the present have been swept away.

   The differences between the two kinds of fools can be exemplified by a comparison of two plays that bear some resemblance to one another. The first is the *Farce moralisee des Gens Nouveaulx qui mengent le Monde et le loge de mal en pire*. The three Gens Nouveaulx represent those who come to power with impossible dreams – 'Faisons oyeaulx voller sans elles' – but who only make things worse. They are ignorant of the means of good government; they care nothing for the wisdom of the past; and they seek only personal agrandizement and financial gain. Promising to protect Le Monde from harm, they begin their own systematic pillaging of his resources. By the end of the play, Le Monde has been totally victimized by his rulers and has had to be moved from his home 'en Mal' to a new home 'en Pire'. The other play is the *Sottie des Rapporteurs*, in which the Prince des Sots calls three of his *sots* together to report on the things they have seen in the world.[11] All the evil that they have seen, however, is turned on its head and reported as good:

> LE SECOND
> Nous avons veu chiens a monceaulx
> Qui s'enfuyoient devant les lievres.
>   LE TIERS
> Sergens ne sont plus larronceaulx,
> Ils sont doulx comme jouvenceaulx
> Et ne boyvent plus mais que bieres. (132–36)

The Prince denies the truth of the report, but, as with the wish to make birds fly without wings, the report of hares chasing dogs has already given the audience a signal that the reports to follow are impossibilities. While *Les Gens Nouveaulx* condemns the abuses of the world by dramatizing their evil effects, *Les Rapporteurs* condemns the same evils with perhaps greater force by making the audience continually compare the world they know with the utopian dream of an ideal society.

Because the subject matter and even some of the lines of the two plays are similar, Droz claims that 'Cette sottie est très voisine de la *Farce nouvelle des gens nouveaulx*. . . . Ce sont les mêmes expressions et les mêmes idées'.[12] Harvey also sees this *sottie* as a 'much-altered version' of *Les Gens Nouveaulx*.[13] We have seen in several instances, however, that the same subject matter can be treated in different genres. In this case, as well, what is important is not the content, but the point of view from which the content is perceived. The Gens Nouveaulx are the malicious fools of the *farce moralisée*. They victimize Le Monde in order to feed their own hunger for money and power. By using the world for their own ends, they destroy that which they are supposed to govern. The *sots*, on the other hand, are the benign fools of the *sottie*. They are observers and reporters of the world's evils. They use their mask of folly (*sottise*) to unmask the folly (*folie*) of the world. The real difference between the two plays, therefore, is a difference in dramatic point of view, which is tantamount to a difference in genre. It is this that distinguishes the *farce moralisée* from the *sottie*.

There is one notable exception to this general distinction, and that is the *Sotise du Monde et Abuz* of André de La Vigne. Here the characters are called *sots*, but they are the malicious fools of the *farce moralisée*: for instance, Sot Corrompu, Sot Trompeur, Sot Ignorant, and Sotte Folle. It should be pointed out, however, that La Vigne always works on the borderline of genres. His *Moralité de l'Aveugle et du Boiteux*, as we have seen, makes use of the farce world to represent the state of man before the reception of God's grace. His *Farce du Munyer* takes advantage of devils from a mystery play, who are already in place in the theatre, to stage a farce trick. It is not, therefore, surprising to find the worlds of the *sot* and the *fol* combined in his *Sottise*. The result in each of his plays is not so much a confusing mixture of genres as it is a probing of the limits of each genre. Medieval drama is all the richer for André de La Vigne's constant testing of its generic boundaries.

Another area in which the *farce moralisée* and the *sottie* tend to differentiate themselves is the representation of time. We saw that in the morality plays time brings the actions of the main characters to fruition, whereas in the farces it is repetitive and sterile. In the allegorical farces the sterility of time often takes on the added characteristic of destructiveness. Time in these plays is frequently personified in one of two forms. Bon Temps is the personification of an ideal time or golden age that existed in the past, for whose return everyone fervently hopes. Le Temps Qui Court is the personification of the corrupt and folly-ridden time of the present, which holds the world in its evil grip. It is in this manifestation that time becomes destructive. In *Marchandise et Mestier*, Grosse Despense explains her arrival: 'De par le Temps suis transmise en ce lieu' (p. 262); and Marchandise complains of a kind of economic depression together with inflation that today sounds all too familiar:

Temps Qui Court, ce n'est pas la loy
De nous bailler tout d'une instance
Pou d'Acquest et Grosse Despense;
Cela me faict craindre et doubter. (pp. 263–64)

This concept of time tends to be dramatized in the *farce moralisée* rather than in the *sottie*. The characters of the *sottie* are all aware of the moral havoc wrought by Le Temps Qui Court, but it is in the *farce moralisée* that we actually see time's destructive forces at work. The *farce moralisée* projects all that is good and ideal into the past and portrays a world in the process of moral disintegration. In *Bien Mondain* both Honneur Spirituel and Pouvoir Temporel are attracted by wealth and worldly goods and reject the virtues of the past exemplified by the Nine Worthies:

Laissons la tous ses anciens;
Ce n'est point de present le temps
Que de vertu on vueille user. (p. 194)

Vertu draws the following lesson from this:

Sy des biens voulez largement,
Faire vous fault du Temps Qui Court
En contrefaisant le billourt,
Et que vertu soit mise au vent. (p. 197)

The great evils that Le Temps Qui Court has brought are Folle Bobance and Grosse Despense. Generally it is Les Gens Nouveaulx who sweep away all the old verities and the proven values, which causes Le Monde to sigh: 'Je regrette le temps des vieulx' (*Gens Nouv.*, 269).

Bon Temps is gone from the world of the *farce moralisée*, perhaps never to return. Some characters, however, try to create their own Bon Temps:

FOLLE BOBANCE
Il n'est au monde telle vie
Que gentillement de s'amacer
Tous les biens sans melancolie.
LE PREMIER FOL, GENTIL HOMME
De soy soucier c'est folie.
LE SECOND
Bon Temps aurons se cest temps dure. (202–06)

The three fools, led by Folle Bobance, set out to transform Le Temps Qui Court into Bon Temps. This, of course, is sheer illusion and the height of folly. They end up in the Chasteau Tout y Fault to spend the rest of their days in poverty. In *Faulte d'Argent* three Gallants try to liberate Bon Temps from prison, but they too ultimately fail and Faulte d'Argent keeps her prisoner secure. Time in the *farce moralisée* is infinitely mutable; but it obeys its own laws and cannot be manipulated by fools for their own advantage. In *Mestier, Marchandise et le Berger*, Le Temps appears in a number of guises. At one point he says to the three characters of the title:

Cuydés vous gouverner le Temps
Et en faire a vostre devise? (p. 17)

He explains that the times are what they are because Les Gens have made them so, and he concludes:

Que le Temps ne se changera
Ne jamais ne desbrouillera
Jusqu'a ce que les Gens se changent. (p. 26)

This is the kind of situation that in the institutional morality would lead to a moral reformation; but in the *farce moralisée* the world remains firmly in the grip of Le Temps Qui Court. The question of moral reform, rather than being treated in the dramatic fiction, is addressed directly to the audience, who undoubtedly understood themselves to be Les Gens.

The world itself is not really different in the *sottie*, but we see it through the eyes of a different kind of fool. The *sots* are acutely aware of what is going on in the world, and they criticize and ridicule the *fols* who are responsible for the sorry state of things; but they tend to be somewhat passive and resigned. There is wisdom in this attitude because, as we have seen, those who try to manipulate Le Temps for their own selfish ends are fools of the worst sort. Bon Temps gives sage advice to the presumptuous Gallants in *Faulte d'Argent*:

Gentilz Gallans, endurer fault
Et dire quelque mot pour rire. (258–59)

This is precisely the attitude that *sots* usually take. They fervently
hope that Bon Temps will return, but they will not themselves try to
take charge of Le Temps Qui Court. They have the insight and wisdom
that madness bestows on certain fools, and their function is to stand
apart from the world and heap ridicule on those other fools who have
corrupted it. But this way of changing the world takes time – what
else? – and the *sots* must wait and have patience. The waiting is
strikingly dramatized in the two *sotties* from Geneva, *Les Beguins* and
Le Monde. Modern readers are tempted to feel that waiting for Bon
Temps is very much like waiting for Godot,[14] though we must take
care not to impose our modern sense of cosmic irony on the medieval
texts. The *sots* are confident that patience will ultimately be rewarded.
At the conclusion of the *Sottie de l'Astrologue*, Le Prince counsels his
sots:

Enfans, nous airons patience
Tant que la revolucion
Du cour du temps a l'influence
Aist austre disposicion. (591–94)

Much has been written on the question of whether or not there is a
difference between the farce and the *sottie*. Aubailly has given us an
ample account of the debate,[15] which it is unnecessary to repeat here.
Suffice it to say that there are generally two positions taken on the
matter. Some critics hold that *sottie* and farce are in principle
completely different genres, though some plays may be difficult to
classify. Picot's edition of the *sotties* was based on this assumption.
Other critics hold that there is no generic distinction between farce and
sottie, the only difference between them being a style of acting. Droz
was the principal proponent of this position. I believe, however, that
the generic paradigm set forth in these pages resolves the problem by
placing it in another perspective. If we see the *sottie* as a sub-genre of
the farce, we satisfy our sense that there is a marked difference
between the *sottie* and the typical farce, while preserving the notion
that they both belong to the same folly-ridden world. Thus all *sotties*
are farces, but not all farces are *sotties*. This perspective clears away
some of the ambiguity that has long surrounded Sebillet's often-
quoted description of the farce: 'Le vray suget de la Farce ou Sottie
Françoise sont badineries, nigauderies, et toutes sotties esmouvantes a

ris et plaisir.'[16] The phrase, 'Farce ou Sottie Françoise', has been read by some as equating farce and *sottie*, making them alternate names for a single genre. It should be understood, however, as naming different aspects (or sub-genres) of the French comic genre that Sebillet compared to the Latin 'Mimes ou Priapées' and that he contrasted to the more decorous morality genre. Just as Sebillet did not intend 'Mimes ou Priapées' to designate a single dramatic genre, so, in all probability, he did not equate 'Farce' and 'Sottie'. This new perspective also explains how playwrights and printers saw no contradiction in titles like: *La Farce ou sotie des vigilles Triboullet* and *La Sotie et farce de Estourdi et Coquillart*.

Droz based her position in large part on passages from two plays in her volume of *sotties* from the *Recueil Trepperel*. In *Les Vigilles Triboullet* we are told that the repertoire of the defunct clown included such farces as *Pathelin* and *Poitrasse*. In *Les Coppieurs et lardeurs* a pair of *sots* goes to the shop of Malostru, the copier, to buy a play. Among those considered are the farces of *Pathelin, Poitrasse, and Le Pouvre Jouhan*. For Droz, the fact that *sots* would play in such farces 'prouve d'une façon irréfutable que la distinction que nous cherchons à établir entre la sottie et la farce n'existait pas dans le texte'. From this she was led to believe that 'un même texte pouvait, au gré des acteurs, être farce ou sottie'.[17] Thus when *Pathelin* was played by regular actors, it was a farce; but when it was played by *sots*, it was a *sottie*. By this same logic one would be forced to classify *La Belle Dame sans Mercy*, which was also part of Triboullet's repertoire, as a *sottie* – an incongruous classification, to say the least.[18] If we pursue this position to its logical conclusion, then every work of literature and every drama, if recited by a *sot*, becomes a *sottie*, at which point the word loses all meaning. Thus, in order for the designation *sottie* to remain meaningful, it must be related to texts rather than to performers.

We noted above that the *sottie* as a sub-genre of the farce provided a distinct point of view from which to observe the folly of the world. In fact, the *sottie* was for the late Middle Ages a kind of magic lens that enabled viewers to see beneath the insignia of rank and behind the mask of respectability to the very core of human folly. One of the constant themes of the *sottie* is that Chascun beneath his outer garb is a fool. To illustrate how this worked, we need only compare a scene from a typical farce with a similar scene from a *sottie*. In *La Farce du vendeur de livres* a bookseller shows his books to two women who are offended by the obscenity of the titles and who ultimately refuse to make a purchase. If a medieval audience saw anything beyond the jokes and the comic situation, it was no more than a mild satire on unscrupulous booksellers and prudish women. But virtually the same scene in the *Sottie des coppieurs et lardeurs* takes on an entirely different significance. In addition to portraying two clients dickering with a bookseller to buy a farce, the play also depicts two fools – Teste Creuse and Sotin – arguing with a third fool – Malostru. Though the client–fools find most of the farces too old-fashioned, they finally select *La Farce des oyseaulx*. What the 'magic lens' of the *sottie* revealed to the medieval audience was the folly buried deep in man's nature, ready to corrupt even the most common of human endeavours. Malostru, the bookseller, is a *copieur*, but *copier* also means, according to Cotgrave, 'to flowt, scoffe, deride, mocke'. Nyvelet, the rotisserie owner, is a *lardeur*, but *larder* also means 'to quip, taunt, breake a jeast on'. In this context nothing could be more natural than to talk about farces, since *farcer* means 'to mocke, deride, flout, or gibe at'. The point is that the farces mentioned in this play remain farces, while the 'magic lens' of the *sottie* enables the spectators to see that even actors who play farces can be fools beneath the skin. To call *Pathelin* a *sottie* because a few *sots* in a play consider acting in it is to mistake the fiction of the farce world for the reality of medieval generic distinctions.

Up to this point no mention has been made of a group of works that were always associated with the theatre in the Middle Ages and were also included in the collections of plays made in the sixteenth century. I refer to the dramatic monologues and the *sermons joyeux*. There is no special place in the generic paradigm for these works, because they are not separate genres in the same sense in which the other genres have been defined. The monologue, like the dialogue and the debate, is a technique of presentation rather than a genre. At first sight, the narrative element of some of the monologues might seem to eliminate them from the dramatic genres altogether. Yet they were played on the stage by actors in costume and were obviously considered to be a form of dramatic discourse in the late Middle Ages. We can account for the narrative dimension by seeing the actor as impersonating a narrator on the stage. Several farces (*Les Coquins*, for instance) have scenes in which characters narrate stories. Moreover, the generic divisions of our paradigm have been made along the lines of the fictional worlds represented, not the number of characters involved in the plays. If we consider the monologues from the same point of view, we will find that they too represent various fictional worlds. Most of them belong to the world of the typical farce, but the *Sermon des foulx*, for example, is a monologue that clearly belongs to the world of the *sottie*. The theme of this work, in which the words *foulx* and *sotz* are used interchangeably to designate people infected with folly, is a commonplace of the *sottie: Numerus stultorum est infinitus*. The preacher invites his listeners to prove it for themselves:

Allez chercher du monde les passaiges,
Vous trouverez plus de foulx que de saiges. (p. 214)

He then launches into a catalogue of states and cities in which fools abound. The list includes most of the countries of the known world, but France is described as especially rich in folly. The homilist next finds fools in all the social ranks from pope to printer. One must, of course, number the preacher himself among the fools of the world, but he is the benign observer–fool of the *sottie* rather than the vicious fool of the *farce moralisée*.

Not all monologues belong to the farce world, however. The *Monologue de Memoyre* is spoken by a figure 'tenant en sa main ung monde sur lequel est escript Foy, Espoirance et Charité, [qui] fault estre abillé en deesse' (p. 1). Memoyre introduces herself at the beginning of the monologue:

Qui veult scavoir comme je suys nommee?
Es haultz secretz et bonne renommee
Mainct bon esprit, par veristable histoyre,
Communement me denomme Memoyre,
La seur du sage et mere de science. (p. 3)

Clearly an allegorical figure, Memoyre plays a role related to that of Raison in the morality plays. She describes each of the theological virtues and explains what the world would be without them. She then pleads with her listeners to make these virtues a part of their lives:

Tres chers seigneurs, ces troys comprins en un
Monstre que l'homme en droicte intention
Doibt avoir Foy, Charité en commun
Avec Espoir et sa salvation. (p. 7)

Thus, at the end of the monologue the members of the audience are asked to make the same kind of moral choice that the main character of a morality play must make. Indeed, the *Monologue de Memoyre* belongs to the morality world.

This manner of classifying dramatic monologues and *sermons*

joyeux as moralities or farces is consonant with the descriptive title of
the La Vallière manuscript. The title, which was placed at the head of
the table of contents, reads in part: 'Ensuyt les farces et moralités qui
sont en ce livre tant a un, deulx, troys, quatre, cinq, six et sept
personnages'.[19] Among the 'farces et moralités' thus defined are four
dramatic monologues and four *sermons joyeux*. We may conclude
from this that there is no need to create a separate generic category for
such works. Thus, *Le Monologue du Franc Archier de Bagnolet*, with
its braggart soldier frightened by a scarecrow, is a 'farce à un
personnage'. Likewise *Le Monologue de Memoyre* is a 'moralité à un
personnage', and *Le Sermon des foulx* is a 'sottie à un personnage'.

Now that the whole generic model has been described and explained,
one may more readily visualize the relationships among the genres by
referring to the accompanying table, which includes representative
examples of each genre and sub-genre. As we noted in the beginning,
however, there is no model without anomalies. These will be taken up
in the next chapter.

Notes

[1]Emile Picot, *Les Moralités polémiques* (1887; rpt. Geneva: Slatkine
Reprints, 1970), p. 2.

[2]Halina Lewicka, *La Langue et le style du théâtre comique français des
XVe et XVIe siècles*, Vol. I, *La Dérivation* (Paris: Klincksieck, 1960), 290–91.

[3]Randle Cotgrave, *A Dictionarie of the French and English Tongues*
(1611; rpt. Columbia: University of South Carolina Press, 1968).

[4]Lewicka, *Etudes*, p. 12.

[5]William Empson, *The Structure of Complex Words* (Norfolk, Conn.: New
Directions, n.d.), p. 111.

[6]Jean-Claude Aubailly, *Le Monologue, le dialogue et la sottie* (Paris: H.
Champion, 1976), pp. 552–54.

[7]Heather Arden, *Fools' Plays* (Cambridge: Cambridge University Press,
1980), pp. 169–73.

[8]The reader of Emile Picot's edition of *Les Sobres Sots* in the *Recueil
général des sotties*, III (Paris: Firmin Didot, 1912), 45–77, should be aware
that the editor silently reverses the words *fos* and *sos* in lines 213, 232, 245,
306, 325, and 375. If Picot is attempting to clarify the distinction between the
two types of fools, his emendations are not always consistent with that goal.

[9]Quoted from L. J. N. Monmerqué, ed., *Le Dialogue du Fol et du Sage*
(Paris: Firmin Didot, 1829), pp. 42–43.

[10]Aubailly, *Le Monologue*, p. 435.

[11]In the Droz edition of this play – *Le Recueil Trepperel: les sotties* (Paris:
Droz, 1935) pp. 53–72 – the word *folz* in lines 69 and 73 should read *solz*.

[12]Droz, *Recueil Trepperel*, p. 54.

Late medieval French drama					
Historical genres	**Fictional genres**				
	Morality plays		**Farces**		
	Personal moralities	Institutional moralities	Typical farces	Allegorical farces	
				Farces Moralisées	Sotties
Biblical history: *Le Mystère de la Passion*	*Bien Advisé et Mal Advisé*	*L'Eglise et le Commun*	*Maistre Pierre Pathelin*	*Folle Bobance*	*Les Coppieurs et lardeurs*
Profane history: *La Destruction de Troye*	*L'Homme Pecheur*	*Les Trois Estatz*	*Le Cuvier*	*Les Gens Nouveaulx*	*Les Vigilles Triboullet*
Saints' lives: *La Vie de Saint Martin*	*Les Enfans de Maintenant*	*La Maladie de Chrestienté*	*Le Savetier et le Moyne*	*Les Cinq sens de l'Homme*	*Le Sermon des foulx*
			Le Franc Archier de Bagnolet		

[13]Howard G. Harvey, *The Theatre of the Basoche* (Cambridge, Mass.: Harvard University Press, 1941), p. 178.

[14]Alan E. Knight, 'The medieval theater of the absurd', *PMLA* 86 (1971), 186.

[15]Aubailly, *Le Monologue*, pp. 280–85.

[16]Sebillet, p. 165.

[17]Droz, *Recueil Trepperel*, p. lxviii.

[18]Arden makes the same point in *Fools' Plays* (p. 6), a penetrating study of the allegorical farce, published after the present work had been completed.

[19]Bibliothèque Nationale, MS. Fr. 24341, fol. 2, r.

CHAPTER V

Anomalous titles and hybrid plays

Ideally one should have to look no further than the titles of the plays to determine their genres. In reality, however, the titles have given rise to a great deal of confusion. We postponed examining the generic designations in the titles until all the other evidence could be reviewed. Now, in the light of what we have found, let us proceed to the examination of the titles.

Late medieval play titles were directed mainly to two audiences. First, they contain essential information for actors, directors, or anyone planning to stage a play. Since new plays were not written for every dramatic performance, a *metteur en scène* in search of a play to produce would presumably look through a group or collection of plays in order to select one appropriate for the occasion. He would want to know at least two things at first glance: the type of play – or genre – in order to set up a balanced programme, and the number of characters, in order to match the number of actors available. We know that in England, where actors in small travelling troupes had to double up on short roles, play titles sometimes indicated both the characters and the number of actors required.[1] In the La Vallière manuscript, a collection of plays belonging to the Conards and other groups of Rouen,[2] the texts are preceded by a table of contents in which each title contains all the information that such groups would need to choose plays to fit the occasion and the resources available.

The other audience to which play titles were directed was composed of readers who would buy copies of plays at printing shops or book stalls. The buyer would want to know what kind of play (genre) was contained in the book or pamphlet, whether it was good (*tresbonne*), funny (*joyeuse*), and especially whether it was new (*nouvelle*). Printers would print types of plays that were popular and likely to sell, and would add such adjectives to the titles to entice buyers. Even the La Vallière manuscript adds descriptive adjectives to the titles of most of its plays, which, together with its late date (second half of the sixteenth century), makes one wonder if they might not have been copied from printed texts.

If we now examine the generic designations of the play titles in the light of the paradigm proposed in the preceding chapters, we will notice that the great majority of the plays are exactly the genre their titles designate them to be. Take, for example, the following title that includes a brief plot summary: *Moralité du Lymon et de la Terre qui contraignent par Raison et la Mort Chascun homme humain de retourner a eulx bon gré mal gré apres qu'il a vescu en peché.* This rather lengthy title is followed by the names of the eleven characters. There is no question but that such a play is a morality play. The titles of morality plays do not distinguish between the sub-genres by calling them personal or institutional as we have done, but the distinction is readily apparent either from descriptive titles or from the cast of characters. The above title, for example, obviously describes a personal morality, while the following title is quite clearly that of an institutional morality: *Moralité a deulx personnages, c'est ascavoir l'Eglise et le Commun.*

In regard to the farce we find the same thing to be true. The vast majority of the plays are precisely the genre their titles designate them to be. It should be remembered, however, that the term *farce* is used in the paradigm to designate a broad category comprising several sub-genres. In the titles the single word *farce* designates the typical farce in most cases. Plays belonging to the category of the allogorical farce are usually designated by terms like *farce moralisée, farce morale,* or *sottie.* A few of the allegorical farces are designated by the single term *farce.* This should not, however, be considered an error in genre designation, since all such plays are farces in the broad sense. Nor should it be considered the result of a supposed indifference to questions of genre, since a reading of the whole title, including the cast of characters, will quickly reveal whether the play is an allegorical farce or not. Today we like short titles and therefore tend to abbreviate the play titles for the sake of convenience. But we must not let our own preferences obscure the fact that in the fifteenth and sixteenth centuries long titles were the norm. It was, moreover, a functional norm. Titles usually included the names of characters and even plot summaries because it was the most convenient way then devised of identifying the plays by type or genre and of determining the use to which they might be put. The following title will serve as an example: *Farce nouvelle a cinq personnaiges, c'est assavoir Marchandise et Mestier, Pou d'Acquest, Le Temps Qui Court et Grosse Despense.* A sixteenth-century reader, noting the presence of allegorical figures and the absence of *sots* and clown-like characters, would immediately recognize a play that attacks social abuses. He could readily classify the work as a *farce moralisée* despite the fact that it is called simply a farce.

Even if almost all the titles accurately designate the genres of the plays, there still remain a few anomalies that must be accounted for before a true generic order among the titles can be demonstrated. There are two types of anomalous titles: those with no generic designation at all and those with one or more generic designations seemingly at odds with the nature of the play. Titles of the first type are anomalous only in the sense that relatively few plays lack genre designations. Four such plays are typical farces, and two of these are confession plays: *La Confession Margot* and *La Confession Rifflart.* It may have been felt that the term *confession* was identification enough for farces of this type, which consist essentially of a dialogue between two characters. A comparison with another confession farce lends credence to this view. The title page of this play reads: *Farce nouvelle a deux personnaiges, c'est asavoir le Brigant et le Curé.* Below the title, however, between two woodblock prints, we find a subtitle stating the subject matter of the play: 'La confession du Brigant au Curé'. On the *verso* the title is repeated as *Farce nouvelle du Curé et du Brigant.* Since the combination *Farce de la confession* does not occur, we may suppose that the word *confession* was analogous to a term like *dialogue*, which was used in farce titles such as *Dialogue de Beaucop Veoir et Joyeulx Soudain.* The third farce without a generic designation is *Le Grant Voiage et pelerinage de saincte Caquette.* Here the title was apparently intended to be a parody of titles commonly found in pilgrimage literature, in which case the word *farce* would be out of place. This leaves only *Colin qui loue et despite Dieu* without an apparent explanation for its lack of generic designation. But in this case even the colophon is unusual, stating simply: 'Cy fine Colin'.

The morality plays without a generic designation in the title present us with a somewhat different problem. In the case of the longer morality plays printed as separate books, it seems that the printing medium itself exerted an influence on the form that their titles took. There was a tendency to think of such works in terms of books with book titles rather than in terms of plays with generic designations in their titles. The shorter plays were most often printed in pamphlet form and in the tall *format agenda*, which would be unwieldy for large books. Apparently these brief works, often printed in haste, were made for quick sale at low cost. Therefore, placing as much information as possible on the title page was a good way to foster sales. Books, on the other hand, were more costly. Buyers would presumably examine their contents with care before deciding to expend the larger sums of money required. The title page of one of the longest moralities reads simply: *L'Omme Pecheur par personnages joué en la ville de Tours*. Below the title is the name of the Parisian printer, Guillaume Eustace. Nowhere is the play called a *moralité*. The colophon reads in part: 'A l'onneur et a la louenge de nostre seigneur Hiesucrist . . . a esté fait cestuy livre appellé l'Homme Pecheur'. Eustace, who composed both title page and colophon, was obviously thinking of buyers who read books and not of those who staged morality plays. The same is true of Anthoine Verard, who in 1508 printed the longest of the extant morality plays, *L'Homme Juste et l'Homme Mondain*. There is no mention of genre on the title page. The prose prologue, written by the author for the printed edition, is addressed to the 'lecteurs et auditeurs . . . dudit livre' (a.iii.r). The colophon begins: 'Cy fine ce present livre intitulé l'Homme Juste et l'Homme Mondain'. In this case both the author and the printer are thinking more in terms of books and readers than of the staging of dramatic genres.

Since printing had created a much larger reading public by the early sixteenth century, the longer dramatic works, especially those of a moral nature, were usually printed for private reading rather than for staging. Nicolas de la Chesnaye, who published his *Condamnacion de Bancquet* in a book with three non-dramatic works, explains in a preface to the play why he did so:

Et pour ce que telles oeuvres que nous appellons jeux ou moralitez ne sont tousjours faciles a jouer ou publiquement representer au simple peuple, et aussi que plusieurs ayment autant en avoir ou ouyr la lecture comme veoir la representation, j'ay voulu ordonner cest opuscule en telle facon qu'il soit propre a demonstrer a tous visiblement par personnages, gestes et parolles sur eschaffault ou autrement, et pareillement qu'il se puisse lyre particulierement ou solitairement par maniere d'estude, de passe temps ou bonne dotrine. (i.ii.v)

He then explains that he has included marginal commentaries and references to the sources of his work in order to elucidate the text for the reader. Such glosses would obviously be useless in a stage production. Moreover, the full title of the book, *La Nef de santé, avec le Gouvernail du corps humain, et la Condamnacion des bancquetz a la louenge de diepte et sobrieté, et le Traictié des passions de l'ame*, identifies the four works included in the volume without any reference to genre. The reader of the title page is not even made aware that one of the works is dramatic in form. Finally, while the author explains in the same preface that he wrote the *Condamnacion de Banquet* 'en forme de moralité', it is evident that in his mind this work is only a subordinate part of 'ce livre nommé la *Nef de santé*'. The extent to which the advent of the printed book modified traditional notions of plays as belonging to dramatic genres is a question that merits further study.

One final morality play with no generic designation in the title is *La Cene des dieux*. The modern editors of this play publish it together with the farces of the Trepperel collection, explaining that '*La Cene des dieux* . . . n'appartient ni aux farces ni aux moralités: c'est un des rares exemples que nous ayons de l'ancien théâtre de collège'.[3] The categories 'moralité' and 'théâtre de collège', however, are not mutually exclusive. What we have in this work is a morality play written for a school production and presumably for a student audience. The dramatic fiction manifestly portrays the morality world and not the farce world. It is a rational world with clearly established moral values and unmistakable sanctions against breaking the moral laws. It is a world in which the choice between good and evil is an act of central significance for the fate of humankind. But unlike the morality plays that trace the life of the human protagonist, *La Cene des dieux* portrays only one segment of that life – the moment of judgment before Death is sent to punish human wickedness. In this regard it is like *Everyman*, which deals only with the moment of accounting for one's life before Death strikes its final blow. But, while in *Everyman* we see the rendering of accounts from the human point of view, in *La Cene des dieux* we see the judgment of humankind from the point of view of the astral bodies – the functionaries of God in the court of divine justice. In both plays the human lives have already been lived and the moral choices have already been made. In *Everyman* the presence of the human character is obviously essential to the dramatic action; but in *La Cene des dieux* his physical presence is not required for the judgment to be made. He is, however, dramatically present. The gods make frequent reference to 'genre humain' and La Vie even makes a direct plea to humankind to turn toward God 'Affin que mort ne vous defface/Pour vos pechés, povres humains' (615–16). The effect on the audience is the same as in any morality play. The spectators see themselves as representatives of Genre Humain in need of repentance and reform.

The second category of anomalous titles includes those titles with one, or even two, genre designations that do not fit the plays in terms of our generic paradigm. Some of these genre designations are errors, sometimes deliberately introduced, while others are apparently local variants of the standard designations. The most obvious errors of genre designations are those attributable to printers' changes. The title, *La Moralité du Mauvais Riche et du Ladre*, appears on the title page of a play that has none of the attributes of a morality play. One might suppose that the printer thought of the biblical parable on which the play is based as a kind of moral *exemplum*, yet there is no prologue or epilogue pointing to an allegorical interpretation of the play as we found in *L'Enfant Prodigue*. On the verso of the title page, however, the printer has preserved what must have been the original title of the play: *La Vie et histoire du Mauvais Riche et du Ladre*. Here the generic designations are in complete conformity with the nature of the play.

The same kind of printer's change is found in the *Moralité de Langue Envenimee*, where the title page reads: *Farce nouvelle moralisee a .xiii. personnages*. Yet there is no question but that the play is a morality and not a *farce moralisée*. This is explicitly stated on the verso of the title page, where we find: *Moralité nouvelle a treze personnages*. This generic designation is repeated in the colophon, which begins: 'Fin de la dicte moralité . . .'. It is clear in this case that Trepperel was setting the type for his edition from an earlier printed edition. We know that the most expeditious way to do this was to distribute the pages of a text among several typesetters, who would then reset each page exactly as it was in the previous edition.[4] Trepperel decided, however, to make one change; he wanted a new title page in large type that would attract the attention of prospective buyers. He knew from experience, no doubt, that farces sold better than morality plays, and for that reason changed the generic designation to *farce moralisée*. This, of course, rendered superfluous the title and cast of characters as they were printed on the first page of the old edition. He excised, however, only the cast of characters, leaving the original title and blank space where ordinarily there would be text.

The erroneous genre designation in the title, *Farce moralisee de deux hommes et leur deux femmes*, is also attributable to the printer. The play has no allegorical characters whatsoever, and one has no hesitation in classifying it as a typical farce of the conjugal variety. The correct designation is printed in the colophon: 'Cy fine la farce des deux marys et de leur deux femmes'. The word *moralisee* is printed on the title page where one would expect the word *nouvelle* as is found in most of the other farces printed in the same *atelier* of Barnabé Chaussard. The designation *Farce nouvelle* does, in fact, appear in the identical font in the title of *Folle Bobance*. It was Chaussard's practice in printing title pages to use xylographic blocks of frequent word combinations, rather than to set them each time in movable type. Philipot has already noted this in the case of *Le Cuvier*.[5] The blocks, often with ornate initials, were composed of frequently used word combinations such as *Farce joyeuse*, *Farce nouvelle*, and *Farce moralisee*. These xylographic portions of the titles are found in several styles and fonts throughout the group of plays printed by Chaussard. In the case of the *Farce de deux hommes*, we may easily conjecture that the typesetter reached for a *Farce nouvelle* block, but picked up a *Farce moralisee* block by mistake. Indeed, the same thing probably happened in reverse in the case of *Folle Bobance*. The latter error, however, does not raise the same generic problem as the former. By the seventeenth century the meaning of *farce moralisée* had been lost. The 1619 edition of the *Farce de deux hommes*, also from Lyon and probably based on Chaussard's edition, is given the incongrous generic designation 'Moralité et farce nouvelle'.[6]

There is one other play whose title contains an obviously erroneous genre designation, and that is *La Farce des theologastres*. The play, with characters like Foy, Raison, and Le Texte de Saincte Escripture, is clearly an institutional morality of a reformist nature. It is easy to ascribe the error to the printer, but there is no concrete evidence on which to base such an allegation, as we found in the plays just examined. The most we can do is to surmise that the printer thought the designation *farce* would sell more copies or that he used the word in a general sense of 'play'. While we are on the subject of this particular work, it should be pointed out that *theologastre* does not mean 'théologien ventru' as Picot[7] and Petit de Julleville[8] both maintained, but 'mauvais théologien'. The *Oxford English Dictionary* defines it as 'a shallow or paltry theologian' (s.v. *theologaster*). The word is formed from *theolog-us* and *-aster*, the suffix 'expressing incomplete resemblance, hence generally pejorative'; (s.v. *-aster*). According to the same source, *theologastrus* was used by Luther as early as 1518. The term is therefore particularly apt in a play supporting Louis de Berquin, whom the theologians of the Sorbonne accused of having Lutheran sympathies.

Not all of the anomalous genre designations are errors; some of them are only variants of the more widely accepted practices of genre identification. The morality play, *Bien Advisé et Mal Advisé*, for example, is called a *mistere* in the colophon. Nowhere does the printed text refer to the play as a morality. We noted above that *Homme Pecheur* lacks a generic designation on the title page and refers to itself only as a *livre* in the colophon. The prologue, however, informs the reader that 'en lisant ce livre et mistere trouverés a plain declaree la matiere par personnages et motz expres'. The word *mistere* seems to be used here in a very broad sense that encompases any significant matter presented to the reader or spectator 'par personnages'. This is the apparent meaning of the word in the prologue of the *Moralité des .iiii. elemens*, where Raison says to the audience: 'Veuillez en paix nostre mistere ouyr'. Thus while the term *mistere* was usually associated with the historical genres, it was occasionally applied to morality plays, where it designated a serious subject matter presented in dramatic dialogue.

The most interesting set of variants is found in the La Vallière manuscript, a collection of plays associated for the most part with the Conards and other confraternities of Rouen. There is a general consistency of genre designations throughout the manuscript, yet the nomenclature differs somewhat from that found in the other collections of plays. First of all, the term *sottie* is never used in a title, even though five of the plays may be classed as *sotties*. These five include *Deux Gallans et Sancté, La Mere de ville, Les Veaulx, Troys Gallans et un Badin,* and *Les Sobres Sotz.* Each of the first four plays is called a *farce*, which conforms to our generic paradigm, since all *sotties* are farces. The fifth play is called a *farce morale*, which also conforms to the paradigm if the term is understood in the more general sense of allegorical farce. It should be noted that virtually all the extant plays with the term *sottie* in the title were printed in Paris. The exceptions are the two *sotties* of the British Museum collection printed by Barnabé Chaussard in Lyon. The two *sotties* from Geneva are found in a manuscript, where they are designated moralities in the titles, though the term *sottie* is found in the preface to the second play.[9] In the survey of contemporary references to play productions described in Chapter III, I found the designation *sottie* used in only seven references – slightly more than one per cent of the sample. Five were from Paris, while the other two came from Lille and Avignon. It would seem, then, that there was a type of fool play practised in many parts of the French-speaking world, but that the genre designation *sottie* was largely limited to Paris.

The next thing one notices about the La Vallière manuscript is that the term *farce moralisée* does not appear in any of the titles, though eleven of the plays clearly belong to that genre. The eleven include the two plays of *La Reformeresse; Eglise, Noblesse et Povreté; Troys Galans et le Monde; Troys Brus; Chascun et Plusieurs; Tout le Monde; Science et Asnerye; Troys Pelerins et Malice; Marche Beau;* and *Mestier et Marchandise*. Five of them are called *farces* and three others are designated by the term *farce morale*. Again, both types fit our generic paradigm without difficulty. What is unusual in the La Vallière manuscript is that the two terms *moral* and *moralité* are used interchangeably. Among the *farces moralisées*, *Tout le Monde* is called a *moral* and *Chascun et Plusieurs* is called a *moralité*. Furthermore, each of the morality plays found in the manuscript is designated by one of the same two terms and sometimes by both, since all the titles are repeated in the table of contents. *Les Quatre Ages*, for example, is called a *moral* in the text and a *moralité* in the table of contents, while the reverse is true for the *Moralité de Nature*. Similarly, *Chascun et Plusieurs* is called a *moral* in the table of contents, and two of the *farces morales* above are there designated *moralités*. This may at first appear to be thoroughly inconsistent, but we must remember that words derived from the Latin *moralis* share a semantic field that includes concepts relating both to allegorical expression and to ethical behaviour. Since the convenient term *moralisée*, employed elsewhere in France to denote an allegorized farce, was not in use in Rouen, the adjective *morale* was used to perform the same function. This apparently led to a confusion with the noun *moral*, a synonym of *moralité*, which resulted in a semantic overlap among all three terms. Despite what might appear to be a gross inconsistency, the problems raised are minor. In the La Vallière manuscript the noun *moral*, which is applied to five morality plays and two *farces moralisées*, is a variant term for both *moralité* and *farce morale*. The only inconsistency in its usage would appear to be its application to a biblical play, *Le Lazare*. Even here, however, the play deals with a problem in domestic morals – that is, the concern of Lazarus and Martha over the wayward worldliness of their sister Mary Magdalen. The only other inconsistencies in the manuscript involve four *farces moralisées* to which the term *moralité* is applied, though in each case but one is it added as a second term to the correct designations of *farce morale* or *moral*. The one exception is *Eglise, Noblesse et Povreté*, which we will examine in the next chapter.

We are left with a few miscellaneous plays whose titles are somewhat anomalous in terms of our generic paradigm. The *Moralité de Pyramus et Tisbee* is not a true morality play, but is given that designation because of the allegorical interpretation of the principal dramatic action. The speeches of a Berger and a Bergiere form a frame play for the central action of the hero and the heroine. In the first scene they explain the separation of the lovers; in the middle scene they prepare the appearance of the lion; in the final scene they explain the Christian symbolism of the tragedy. Henry de Barran's *Tragique comedie de l'homme justifié par Foy*, published in 1554, is a true morality play. The author, who was familiar with the dramatic genres of Antiquity, was already trying to fit medieval genres into the ancient categories of comedy and tragedy. In a preface to the play he refers to 'Comedies, Tragedies, et autres semblables histoires prinses de l'Escriture sainte' (a.2.r). He was aware that the morality play does not fit into either category, hence the designation *tragique comedie*. The *Comedie du Pape malade*, published in 1561, is also a morality play. In this case the author clearly explains in the preface why he calls it a *comedie*. The corruption of the papacy, as depicted in the play, has reached such an advanced stage, he claims, that it will soon destroy itself 'et lors il y aura matiere de joye, comme c'est le naturel des Comedies d'avoir comencement fascheux, et issue joyeuse' (p. 6).

Our examination of the play titles has revealed a general consistency in the genre designations found in them, as well as a remarkable conformity to the generic paradigm outlined in the previous chapters. Moreover, virtually all anomalies are explicable in terms of printers' errors or variant usages. Once the anomaly is explained, the play fits easily into one of the categories of the paradigm. There are a few plays, however, that do not readily fit the paradigm because of anomalies, not in their titles, but in their form. These are the hybrid plays.

A hybrid play is one in which there is a mixing or blending of two or more previously distinct dramatic genres. We encounter numerous hybrid plays in the second half of the sixteenth century, a period when playwrights were experimenting with the genres of Antiquity. But even before the impact of the ancient genres was fully felt, there was an occasional blending of traditional medieval genres in a single play. We see this in the *Moralité d'ung Empereur qui tua son nepveu*, which, as we noted earlier, is a blend of miracle and morality plays. It is a true blend or hybrid in that the two genres involved cannot stand independently of each other, thus making their distinction to be a matter of point of view. If we consider the play from the perspective of the nephew, it is a morality play; but if we see it from the perspective of the emperor, it is a miracle play. Furthermore, because the play deals with the Roman empire, it has historical dimensions. The practice of dramatizing incidents from Roman history (or legend) as opposed to biblical history dates back at least to the mid-fifteenth century.[10] Roman historical plays served often as moral *exempla* and were therefore susceptible to an admixture of morality play elements. The *Histoire de l'orgueil et presumption de l'Empereur Jovinien*, printed around 1580, but possibly written earlier,[11] is a hybrid of this kind. Here the emperor, like the protagonist of a morality play, falls into the sin of pride for which he is punished. Ultimately he repents and is reconciled with those around him. In spite of the morality-like structure, the play presents itself as a history play and is nowhere called a *moralité*. The hybrid nature of such plays is openly acknowledged in the title, *Moralité ou histoire rommaine d'une femme qui avoit voulu trahir la cité de Romme*. This moral *exemplum*, taken from Valerius Maximus, teaches a lesson of filial love and devotion. In none of these hybrids do we find the allegorical characters usually associated with the morality plays.

Another hybrid play is the *Moralité d'une pauvre fille villageoise*, printed in Paris by Simon Calvarin. There is no date on the title page, but the *British Museum General Catalogue of Printed Books* gives '1550?' as the year of imprint. The play concerns a virtuous peasant girl whose beauty attracts the attention of her Seigneur. When she refuses his pleas, he decides to take her away by force, but first grants her a few moments alone with her father. The girl begs her father to kill her in order to prevent the defilement of her body. If he refuses, she will be forced to kill herself and thus be damned forever. The Seigneur overhears this pathetic scene and is turned away from his evil intent.

In order to reward such virtue, he raises both father and daughter
from their peasant status, making the father an overseer in his castle.

As one may readily see, the *Moralité d'une pauvre fille villageoise* is
not a full-fledged morality play. There are no personified abstractions
representing virtues and vices, and there is no psychomachia in which
the heroine must choose between good and evil. The *moralité*
designation in the title refers more to the dramatized moral lesson than
to a morality play structure. Still, the playwright has incorporated
several elements of the morality structure in his work. Though not
torn between virtue and vice, the heroine must nevertheless make a
choice between two evils. She does not hesitate to choose death over
defilement. In this, she is somewhat like Bien Advisé, who, though
faced with vices of all sorts, is never once tempted by them. The
peasant girl is thus analogous to the good half of the divided morality
protagonist. This, however, cannot obscure the fact that the principal
structure of the work is derived from the miracle play. Like the miracle
genre, *Une pauvre fille* is peopled with human characters, rather than
personifications, placed in a 'realistic' setting. In addition, there is a
prayer to the Virgin, and the heroine is pushed to an extreme act by
circumstances beyond her control. Most important, however, is the
fact that the moral conflict at the centre of the drama is between two
characters rather than within the soul of the protagonist. Ultimately
the virtuous young girl is saved by the 'miracle' of the Seigneur's
dramatic change of heart brought about by the grace of God. In this
way the playwright was able to incorporate the divine intervention
that the miracle genre requires, while keeping the laws of nature
intact.

We should also include in this group of hybrid plays the *Tragedie de
l'amour d'un Serviteur envers sa Maistresse* (1571). In spite of the late
date, Jean Bretog was still strongly influenced by the morality form.
There are, for example, three personified abstractions among the
characters of the play. The Serviteur, like the morality protagonist, is
placed in a struggle between good and evil (Chasteté and Venus) and
chooses the latter. The husband, goaded by Jalousie, exposes the lovers
and then dies of humiliation. The Serviteur is condemned to death, but
there is no 'miracle' to save him at the end. His death, like that of
Homme Mondain, is directly brought about by his sinful life. Yet
Bretog, who claims that the story is true, believed the death penalty to
be too severe for so common a crime as adultery. For this reason he
treats the story as a tragedy and, in the process, brings about a

relationship between audience and protagonist that is completely different from that which one finds in the morality plays. Indeed, he is on the verge of creating a genuine tragic hero.

The hybrid plays discussed so far apparently resulted from deliberate attempts at generic innovation. Playwrights were seeking ways of expressing new concepts in dramatic form by combining structural elements from two or more previously distinct genres. No doubt the impetus for seeking new forms of dramatic expression came indirectly from some of the troubling social issues of the time. *L'Empereur qui tua son nepveu*, for example, was almost certainly influenced by contemporary questions about the nature of kingship and the source of royal authority. Moreover, Bouchetel saw tragedy as originating in order to instruct princes in virtue.[12] The same concern for the instruction of princes may also have influenced the creation of historical–fictional hybrids of the morality play. Not all hybrid plays, however, resulted from authorial experimentation. There are some hybrids whose generic structure was determined by the nature of the public occasion for which they were written. In the late Middle Ages there were three kinds of collective observances whose significance was great enough to exert a modifying influence on plays performed in conjunction with them. These were wedding feasts, carnival celebrations, and royal or princely entries.

The staging of plays at wedding feasts was apparently not at all uncommon. If we may judge from the wedding scene in *L'Histoire de l'Enfant ingrat*, some form of entertainment in addition to the music was generally expected. In this scene the Seigneur, whose daughter is marrying L'Enfant, gives orders for the festivities:

Maistre d'hotel, expressement
Que nous soyons bien festoyez;
Et quoy qu'il soit, nous pourvoyez
De menestriers et de farseurs
Pour resjouir ou de danseurs. (F.6.r)

The banquet itself is presumably a representation in miniature of a real wedding feast:

LE MAISTRE D'HOTEL
Sus! Que chacun s'assee empres
Et qu'on sonne les instrumens;
Et puis on aura par expres
Quelques joyeux esbatemens.

LE SEIGNEUR
Nostre espousé, servez les gens
De voz nopces. C'est la maniere.
LE FILZ
Si bien qu'ils seront contens.
Que chascun face bonne chere!
>   *Nota que les instrumens sonnent*
>   *ce qu'ilz voudront.*
LE SEIGNEUR
Sus, sus! Menons joye planiere!
Voicy nostre esjouyssement.
LE PERE
C'est ma liesse singuliere
Et l'espoir de mon sauvement.
LE CURE
Nous aurons quelque esbatement,
Ce croy-je.
>   LE VOISIN
>   Quelque farcerie.
>   LE SECOND VOISIN
Feste ne vaut rien autrement,
S'il n'y a farce ou mommerie.
>   *Icy jouent une farce.* (F.7.r-v)

The farce is not named, but in keeping with the joyous spirit of this
wedding feast, one would expect a farce embodying the happy lyricism
of *Le Mariage Robin Mouton*, or perhaps even the good-natured
twitting of *Le Nouveau Marié qui ne peult fournir a l'appoinctement
de sa femme*. In any case, if we are to believe the fools of *Les Coppieurs
et lardeurs*, there existed a whole corpus of 'farces de nopces', not to
mention monologues and *sermons joyeux*, for playing at such joyous
occasions. There are four works that specify in their titles that they
were written 'pour jouer a une nopce'. Two are monologues – the
Sermon du mesnage and Roger de Collerye's *Sermon pour une nopce* –
both of which comically exploit the anti-marriage themes of the farce
world. It is paradoxical, however, that the other two works, which are
multi-character plays, are not lively, comical farces of the kind
mentioned above, but allegories of a more serious and thoughtful
character. One is *Le Dict des jardiniers* (the title is supplied by the
modern editor), which was written around 1530 'pour les nopces M.
Disemieux du Daulphiné et Madamoyselle de Montvaignard dite de
Boege'. The author refers to the play as a 'farce' in one place and as a
'farce mor . . .' in another. Regrettably, part of the designation has
been lost because of damage to the manuscript. We may surmise,

however, that the truncated word was *morale* or *moralisee*, indicating
the allegorical nature of the play. The bride is seen as a Rose in need of
a gardener to care for her. The action of the play consists of a contest
among three gardeners – Loyal Desir, Franc Vouloir, and Coeur
Valleureux – to determine who can recite the best 'dicts' in praise of
the Rose. The winner will become gardener to the flower, enabling her
to bear fruit. The judges are Nature, who made the Rose, and
Prudence, her guardian. In the text there are sexual *double-entendres*
that are characteristic of both the farce genre and the wedding feast.
Yet the sustained allegory and the somewhat elevated style are
characteristic of the morality genre and are more in keeping with the
rank of the aristocratic young couple. The result is a play that belongs
fully neither to the farce world nor to the morality world.

The other play designated as a wedding play is the *Farce nouvelle de
l'ordre de mariage et de prebstrise treshonneste et joyeuse pour joer a
toutes nopces*. It begins with a debate between Le Marié and
L'Ecclesiastique on the merits of their respective callings. Each tries to
influence Le Gallant in his choice of a state of life. The latter is
persuaded to choose marriage, not on the strength of the argument,
but by the appearance of La Fille, a beautiful young girl standing next
to the Tour de Mariage. The young lovers become engaged and receive
moral instruction from the first two characters. They are then married
and are given additional moral lessons. The bride presents her
husband with a wreath of pansies, which are the Pensées de Mariage.
With this the Gallant becomes suddenly aware that he has given up his
former freedom and has assumed the heavy responsibilities of
marriage. 'Pour Dieu', he cries, 'qu'ilz me soient ostees;/Ilz me
rompent toute la teste' (328–29). He cannot be consoled for his loss
until L'Ecclesiastique brings a little girl named Paix to live with the
young couple in the Tour de Mariage. The Gallant eventually becomes
accustomed to the Pensées de Mariage and shoulders the
responsibilities of his new state. This transformation is explained in
the following way:

LA FILLE
Ce qui l'a fait ainsi sauvage
C'est folie qui l'a gouverné.
LE GALLANT
Il sembloit que je fusse estonné,
Mais raison a tout retourné
Sa folle emprise malheureuse. (392–96)

This is clearly the morality world. In choosing to marry, the protagonist makes a moral choice that brings consequences far beyond the simple retributive justice of the farce world. He is temporarily led astray by Folie, but her hold on him is ultimately broken by Raison, who then asserts her rightful dominion. Despite these characteristics, however, the play does not wholly belong to the morality genre. In the preceding résumé I have deliberately stressed the morality aspects of the work in order to contrast them more easily with its numerous farce elements. The opening debate draws its anti-marriage arguments from the farce tradition, and the Gallant's reaction to the Pensées de Mariage is reminiscent of many a farce husband. Like Jacquinot of *Le Cuvier*, he blames his troubles on the devil:

Le dyable me fist tant amasser;
Tousjours je pense sans cesser:
'Vecy terrible seigneurie'. (333–35)

In addition, the language, the jokes, and the puns are all more characteristic of the farce than of the morality play.

Though it is not mentioned in the title, *Regnault qui se marie a Lavollee* was probably written to be played at a wedding feast. It is filled with the comic gibes against marriage and the juvenile teasing of the bridegroom traditionally associated with weddings. While the play certainly belongs to the farce genre, there is the unusual presence of two personified abstractions from the morality tradition. Regnault's two companions are Franc Arbitre and Godin Falot (Goodfellow), who must of course be abandoned when he marries. In *Homme Pecheur*, Franc Arbitre is 'habillé en Rogier Bon Temps', which tells us something about what Regnault had to give up. As the newly-weds retire to 'coucher dedans quelque beau lit' (293), the saddened former companions sing an ironic 'Requiescant in pace'.

Such plays reflect the two principal affective elements of wedding celebrations: joy and moral concern. The joy is of course obvious and is expressed not only in the wedding farces, but in the general high spirits, the jokes about marriage, and the teasing. Yet a wedding is also a time of concern for the future welfare of the couple. It is the last chance to make certain they know the moral foundations of marriage. Instruction may be given in the wedding homily, but it may also be given in a play, as we saw in the *Ordre de Mariage*. The wedding celebration may thus be seen as a ritual blending of the jokes and teasing characteristic of the farce world with the moral instruction associated with the morality world. It is hardly surprising, then, to find this same blending of generic elements in the hybrid wedding plays.

In the Middle Ages the season of feasts and public celebrations that began with Christmas and the Feast of Fools and ended with Mardi Gras and Ash Wednesday was, in the broad sense of the term, the carnival season. The winter solstice marked the end of the old year and the lengthening days signaled the birth of a new cycle. Within this period, parallelling the infancy of the new year, were a number of feasts relating directly to infancy or childhood. In the religious calendar we find Christmas, the Circumcision, Epiphany, and so on, while in the popular tradition we note the hierarchical inversions and the reversions to childhood that marked the Feast of the Innocents, the Feast of Fools, and the *jours gras* preceding Lent. These characteristics prompted Claude Gaignebet in his essay on carnival to term the whole season a 'royaume d'enfance'.[13]

An integral part of the festivities of the carnival season was the staging of plays in the streets and squares of the towns, especially the towns of the northern provinces. Many types of plays were produced, but particularly popular were the genres that reflected the spirit of the season – farces, *sotties*, and comic moralities. Occasionally we find references to carnival in the plays that have come down to us. Le Ventre in the *Moralité du Ventre* calls for wine: 'Qu'on boyve en Enfant Sans Soulsy'. Then to justify his behaviour he asks: 'Est il pas mardy gras demain?' (p. 13). In *Les Sobres Sotz* one of the Sots says: 'A ces jours sy y fault tout dyre' (288). Carnival, of course, gave everyone licence to say things that would be punishable at other times, rendering such talk as harmless as the babble of fools or the prattle of children. In the same play the Badin claims the right to speak out, even though his words are spiteful:

Que sy ma parolle est despite,
Je seray tousjour franq et quicte
Comme le jour du mardy gras. (179–81)

The Badin was a comic character type who appeared in many of the farces of the fifteenth and sixteenth centuries, playing the role of the idiot or the naive fool. His costume usually included a baby bonnet, suggesting that he was in essence a grown-up child.[14] Farces and *sotties* that included the childish Badin were particularly apt for the carnival season when the year was in its infancy.

There is much of the carnival spirit in the farce world. For one thing, social ranks are abolished in the typical farces, where the characters must live by their wits. Just as the pranks and mummings of carnival are free of the deference due to rank, so the tricks and deceptions of the farce world tend to efface all social distinctions. A peasant can deceive his lord with impunity (*Le Gentilhomme et Naudet*) and a cobbler can trick a monk with neither regret nor fear of reprisal (*Le Savetier et le Moyne*). It is true that the social ranks are not always abolished in the *farce moralisée* and the *sottie*, because the upper levels of society are often the object of satirical attack. Yet these genres, too, share the carnivalesque spirit in that their satire is closely related to the ritual mockery and invective characteristic of both carnival and its ancestor, the Roman Saturnalia.

In the medieval scheme of things carnival and Lent represented opposing views of the world. If the farce world exhibits some of the characteristics of carnival, then one would expect its opposite, the morality world, to manifest something of the spirit of Lent. Indeed, this is the case. The moral lessons, the struggle against evil, the individual responsibility for moral choices, and the repentance and confession of sin that characterize the personal morality play are all given particular emphasis in the season of Lent. In this light one begins to see that many dramatic and literary genres, perhaps all of them, are reflections of broad cultural conceptions of the world or of certain aspects of the world. This is why genres are, in the long run, unstable. As a culture's broad, underlying conceptions of the world change, so its literary and dramatic genres are transformed to reflect the culture's new vision of itself and its place in the world.

The renewal of the year cycle in the Middle Ages was not all childish pranks and carnivalesque folk customs. In order to insure prosperity and God's blessing for the community, there had to be a purification in the form of prayer, fasting, and sacrifice. Carnival, therefore, had to be superseded by Lent and, because carnival derives its strength from the deepest life-sustaining forces of the psyche, it also had to be conquered and judged by Lent. The struggle between carnival and Lent was acted out during Shrovetide in numerous folk customs and traditional rites. These were popular analogues, not only of the seasonal struggle between summer and winter, but of the ancient conflict between life and death. The latter conflict found its most common expression in the Lenten and Easter liturgies and is succinctly described in the Easter hymn, *Victimae paschali*:

Mors et vita duello
Conflixere mirando;
Dux vitae mortuus regnat vivus.

It is not unexpected that, with two such fundamental forces in conflict, the late Middle Ages would create dramatic as well as other symbolic representations of the struggle. Furthermore, if the two forces are related to two different generic worlds, then it would not be surprising to see a hybrid dramatic genre evolve. This is undoubtedly what happened in the development of carnival plays such as *La Bataille de Sainct Pensard a l'encontre de Caresme* and *Le Testament de Carmentrant,* for in these two plays the farce and morality worlds confront each other directly. In both plays, on the side of the carnival characters, there is the constant quest of immediate gratification without regard for consequences that is typical of characters in the farce world. This kind of quest in the farces often involves food, which is of course the central concern of the carnival plays. *La Bataille de Sainct Pensard* with its catalogues of rich foods is strikingly reminiscent of *Le Capitaine Mal en Point* with its fantastic imaginary banquet. Many of the characters' names, too, belong to the farce world. Maistre Aliborum is a character in *Les Queues troussees* and Maistre Accipé is a sobriquet given at one point to Le Capitaine Mal en Point. But while these carnival characters are oblivious to the consequences of their actions, there is another world that they have to deal with – the world of fasting and Lenten privation. The arrival of Lent unleashes a battle that resembles in many respects the battles between the virtues and vices of the morlaity plays. *La Bataille de Sainct Pensard* leans more toward the farce genre, as one might expect in a Basoche play, and the battle ends in a victory for Charnau and his cohorts. Nevertheless, they negotiate a truce by which Caresme is allowed to remain for a period of time. As Charnau explains:

D'aujourdhuy en quarante jours
Je viendray en mon hault estat
Et mettray Caresme a rebours. (1213–15)

But in *Le Testament de Carmentrant,* which leans more toward the morality genre, Carmentrant is soundly defeated and a judgment of banishment is immediately pronounced against him.

We recognize the same carnival scenario incorporated into the morality play, *La Condamnacion de Bancquet.* This play is a type of personal morality, though it has no human protagonist. In this regard

it resembles *Langue Envenimee,* where the vice is personified to show
its harmful effects on a personified virtue rather than on a human
character. Bancquet and Soupper are clearly vice characters. They
scheme to betray their guests, who are personified attributes (Bonne
Compaignie) or activities (Je Boy a Vous) of banqueting, and they
delight in seeing their guests suffer. Though the excesses of Bancquet
may seem to represent a social or collective vice, the lesson of the play
is clearly directed toward personal morality and not the reform of
institutions:

C'est peché, c'est blasme, c'est vice,
C'est oultraige et difformité
De faire au corps tant de service
Qu'on en aquiert infirmité. (p. 271)

La Condamnation de Bancquet resembles *Langue Envenimee* also in
the fact that Bancquet, toward the end of the play, becomes less an
abstract vice and takes on certain human qualities. He repents of his
misdeeds and confesses to a priest, both acts implying the moral
responsibility that a human protagonist would have. But the judgment
and condemnation of Bancquet are obviously patterned on the folk
ritual of the judgment and banishment of carnival. In this case
Bancquet is condemned to death, but his farewell to the world and its
pleasures echoes the traditional *Adieu* that closes the *Testament de
Carmentrant.*[15] Here, however, the author, Nicolas de la Chesnaye,
humanized the vice character in order to make the play and its lesson
more immediate and more personal. This is the same principle, though
with different aims and results, that Shakespeare used in creating
Falstaff from the vestiges of the carnival and vice traditions.

The *bergerie* is a pastoral morality play that blends characteristics
of both the personal and institutional moralities. It is a sustained
pastoral allegory in which the miseries of the present time are
contrasted with a past Golden Age or an idealized future. Its most
prominent theme is a fervent hope or plea for peace and an end to the
suffering caused by war and dissention in high places. The pastoral is a
traditional mode of literary expression going back to Antiquity, which
medieval writers adapted to their own purposes. In pastoral works
shepherds gave voice to the complaints of the people, who had to
endure many hardships and suffer many privations. This became a
topos of the nativity plays, where a catalogue of the world's woes
traditionally preceded the coming of the saviour. Pastoral works also

represented a world to which the aristocracy and the bourgeoisie could escape in fantasy from the power struggles of court and marketplace. Finally, the pastoral world was for all people a place of peace and, because peace was a *sine qua non* of an ideal society, some pastoral works came to express the collective hope for an ideal ruler (or shepherd), who would guard his people from dangers of every kind. This is the hope for peace that is dramatized in the pastoral morality play.

There are two early pastoral moralities, dating from the first half of the fifteenth century, which exhibit some of the traits of the later *bergerie*. The *Alliance de Foi et Loyauté* is basically a plea for peace. Foi, the shepherd, and Loyauté, the shepherdess, have abandoned the three estates because of their general corruption. In the pastoral setting of the play they meet and are married. Their constant companion is Paix. We thus learn that where Faith and Loyalty are united, Peace is always to be found. The lesson is general and apparently directed to all levels of society. In the *Moralité du Petit et du Grand* the two shepherds represent the common people and the nobility respectively, both of whom complain of the ravages of the war with England. There is also an urban theme in the play, since the people will ultimately be under the protection of Paris, aided by Justice and Conseil.

There are two pastoral morality plays from the late fifteenth century that are designated *bergerie* in their titles. The *Bergerie de l'Agneau de France* was almost certainly written for an entry of Charles VIII, still a minor, into one of the cities of France shortly after his coronation.[16] It is quite possible, though there is no direct evidence for it, that the *Bergerie de Mieulx Que Devant* was also played at a royal entry. We know that pastoral plays, as well as *tableaux vivants*, were regularly presented before kings or nobles at solemn entries into cities. The allegory of the shepherd as leader of his sheep made the pastoral theme an apt one for such occasions. At the entry of Charles VIII into Rouen in 1485, the organizers of the ceremonies produced a play 'faicte sur pastoureries'.[17] Also in Rouen at the entry of the Duke of Orléans in 1492, a wagon preceded the Duke in the procession, on which was played 'un esbatement joyeux de pastorerie'.[18] *Bergeries* were played at solemn entries at Bayonne and Le Puy in 1530 and at Paris in 1531.[19]

Royal entries were, among other things, occasions for the bourgeoisie of a city to display in a dramatic fashion the prosperity of their town and its importance in the kingdom. But it was also an occasion on which the city was, as Konigson says, 'confrontée au prince'.[20] The burghers offered praise and obedience to the king in exchange for his recognition of the city's ancient priviledges. The *tableaux vivants* along the route of the procession, particularly from the late fifteenth century on, presented the king with laudatory images of himself as protector, healer, and shepherd of his people. At the same time the *tableaux* necessarily made manifest the needs and desires of the people, thus serving also as petitions for his protection and guidance. It is in this regard that the *bergeries* are hybrid plays influenced by the occasion for which they were written. Because of their special audience – the king – they cannot teach either personal or institutional morality in the same way that other morality plays do. Instead, they must petition by showing clearly to the sovereign what the needs of the people are. In the late Middle Ages the most pressing need of the cities to insure their prosperity was peace.

In the *Bergerie de l'Agneau de France* the Agneau is Charles VIII, still in his minority, who must be protected by the three shepherds, presumably the princes of the blood. Picque, who represents war or dissention, gains control of the Agneau. Remede arrives and the shepherds beg him to remove Picque, but she is too strong for him at the present time. He therefore departs, enjoining the shepherds to have patience until his return:

Enffans, je vous jure mon ame
Que quant je reviendray icy
Je l'osteray. (402–04)

Remede will thus be more powerful when he returns, suggesting that when the king comes into his majority he will quickly dispel war and dissention. In one sense this is a lesson about the duties of kings, but because the future king is in the audience and only he will have the power to bring an end to strife, it is also a petition for peace. 'Ne nous laissez pas au besoing' (395), pleads the third shepherd. Similarly, the *Bergerie de Mieulx Que Devant*, rather than being a lesson in personal or institutional morality, is a play that expresses the suffering and miseries of war and the deeply-felt hope for peace. This play too was probably written to be performed before a king, because Mieulx Que Devant, resembling the ancient gods, represents the kind of ideal society that only a king could bring into being.

The *bergerie* is therefore a petitional genre related to the *tableau vivant* of the solemn entry. There is a close relationship between the theatre of the mystery and morality plays and the theatre of the entries. Indeed, as Konigson suggests, there is between the two a unity of conception as well as a unity of urban setting.[21] In addition, there is a structural unity that we shall examine in the next chapter.

In our study of genre thus far we have approached the question from a conceptual point of view. We have seen how the late medieval concepts of history and fiction, of reason and folly were reflected in the dramatic genres of that period. Medieval genres, however, may be productively examined from other points of view. We shall next turn to a formal approach in which we compare the processional pattern found in religious and civic ceremonies with an analogous pattern found in dramatic productions. This will require shifting the focus of our attention to a higher level of abstraction, so that we may view all of late medieval drama as one type of spectacle (or genre) on the same level with other organized spectacles such as jousting, royal entries, and carnival parades. We shall see that the processional structure shared by all such spectacles is tantamount to a single overarching genre that embraces virtually every collective act of late medieval society.

Notes

[1] David M. Bevington, *From Mankind to Marlowe* (Cambridge, Mass.: Harvard University Press, 1962), pp. 265–73.

[2] See Emmanuel Philipot, ed., *Six farces normandes du recueil La Vallière* (Rennes: Plihon, 1939), pp. 5–7; and Raymond Lebègue, 'La Vie dramatique à Rouen de François Ier à Louis XIII', *Bulletin Philologique et Historique du Comité des Travaux Historiques et Scientifiques* (1955–56), pp. 400–6.

[3] Eugénie Droz and Halina Lewicka, eds., *Le Recueil Trepperel: les farces* (Geneva: Droz, 1961) p. 97.

[4] Alan E. Knight, 'Fragments de trois farces du Recueil de Florence' *Romania*, 94 (1973), 548.

[5] Emmanuel Philipot, ed., *Trois farces du Recueil de Londres* (1931; rpt Geneva: Slatkine Reprints, 1975), p. 41.

[6] Emile Picot and Christophe Nyrop, eds., *Nouveau Recueil de farces françaises* (1880; rpt Geneva: Slatkine Reprints, 1968), p. lxi.

[7] Picot, *Les Moralités*, p. 30.

[8] Petit de Julleville, *Répertoire*, p. 245.

[9] Picot, *Recueil*, II, 327.

[10] Raymond Lebègue, *La Tragédie religieuse en France* (Paris: Champion, 1929), p. 105.

[11] Lebègue, *La Tragédie*, p. 100.

[12] Bernard Weinberg, *Critical Prefaces of the French Renaissance*

(Evanston: Northwestern University Press, 1950), p. 108.

[13]Claude Gaignebet, *Le Carnaval* (Paris: Payot, 1974), pp. 41–56.

[14]Michel Rousse, from the 'Discussions' following 'La Farce jusqu' à Molière', *Cahiers de l'Association Internationale des Etudes Françaises*, 26 (1974), p. 303.

[15]Aubailly, *Le Théâtre*, p. 73.

[16]Halina Lewicka, ed., *Bergerie de l'Agneau de France* (Geneva: Droz, 1961), p. 16.

[17]Petit de Julleville, *Répertoire*, p. 346.

[18]Elie Konigson, *L'Espace théâtral médiéval* (Paris: Centre National de la Recherche Scientifique, 1975), p. 195.

[19]Lewicka, *Bergerie*, p. 17.

[20]Konigson, *L'Espace théâtral*, p. 201.

[21]Konigson, *L'Espace théâtral*, p. 203.

CHAPTER VI

The processional context of medieval drama

One of the salient characteristics of late medieval culture was the progressive theatricalization of important festal and ceremonial occasions, a trend that continued well into the sixteenth century. Traditional times of rejoicing became occasions for dramatic spectacle on a grand scale. Indeed, whole holidays were theatricalized in one form or another, thereby giving drama and spectacle pride of place among the expressions of collective feeling. Though the dramatic legacy of the earlier centuries was by no means insignificant, the fifteenth and sixteenth centuries saw a veritable explosion of popular demand for dramatic representations. As a result, there was not only a rapid increase in the number of plays written, but also an expansion of the types of communal occasions for which dramatic spectacles served an expressive function. By the mid-sixteenth century this medieval dramatic tradition had become so deeply rooted among the people and such an integral part of holiday celebrations and ceremonial observances that the disdain of that small band of avant-garde poets called the *Pléiade* had little immediate influence on its fortunes. Neither did the growing body of classical learning in the schools alter significantly the popular demand for the old, familiar plays. Even the decree of the Parlement of Paris in 1548 forbidding the playing of mystery plays had little more than a local effect. So strong, in fact, was the hold of dramatic spectacle on the populations of the fifteenth and sixteenth centuries, that the decline and eventual demise of the medieval theatrical tradition was a long, gradual process continuing in some areas well into the following century.

One of the most common forms of expression for late medieval social rituals and holiday celebrations was the procession, a festive and ceremonial form lying midway between life and art, between literal act and play. Its structure provided a formal context for the various modes of dramatic representation. We have previously considered dramatic genres as reflections of the several facets of the medieval conception of the world. Now, in order to understand better how the drama as a whole fits into the real world of the late Middle Ages, we shall view it as a single spectacular genre distinct from other spectacles in the context of a processional structure. Indeed, the processional form of this period was a broad ritual pattern of which the drama, more strictly defined, was only a part. From this point of view, the processional pattern was a kind of overarching dramatic genre that we must see as such in order to place the medieval theatre in its proper social perspective. It is this processional genre or context that we shall examine here.

The importance of the procession, particularly of royal and noble entries, in the study of the medieval theatre has long been noted. Kernodle studied the *tableaux vivants* of the entry as links between medieval art and the theatre of the Renaissance, but he took little interest in the procession itself, which he considered to be a primitive form of expression.[1] Moreover, he considered medieval drama to be so closely tied to its processional origins that it, too, seemed to him a primitive form, lacking all sophistication in its organization of theatrical space.[2] Konigson has recently corrected this view, but at the cost of making too radical a separation between the medieval theatre and the procession: 'Aucune scène ... ne peut aligner les lieux dramatiques ou les décors ... selon l'ordre processionnel, pour la simple raison qu'aucun texte écrit entre la fin du XIVe siècle et les temps modernes n'exprime une telle linéarité spatiale.'[3] This is no doubt true in the limited, spatial sense that Konigson means it. There is no sustained continuity of physical movement in medieval plays in terms of characters processing from one decor to another. Yet we have noted a certain conceptual linearity in medieval plays, as opposed to the crisis structure of tragedy and comedy, that is probably not unrelated to the pervasiveness of the processional form in medieval society. In order to see how medieval plays are related to real processions, however, we must view them, not as isolated and self-contained productions, but as part of a larger structure of collective activities and ceremonies that were both processional in form and theatrical in nature.

Obviously the procession was not unique to the Middle Ages. Probably as old as human culture, it is one of the few fundamental ways of organizing the observance of significant moments in the life of a people. Because the peoples of the past generally attached the greatest significance to religious events, processions have tended to be mainly religious in nature. In the earliest days of the church, Christians in Jerusalem began collectively retracing the steps of Jesus to Golgotha, and in churches everywhere processions were integrated into the liturgy to commemorate this and other events in the life of Christ or to symbolize the passage from one spiritual state to another. What was commemorated symbolically in the liturgy was acted out literally by pilgrims making journeys to holy shrines. Pilgrimages were less formalized than liturgical processions, but were nonetheless collective acts of devotion. From this point of view, Chaucer's Canterbury pilgrims were actors in a processional drama and their tales were 'insubstantial pageants' in a winding march from the Tabard Inn to Becket's shrine. One might also see the crusades as massive armed processions whose participants, at least in the beginning, collectively played the role of Christ the liberator. Indeed, each crusade took the shape of an enormous Harrowing of Hell, reaching from one continent to another, whose goal was to release the Christians imprisoned in the Saracen limbo.

The church, however, was by no means the only domain in which the established rituals showed a marked tendency toward theatricalization. By the end of the Middle Ages, virtually every kind of traditional ceremony had been invested with a highly dramatic character and in some cases the ceremonies were dramas in their own right. A particularly striking example may be found in those splendid and brilliant tournaments in which the late medieval nobility acted out their highest ideals and their most deeply-held values. Instituted as a training exercise for war, the tournament developed over a period of about five centuries into one of the most colourful and dramatic spectacles of the late Middle Ages.[4] Participation in these elaborate ritualized contests was limited to members of the nobility, but anyone could be a spectator. Indeed, when the lists were constructed, particularly the closed lists surrounded by scaffold seats, they must have borne a striking resemblance to the enclosed theatres in which many of the mystery plays were produced. The audience, too, must have been virtually the same for both types of events. Moreover, the similarity between the two spectacles must have been all the more striking on those occasions when jousting lists, like mystery-play theatres, were set up in the main square or market place of a town, with the encircling buildings providing additional viewing places.

The *Comptes de la ville de Cambrai* contain a number of references to both tournaments and dramatic entertainments held in the market place of that city. The construction of the lists and stages (*hourds*) for these events involved making holes in the ground, which then had to be refilled. In 1434 a certain sum was paid to 'Jehan Le Wery, cauchieur, pour avoir ouvré a recauchier plusieurs traux estans sur le marquiet, qu'on avoit fais a mettre les lices la ou on jousta'.[5] Every year at this period the city of Cambrai celebrated the twentieth day after Christmas (January 13) as a special day of merriment. The celebration usually lasted three days, during which time farces were played by a *société joyeuse* called Lescache Profit. An entry in the account book for 1448 records a certain sum paid again to 'Jehan Le Wery pour ... avoir restoupé les traux et remis a point le cauchie du marquiet qui, par les hours et habilements de l'abbaye descache pourfit, avoient esté fais a le feste du XXe'.[6] It is apparent from these accounts that tournaments and plays resembled each other greatly in their utilization of theatrical space. It is also apparent that the municipality of Cambrai, by contributing financially to tournaments and dramatic presentations, treated both equally as public entertainments.

The tournament was not always just a test of prowess in colourful garb; it was sometimes performed as a dramatic re-enactment of a historical or allegorical contest with the participants dressed in appropriate costumes. In Tarascon in 1449 René d'Anjou organized the *Pas de la Bergière*, in which the participants were costumed as shepherds. René's wife, Jeanne de Laval, played the shepherdess.[7] The tournament could thus be a drama in its own right with its own dramatic conventions and theatrical traditions.

As striking as the parallels are between tournament events and dramatic productions, it is the procession that most closely links the tournament with all the other medieval social dramatizations. The parade of heralds and richly dressed knights leading their ladies on brilliantly caparisoned horses to the arena, the parade of victors returning to the castle, the ceremonial banquet, and the awarding of prizes were all integral parts of one long processional drama. The stylized combat was thus only a part of the whole spectacle, though a significant part, to be sure. It formed a kind of fixed or stationary node of activity in the linear structure of the event. The banquet with its entertainments was another such node of activity. If the tournament lasted several days, with all the participants processing to and from the lists each day, it was still a single processional spectacle with added nodes of activity. It is precisely this processional element that makes the tournament structurally analogous to all the other collective dramatizations of the late Middle Ages, including the mystery plays, as we shall see; for the processional form was the underlying pattern of almost all organized public spectacles of that time. It was adapted to the requirements of the occasion or modified according to the needs of the group involved, thus manifesting itself in different genres, but the basic structure of the processional dramatic spectacle remained constant.

The processional form linked the theatre to life. If we understand this relationship, we will come to see formal drama as an integral part of the whole psycho-social complex of late medieval culture. The dramatic spectacles of those days had not yet been severed from everyday reality by the proscenium arch. Drama had not yet been relegated to the tenebrous world of dream and fantasy as it has been in today's darkened theatres and cinemas. It was, instead, an essential part of the rhythm of life, the constantly recurring rhythm of fast and feast, constraint and release, work and play. That which in modern times we isolate from the rhythm of everyday existence, set in a frame, and call theatre was in the late Middle Ages integrated into collective acts of self-affirmation that frequently took the form of processions. Just as the combat was a stationary node in the processional structure of the tournament, so the various types of stage plays formed nodes of more intense dramatic activity in the processional observance of holidays and important events. Perhaps it is because of their close relationship with a linear pattern of this kind that so many of the plays themselves incorporate the linear structure, figuratively speaking, of historical narrative or moral pilgrimage.

Probably the most spectacular of the late medieval processions was the royal or noble entry. When kings or nobles made official visits to their cities, the ceremonies took the form of the solemn entry, a kind of processional drama marked by a magnificent spectacle and a holiday atmosphere. In the royal entry a formal exchange between king and burgesses was acted out, the city pledging its allegiance and its financial resources to the king in return for certain favours and privileges.[8] It was a highly theatrical ceremony, existing, as we have noted, on the borderline between literal act and play; yet there *was* role-playing and dramatic representation. The king played the role of the ideal ruler, while the burgesses acted out an idealization of the city's relationship to the monarch. Even though the *représentants* and the *représentés* were very nearly identical, there was still enough difference – each side representing itself in an idealized state – to justify speaking of the solemn entry as a type of drama. Indeed, we may view the processional entry as a broad generic category corresponding to drama proper. Moreover, the exchange involved in the ceremony was paralleled by a double dramatic perspective. The king and his retinue were 'actors' in a drama that moved through the streets of the city, while the townspeople were 'actors' in a stationary drama along the route of march. In addition, stages were set up at intervals, on which were played 'true' dramas or which contained *tableaux vivants*, both involving full impersonation. Because the moving audience (the king) would stop before these stages to witness the play or *tableau*, they constituted nodes of dramatic activity in which the drama was of a somewhat different character from that of the procession. Let us examine more closely these nodes of dramatic activity and their function in the procession as a whole.

It was, so far as we know, for the entry of Charles VI in 1380 that stages were first erected in Paris for 'divers personnages et plusieurs hystoires'.[9] The stages came to be established at particular sites along the procession route and throughout the following century the pattern of royal entries into Paris remained essentially the same. The king would go first to the royal chapel at Saint Denis, a short distance north of the city. He would then ride with his entourage to the Porte Saint Denis, where he would be met by an honour guard of municipal soldiery and the notables of the city, who would present him with a key and then join the royal procession. The gate itself was always decorated with large replicas of municipal or royal arms, surrounded by living figures costumed in various allegorical guises. The procession would then follow the Rue Saint Denis to the Châtelet, from which point it would cross the river to stop at the Cathedral and then proceed to the Palace.

At the entry of Charles VII into Paris in 1437, the procession route was studded with stages, placed at fixed intervals, on which were presented *tableaux vivants* or *mystères mimés*, mostly of a religious nature. The herald Berry describes the stages in the following way:

Tout au long de la grant rue Saint Denis, enprés le giet d'une piere l'un de l'autre, estoient faitz eschaffaulx bien et richement tendus ou estoient fais par personnages la Nonciation Nostre Dame, la Nativité Nostre Seigneur, sa Passion, sa Resurection et sa Pentecouste, et le Jugement, qui estoit tres biau, car il se jouoit devant Chastellet ou estoit la Justice du roy.[10]

The *Chronique d'Enguerran de Monstrelet* describes the same procession in greater detail.[11] After passing through the Porte Saint Denis, the king stopped first at a fountain flowing with 'bon ypocras, vin et eaue', where a choir of angels sang to him. The procession halted next at the Hôpital de la Trinité, where the Confrères de la Passion recreated the major incidents of the Passion: 'Et ne parloient riens ceulx qui ce faisoient, mais le monstroient par jeu de mistere.' At the Ancienne Porte Saint Denis the king saw representations of several of the patron saints of France; at the Eglise du Saint Sépulcre he witnessed the Resurrection; and at the Hôpital Sainte Catherine he beheld the events of Pentecost. On arriving before the Châtelet, an ancient fortification built to protect the island city from invasion, the procession halted long enough to observe three *mystères*: the Annunciation on one side; the Last Judgment on the other; and at the gate of the fortress, through which all traffic had to pass to gain access to the Cité, an allegory of the *Lit de Justice*. The two latter *mystères* were appropriate for the site, because the Châtelet was the seat of criminal justice administered by the Provost of Paris. This site, moreover, was the most important node of dramatic activity along the route of the procession, since in every royal entry there were two or more stages erected here. Charles VII and his entourage then proceeded to the Cathedral and finally to the Palace, where a ceremonial banquet had been prepared.

Not all of the costumed mysteries were on fixed stages along the procession route. Some of them rode in the parade itself. When Henry VI made his first entry into Paris in 1431, he was met outside the city by the goddess Fama, 'acompaignee de personnages representans les anciens IX preux et IX preuses . . . tous armés et montés sur coursiers'. A herald wearing the arms of the city of Paris 'menoit et conduisoit le dit mistere'.[12] After welcoming the king to Paris, this mounted mystery preceded him to the end of the route. Similarly, the procession of Charles VII into Paris in 1437 included 'les personnages des Sept pechiés mortelz et des Sept vertus, montés a cheval, et estoient tous habilliés seloncq leurs proprietés'.[13] There were other forms of processing mysteries, as we shall see later. The point to be noted here is that the moving procession and the fixed stages comprised a theatrical spectacle where real persons interacted with dramatic characters. There was no clear dividing line between life and drama.

The subjects of the *mystères mimés* and the *tableaux vivants* presented at solemn entries in the early fifteenth century were usually taken from sacred history. In the course of the century, however, there was a gradual change in the subjects and types of representations. At the entry into Paris of Louis XII in 1498, only the Confrérie de la Passion maintained the old custom of staging events from biblical history. They presented the sacrifice of Abraham and the crucifixion. All the other *tableaux vivants* were representations of the king surrounded by kingly virtues, images of the royal family tree, or allegories of the submission of Paris to the new monarch and of the peace and good times that everyone hoped he would bring. Thus, as the royal entry became progressively more theatrical in the course of the fifteenth century, its dramatic elements came to reflect the increasing centralization of power in the person of the king:

D'abord simple fête, puis aussi spectacle, puis aussi solennité quasi religieuse, une entrée royale est de plus devenue à la fin du XVe siècle un grand théâtre où le sentiment monarchique est de plus en plus exalté et la politique royale de mieux en mieux justifiée. L'entrée royale est bien désormais un moment important de la vie politique française, que les Français viennent contempler de loin, ou dont ils écoutent avec passion les longs récits imprimés.[14]

The appearance of these 'longs récits imprimés' marked another kind of change in the character of the royal entry. Previous written descriptions of entries had been made by chroniclers, whose audience probably did not extend much beyond the court. The introduction of printing into France made it possible to extend the political message of the royal entry to a much wider audience. People unable to witness the great spectacle at the time it occurred were now able to read a detailed description of it. In addition, those who had seen the procession were enabled to relive a memorable experience. But the translation of a visual spectacle into a verbal text transforms a living, literal act into literature. The result of such a transformation is that both the procession and the *tableaux vivants* exist on the same level of reality in the written text. Though there is a difference of dramatic density between the procession and the *tableaux*, the reader must perform the same mental operations to transform both elements of the royal entry into a spectacle of the imagination. Let us examine one of the printed texts describing a particularly magnificent entry and note how the writers deal with the dual perspective involved, that is, with the moving and fixed aspects of the spectacle.

In 1539, when the Emperor Charles V was ready to embark from Spain to go north by way of Genoa, Francis I offered him passage through France, which he readily accepted. It was a period of truce in the long hostilities between king and emperor, and a time when Francis was hoping that Charles would consider marriage with his daughter, Margaret. The king met the emperor's cortege in the Loire Valley, after which there ensued a series of processions from one chateau to another and a series of entries into the towns along the way that were unrivaled in their splendour and magnificence. On 1 January 1540 (N.S.), His Imperial Majesty entered the city of Paris in an especially brilliant procession, the order and description of which were set down by Normandie and Champaigne, two of the king's heralds. The text, entitled *L'Ordre tenu et gardé a l'Entree de ... Charles Empereur ... en la ville de Paris*, was printed almost immediately after the event.[15] The account of the entry begins thus:

Apres que la sacree majesté Imperialle Charles cinquiesme de ce nom, tousjours Auguste, eut esté en grand honneur festoyé par le roy de France a Fontainebeleau, et qu'il eut esté aucuns jours au chasteau du boys de Vincennes ou on luy feit toute la bonne chere qu'il est possible de faire, le Jeudy premier jour de Janvier l'an mil cinq cens trente neuf il partit dudit chastel de Vincennes entre huyt et neuf heures du matin avec le Roy nostre sire, messeigneurs le Daulphin et le duc d'Orleans ses enfans, les princes, seigneurs, et officiers de leurs hostelz. Et vindrent descendre a sainct Anthoine des champs lez Paris. (a.ii.r)

Here the emperor was saluted with more than 300 rounds of artillery and was presented with the keys to the city. It is interesting to note that the king took part neither in the municipal welcome nor in the procession through the streets, respecting, apparently, the separate domains of city and palace:

Durant ce temps le Roy alla disner au logis de Montmorency en la rue sainct Anthoine ou il veit l'ordre du triumphe. . . . Et apres l'avoir veu, s'en alla au palais pour recevoir ledit Empereur quand il arriveroit. (a.ii.v)

The procession into the city began between two and three in the afternoon to the accompaniment of more artillery 'laquelle feit ung grand bruit et tempeste'. Leading the procession were the four mendicant orders, 'Cordeliers, Jacobins, Augustins et Carmes', as well as other religious orders of the city with processional crosses and reliquaries. Next came the rector and members of the university and the beadles of the 'nations' bearing golden maces. There followed three contingents of archers and other soldiers, numerous officials of the city of Paris, and several groups representing the various orders of justice, including 'la justice ordinaire pour le Roy au chastellet de Paris', 'la justice des Aydes', and 'la court de Parlement'. Then came the

members of the king's household, followed by seven cardinals and
Anne de Montmorency, the Constable of France. 'Venoit apres la
sacree majesté imperialle', accompanied on the right by the Dauphin
and on the left by the Duc d'Orléans. The emperor was followed by a
large company of nobles and finally the four Captains of the Guard
and their archers 'lesquelz gardoient lesditz seigneurs de la foulle du
peuple qui estoit merveilleuse'.

The procession stopped at the cathedral where the emperor was
received by Cardinal Du Bellay, the Bishop of Paris. After saying a
prayer, he proceeded to the palace, where the king received him with
great pomp and led him to the magnificent banquet prepared in the
Grande Salle. The king and the emperor sat together and were served
by members of the nobility acting the parts of the chief servers in the
royal household.

Et apres le soupper vindrent plusieurs princes et seigneurs en masques tous
vestuz de drap d'or, broderies et autres habitz de valeur inestimable, et furent
faictes morisques, dances et autres esbatemens les plus triumphantz qu'il est
possible de veoir. Et icelles finies, l'Empereur se retira en la chambre pour luy
ordonnee. (c.ii.v)

The remaining days of the emperor's visit were marked by
tournaments and jousting at the Louvre, after which he left Paris with
the king for a visit of several days at Chantilly.

The *Ordre tenu et gardé a l'Entree* is followed by a second account
entitled *Description des Magnifficences, Theatres et Misteres faictz en
la ville de Paris pour la reception de l'Empereur*. Here the authors
describe the decoration of the streets and the houses along the route of
march, the five triumphal arches through which the procession passed,
and the two stages or theatres, each containing an elaborate *tableau
vivant*. The first *tableau* was an allegory of War and Peace. It consisted
of a garden with two gates: the gate of War, which was barred, and the
gate of Peace, which was open. There were symbols of both king and
emperor in the garden, signifying the peaceful coexistence of the two
rulers. No words were spoken, but 'une belle fille nommee Aliance . . .
feit reverence a l'Empereur quand il passa'. Her message was written
on a placard above her head:

Bien soit venu en ce verger de France
L'imperialle et majesté sacree,
La peur des Turcz, des Chrestiens la deffence,
L'Aigle vollant en chascune contree. (d.iii.r)

The second *tableau* was an allegory of Concord and Discord. It consisted of a large pair of elaborately decorated, two-headed eagles, symbols of imperial majesty. Between the eagles 'estoit assise une belle dame nommee Paix . . . laquelle tenoit ung rameau d'ollivier'. Above the figure of Peace was written the following quatrain:

Je suis la paix, fille de Dieu vivant.
Quiconques est mon honneur poursuyvant,
Dieu est pour luy et sa maison augmente.
Qui guerre suit, la destruict et tourmente. (d.iv.v)

Tableaux vivants of this kind are in reality dramatized emblems, yet they bear a marked relationship to the morality play. They have some of the allegorical and ethical dimensions of a morality play, but because of the rank of the principal member of the audience, they must petition rather than preach. In this characteristic they also resemble the *bergerie*.

In addition to the *tableaux vivants*, the streets were hung with storied tapestries, which formed a series of *tableaux morts*, so to speak. The Grande Salle was also hung with 'riches tapisseries a personnaiges tant des histoires sainctes que poetiques'. The text mentions only two of these tapestries: the story of the Iliad and the Acts of the Apostles. The king and the emperor dined at the 'table de marbre':

Aux deux costez de ladicte table estoyent deux eschaffaulx a deux estages, et autant plus bas vers les cheminees, pour veoir les mommeries, jeux et dances des Princes et gentilz hommes. (e.ii.v)

The four scaffolds, two on each side of the hall, and the elevated table provided places for the spectators and probably the musicians as well. Presumably all the guests except those at the 'table de marbre' moved up to the scaffolds after dinner. The tables were then removed, creating a central arena for the mummings, plays, and dances. The shape of the theatre thus formed was much like that of many theatres constructed for tournaments and mystery plays.

The royal entry was thus composed of two distinct, but wholly integrated, simultaneous dramas, each having a different audience. 'La foulle du peuple', lining the streets and crowding the windows of the parade route, comprised the audience of a processional drama that the emperor and the representatives of all the major social institutions were acting out. The content of the drama was not a story, but an ideal order of social relationships. At the same time the emperor and other notables in the procession were the spectators of a stationary or fixed

drama in which the people demonstrated their feelings of respect and
reverence by dramatizing allegorical petitions for peace and
prosperity. It is this dual nature of the royal entry that the authors of
the *Ordre tenu* and the *Description des Magnifficences* reflect by
dividing their account of the ceremonies into two parts. While their
explicit distinction is between action and decoration, there is an
implicit recognition of two well-defined spectacles interwoven in the
same processional drama. This is what Konigson refers to as 'la fusion
de deux espaces'.[16] At the same time, we still recognize the periodic
nodes of dramatic activity in the linear structure that we have
observed in other processions. The nodes may be thought of as
paradigmatic axes that intersect the syntagmatic axis of the procession
at various intervals.

There were many other types of civil, religious, and holiday
processions in France in the fifteenth and sixteenth centuries. Funeral
processions, which were among the most common types, were often
both civil and religious in nature. They were also highly dramatic
reminders of the eternal contest between life and death. Among the
most impressive in this regard were the royal funeral processions, in
which the dead body and a life-like effigy of the king were borne
together in startling and dramatic contrast. In royal funerals
throughout the period under consideration the effigy was accorded, to
an ever increasing extent, the honours given to the living sovereign –
so much so that a contemporary account of the funeral procession of
Francis I in 1547 could refer to its passage through the streets of Paris
as 'l'antree dudit triumphe en ladite ville'.[17] Here we may look upon
the effigy as an 'actor' playing the role of the king in a processional
drama. Again we note how unclear the distinction was between drama
and literal act in public ceremonies.

Henry III, attempting to influence Providence in the matter of an
heir to the throne, both fostered and participated in penetential
processions. Frances Yates has called attention to a series of twenty-
two drawings made in 1583 depicting the king in a procession of this
sort.[18] Many of the participants are costumed to represent biblical
characters and, while some of the background scenes include
recognizable Paris landmarks, others are discernible representations
of biblical events. Yates interprets the latter scenes as *tableaux vivants*
that were set up along the procession route. Moreover, the king
himself, impersonating the penitent King of Nineveh, takes part in a
processional dramatization of the story of Jonah. Jonah is represented

both in the procession, where he is carrying a large fish, and in the background scene or *tableau vivant*, where he is emerging from the mouth of a whale on a seashore. Yates suggests that the whale may also be seen as a dolphin, which would express inconographically the theme and purpose of the procession: that is, the advent of a Dauphin.[19]

In 1588 a procession marched from Paris to Chartres in which Frère Ange, a Capuchin monk, impersonated Christ bearing the cross to Calvary. He was led by Roman soldiers and was accompanied by Mary, his mother, and Mary Magdalene. It is noteworthy that what had been banned from the stage in Paris for 40 years was permitted in a procession. Still, some of the contemporary observers found such a walking mystery play to be excessive. Others, however, were deeply moved by it. Yates feels that the procession of 1588 may have been an extreme development of a more general 'tendency towards processional rendering of sacred drama'.[20] Indeed, the tendency was already quite evident a generation earlier in the annual Corpus Christi procession of Draguignan, during which the marchers re-enacted brief scenes from the Old and New Testaments. An ordinance of the city council dated 8 May 1558 states:

Le dit jeu jora avec la procession comme auparadvant et le plus d'istoeres et plus brieves que puront estre seront et se dira tout en cheminant sans ce que personne du jeu s'areste pour eviter prolixité et confusion tant de ladite prosession que jeu et que les estrangiers le voient aisement.[21]

These are rather late processions relative to our period of inquiry, yet we find in them at least two distinctly medieval dramatic traits. First is the use of drama as an act of piety. This is all the more apparent in the king's procession, which was an act more of personal than of collective piety. The mystery plays of the Middle Ages, as we noted earlier, were frequently produced as acts of piety – thanksgiving for the return of peace or deliverance from the plague; petitions for protection against an enemy or some other imminent danger. The second medieval trait found in these late sixteenth-century processions is the integration of drama into the processional structure. This is all the more striking in that the processions of 1583 and 1588 came in the midst of the revival of ancient theatre a generation after the prohibition of religious plays in Paris. We may infer that processional drama was a structure so deeply embedded in late medieval culture that it could not be decreed out of existence.

All serious processions, religious or civil, had their comic analogues in the holiday processions of various *sociétés joyeuses*. These comic confraternities were particularly active in the northern provinces and include such groups as the Abbaye de Lescache Profit of Cambrai, the Mauvaises Braies of Laon, the Trompettes-Jongleurs of Chauny, and the Conards of Rouen. Their repertories included a number of dramatic activities such as plays and processions that took place on certain holidays during the year. The period of the most intense activity for these groups was the carnival season, which, in its broadest sense, extended from the darkness of the winter solstice through the delirium of Mardi Gras.[22]

The carnival procession was the antithesis of the royal entry in the sense that the rigid social hierarchy dramatized in the entry was deliberately reversed or shattered in the Saturnalian misrule of carnival. Moreover, if the civil and religious processions are formally related to the mystery and morality plays, then the comic processions are generically akin to the farces and the *sotties*. Characterized by folly and a general attitude of mockery, they constitute the satirical underside of the medieval processional tradition.

Les Triomphes de l'Abbaye des Conards, printed in Rouen in 1587, is a descriptive account of the Conards' activities of 1541 (N.S.), which included a magnificent procession. The style of the account is reminiscent of Rabelais in that the author has employed a number of comic devices familiar to the readers of *Pantagruel*: comic names, accumulations, inflated numbers, exaggerated precision, etc. The account narrates the month-long carnival preparations, which began on 30 January – Mardi Gras fell on 28 February that year. These included meetings of the 'gras Conseil', announcements, minor processions, petitions to the Parlement, calls to assembly, and cries in the streets. The major procession of the year took place on the Sunday before Lent:

Le dimenche gras sur le midi, se trouverent au vieil palais de ladite ville de Rouen, place dediee à faire telles assemblez, ledit sieur Abbé avec ses resveurs en decimes Cardinaux, Patriarches, Chancelier, Pronotaires et autres du college, accompagnez des neuf vices du couvent, au nombre de xxiiii ou xxv cens personnes accoustrez et masquez de si diverses sortes et conduits d'une si haute gaine qu'impossible est faire mieux sans art d'ennemy. (C.ii.r)[23]

Almost at the beginning of the parade came 'Le Pompe funebre de marchandise morte', literally a procession within a procession. The funeral cortege was led by a figure on horseback, who was dressed in mourning with symbolic tears of silver sewn to his garments, and who carried a banner on which was written: 'Alchofribas le disoit bien'. The cortege was a satirical comment on the state of business in Rouen and included such characters as Pauvre Commun, Avarice, Credit, and Trafique. There followed a long parade of the officials of the 'Abby' in which all notion of hierarchy had been deliberately turned upside down. As a consequence we find such unexpected pairings as 'les enquesteurs avec les accusepets ... les gens de l'Abbé avec les gouverneurs des lieux dangereux comme ... Bas de Fesse'. We also encounter names that belong to the comic world of farce and *sottie*: Frappecul, Baillevent, Maupencé, Maumisert, Rien Ne Scait, and Plattebourse. Then, preceded by torches, drums, fifes, and trumpets, came 'le grandissime, magnifiquissime et potentissime sieur Abbé' and his train.

Toward the end of the procession a satirical allegory entitled *La Buee ou laissive de l'Abbé* was mounted on seven floats:

Suivoyent en grande magnificence de pompe et triomphe sept chariots faits par bon art d'architecture en forme de theatres d'antique, conduits subtillement par certains instrumens, estans dedans lesdits chariots, qui n'estoyent veuz pour les enrichissemens et syrages d'iceux. (E.i.v)

Preceding the floats on horseback was a richly costumed 'personnage nommé Affection Mondaine ... lequel en passant dispersoit aux regardans un Dizain, et en certains lieux faisoit lecture d'iceluy, et d'une Ballade' (E.ii.r). The *dizain* was a descriptive summary of the dramatic actions that would be seen on the floats:

Religion assemble les drappeaux,
L'Eglise eschange et Foy et Verité
Y teurdent fort. Simonie en fardeaux
Le linge baille et dame Pauvreté
Le linge estend. Puis, par activité,
Ambition assiet et Avarice
Le feu allume. En tout plie Justice.
Faveur, Richesse y lavent par esbat;
Hipocrisie a de verser l'office.
Folle Amour seiche et Noblesse apres bat. (E.iv.v)

There were no spoken words in the processional allegory other than the periodic readings of the two poems by Affection Mondaine. On each float were one or two allegorical scenes in which the actions named in the *dizain* were repeated throughout the procession, the whole constituting a mimed *farce moralisée* of the Abbot's laundry. The mimed actions were distributed on the seven floats as follows, with the captions written on placards below each scene:

1. Religion assemble. L'Eglise eschange.
2. Foy et Verité teurdent.
3. Ambition assiet. Simonie baille le linge.
4. Avarice allume. Hipocrisie verse.
5. Faveur et Richesse lavent.
6. Noblesse bat. Pauvreté estend.
7. Folle Amour seiche. Justice plie.

There followed immediately another mimed *farce moralisée*, eloquent in its simple repeated action:

Apres lesdits chariots marchoyent quatre hommes accoustrez de differentes sortes en semblance des quatre estats. . . . Ils conduisoyent un petit chariot carré . . . au dedans duquel estoyent quatre personnages de grande estime et representation, l'un habillé en Pape, l'autre en Empereur, le troisiéme en Roy et le quatriéme en Fol. Lesquels jettoyent un Monde rond de l'un a l'autre en mode du jeu du pot cassé, et portoyent derriere leur dos, chacun a part soy, differemment ces mots: Tien-cy, Baille-ça, Rit-t'en, Mocque't'en. Et margoüilloyent ce pauvre Monde assez rudement, de sorte qu'il eust beaucoup a souffrir entre leurs mains. (F.i.v)

The banquet and entertainments that traditionally followed a procession took place two days later on Mardi Gras. The tables for the banquet were set up in 'la halle aux draps nouveau bastie, la plus belle et espacieuse qui soit en France' and arranged so as to form a theatre:

Au milieu y avoit un eschaffaut pour jouer les farces, comedies et morisques, fait de sorte qu'on pouvoit passer par dessoubs pour le service dudit disner; et dessus y avoit un personnage abillé en Hermite, assis sus une chaire, lequel en lieu de Bible lisoit continuellement durant ledit disner la Cronique Pantagruel. Au bout de ladite salle y avoit un theatre haut eslevé, richement tapissé, sur lequel estoit le sieur Abbé au milieu, et aux deux costez le Chancelier, Patriarche et Cardinaux. . . . Au[x] deux bouts les trompettes et haubois et en bas estoyent les phiffres et tabours. . . . A la fin du disner . . . furent faits plusieurs farces et comedies, dances et morisques en grant nombre avec bonnes moralitez et de bonne audace. (I.i.v–ii.r)

Note that the word *eschaffaut* in the preceding text refers to the playing stage, while the word *theatre* refers to the elevated platform where the dignitaries dined and from which they watched the plays after dinner. Its principal function, though, was to provide a place for them to be seen, for they too were part of the spectacle. Thus the structure of this theatre (in the modern sense), with two elevated stages – one for the dignitaries and one for the players – reflects the same dual perspective characteristic of the procession. We cannot, therefore, separate the banquet and its dramatic entertainments from the procession proper. The latter is a moving drama with a double perspective; the former is a stationery node of dramatic activity that maintains the processional perspective.

It seems virtually certain that one of the 'moralitez de bonne audace' played at the carnival banquet was the *Moralité de l'Eglise, Noblesse et Pauvreté qui font la lessive*. Not only is the metaphor of washing in this play identical to that of the processional allegory, but the fourteen personifications who do the washing are the same with one exception: Simonie has been replaced by Rapine. The play is quite simply a spoken version of the mimed *farce moralisée*. Verbal description, however, replaces the mimed actions, which makes possible a great economy of actors. The characters are therefore limited to the three of the title. Moreover, the virulence of the attack on the abuses of the first two estates is strengthened by its translation into a verbal mode of expression. This is undoubtedly what was meant by 'bonne audace'. Furthermore, viewing the play from the generic perspective of the preceding chapters, we see a virulent institutional satire with no provision for reform within the action of the play, which clearly places the work in the farce world rather than in the morality world. The 'moral' of the play is external to the dramatic action and is spoken by Eglise to the audience:

Aucun poura y prendre bonne exemple
Et de mal faict en bien se coriger. (p. 15)

Therefore, despite the fact that the play is called a *moralité* in the title, it should be classed as a *farce moralisée*. We noted in the previous chapter that the Conards of Rouen tended to interchange the terms *moralité* and *farce morale*, which might explain the anomalous genre designation of the title. In any case, now that we see the play in its context of satirical carnival procession, it is all the more apparent that it belongs to the farce world.

One of the things we have noted in our survey of processions is that in the late Middle Ages there was no clear distinction between pure drama, so to speak, and public ritual act. Not only were regular plays an inseparable part of late medieval processions, but the procession itself had been so theatricalized that it came to resemble what we would normally call drama. The plays involved in the processions that we have considered up to this point have all been short works played either in movement or at fixed nodes of dramatic activity along the parade route. If we turn now to the lengthy mystery plays, they too may be seen as stationary nodes of dramatic activity in a larger processional context. The great mystery plays were always preceded by a parade, called a *montre*, which served to advertise the coming spectacle. The costumed actors would process through the streets, accompanied by heralds and trumpets, giving the townspeople a preview of the marvels they would see in the theatre. In addition, each day, or *journée*, of the production was likely to open with a procession of all the actors marching to the theatre in the morning and from the theatre in the evening. The proportions, of course, are changed, but the processional structure remains. The brief pauses for dramatic activity characteristic of the other processions have been expanded to the *journées* of dramatic activity characteristic of the mystery plays. Let us see how this worked in actuality.

In 1496 the town of Seurre in Burgundy hired André de La Vigne to compose a play on the life of Saint Martin, patron of the community. He also wrote a brief morality play and a farce to accompany the mystery play. Even more important for us is the fact that he drew up an account of the significant events related to the production. Delayed at first by threat of war, the mystery play was finally scheduled to begin on Sunday, 9 October, of the same year. The *montre*, which was held on the preceding Tuesday, was a procession of all those who had a part in the play, riding on horseback in their costumes through the streets of Seurre. They processed in cosmological order, the devils first and the court of heaven last. In all, there were 180 horses in the parade.

After several days of clear weather, Sunday brought a heavy rain that lasted until about three o'clock in the afternoon. By that time those who had come to Seurre to see the play were growing restive. The mayor and the aldermen, in order to keep the visitors from leaving, decided to 'jouer une farce sur le parc pour les contenter et aprester'. The word *parc* in this and the following passages refers to the playing space or arena of the circular theatre.[24] The text continues:

La trompecte fit le cry que tous joueurs se rendissent incontinent habillez de leurs habitz en la maison monsieur le Marquis et tous les aultres allassent sur les eschaffaulx. Ledit cry fait d'une part et d'aultre, chacun fit son debvoir. Lors on mist les joueurs en ordre et yssirent de chelz mondit sieur le Marquis les ungs apres les aultres si honnourablement que quant ilz furent sur le parc, tout le monde en fut fort esbahy. Ilz firent leur tour comme il appartient et se

retira chacun en sa loge, et ne demeura sur ledit parc que les personnages de la
farce du Munyer. (fol. 262 r)

When the farce ended, the larger processional drama was not yet
finished:

Au partir dudit parc tous lesdits joueurs se myrent en arroy, chacun selon son
ordre, et a sons de trompetes, clerons, menestriers, haulx et bas instrumens
s'en vindrent en ladite eglise monsieur sainct Martin devant Nostre Dame
chanter ung salut moult devostement affin que le beau temps vint pour
executer leur bonne et devoste entencion en l'entreprise dudit mistere. (fol.
262 v)

What strikes one immediately in this text is the fact that the entire
cast of almost 200 players was called out in costume to present a short
farce with eight characters, five of whom were devils from the hell
scenes of the mystery play. While there is an element of advertising
here in what amounts to a second *montre*, this elaborate procedure
provides a significant insight into the importance of the procession in
the production of medieval mystery plays. A production of this kind
was not just an amateur entertainment of gigantic proportions; it was
a collective act of piety, a communal affirmation of the Christian order
of the cosmos. In each procession the players were 'mis en ordre' in
imitation of the chain of being from the devils through all the
characters of the play up to God. Each procession was cosmology made
flesh; each was a visible mimesis of metaphysical reality, requiring the
participation of all spectators in the form of their intellectual and
emotional assent. The processional form was not only one of the best
means of demonstrating the universal chain of being, it was also one of
the most effective ways that human culture has devised of integrating
the individual life into the life of the community. At the same time, we
should not be unaware that these plays were also good business. The
mayor's concern over the possible departure of the visitors was
prompted by his fear that the town would lose revenue. Because of
their size, the mystery plays often required a large capital investment,
but they also provided in some cases a good rate of return.[25] There was
no conflict of allegiance between good business and piety, nor was
there any suspicion of hypocrisy in the combination. The two
approaches were quite compatible in the late Middle Ages.

The good weather did return to Seurre and the whole town devoted
the next three days to re-enacting the life of its patron and guardian,
Saint Martin. André de La Vigne describes the opening procession of

the mystery play in a prose that is itself a mimesis of the processional
rhythm as he orders the preparatory events and lines up the musical
instruments for the march:

Commandement fut fait a son de trompete par mesdits sieurs les maire et
eschevins dudit Seurre que tout le monde cloyst boutique et que nul ne fust si
osé ne hardy de faire euvre mecquanique en ladite ville l'espace de trois jours
ensuivant, esquels on debvoit jouer le mistere de la vie monsieur sainct
Martin, et que tous joueurs se rendissent au moustier dudit Seurre
incontinant. Le monde se retira aux eschaffaulx, lesdits joueurs aussi ou il
debvoient et puis furent mys en ordre par ledit maistre Andrieu selon le
registre et marchoient avant a sons de trompetes, clerons, bussines, orgues,
harpes, tabourins et aultres bas et haulx instrumens, jouans de tous costez
jusques sur ledit parc, faisant leur tour comme en tel cas est requis, qui estoit
une si gorriere et si tressumptueuse besongne qu'il n'est possible a
entendement d'omme de le scavoir escripre ne [dire], tant estoit la chose belle
et magniffique. (fol. 262 v)

Thus the players processed to the theatre each morning, and thus
each evening they processed from the theatre to the church, where they
devoutly sang a *Salve Regina* in thanksgiving. We must see the play,
the procession, and the ceremony of thanksgiving as being integral
parts of a single collective spectacle that, taken together, formed a
broader dramatic genre.

Another characteristic of the procession that we find in the
production of the great mystery plays is the dual dramatic perspective.
The principal spectacle was, of course, the mystery play itself; but, in
consonance with the increasing theatricalization of public events in
the late Middle Ages, the order and arrangement of the audience in the
theatre came to be a significant spectacle as well. When one thinks of
the kind of circular theatre depicted by Fouquet in his painting of the
martyrdom of St Apollonia, presumably the kind that was constructed
in Seurre, one sees immediately that the members of the audience
constitute a parallel spectacle – a *tableau vivant*, as it were, of the new
social order. Konigson notes how the beginnings of a social structure
based on economic classes were reflected in the distribution of
spectators in the theatre:

A l'immobilisme d'ordre divin du corps social, qui a été battu en brèche par les
marchands, les financiers et les maîtres de métiers succède un immobilisme
conservateur que la place respective des spectateurs sur les gradins ou dans les
loges exprime visuellement. Pour la première fois les places payantes
introduisent le spectacle également dans la salle en ordonnant le corps social
selon sa fortune.[26]

What had been a mixture of the various social ranks, whose members were distinguished by dress and insignia, became, in the course of the fifteenth century, a spectacle of the community divided into economic classes. With this change the dual perspective of the medieval processional drama was brought into still greater relief.

One ordinarily thinks of the shorter dramatic forms – farces, *sotties*, and morality plays – as being performed independently of public ritual ceremonies such as processions. Indeed, this was often the case. Yet they were just as frequently performed in the context of a larger processional structure. Municipal records from cities of the northern provinces bear witness to an intense dramatic activity in the fifteenth and sixteenth centuries.[27] Every city and town had a number of confraternities and *sociétés joyeuses* who entertained themselves and others on holidays by staging plays. Many of these groups were subsidized by their municipal councils to travel to neighbouring cities 'affin d'entretenir amour et soscieté aveuques les bonnes villes voisines', as a document from Laon expressed it in 1496.[28] One must not imagine that such groups of amateur actors travelled informally and incognito as they would today. They went in procession on horseback, with heralds preceding them and sometimes accompanied by aldermen of the city or wealthy members of the patrician class. They were not just travelling players; they were also representatives of their city. One of their major functions was to demonstrate by the brilliance of their procession the wealth, honour, and dignity of the city from which they came.

One of the most spectacular of such processions took place in 1548, when the aldermen and council of Lille subsidized the Prince d'Amour and his troupe to go to Valenciennes for the annual festival of the Prince de Plaisance. The procession included other *sociétés joyeuses* and numbered over 200 people. It was escorted by noblemen and accompanied by heralds, trumpets, and pages. The procession was met at the gates of Valenciennes by the Prince de Plaisance and his court, together with delegates from the trade guilds of the city. From there they processed through the city to their lodgings and then to a banquet at the city hall. In the evening all the troupes played farces by torchlight in the streets and squares of Valenciennes. The next day being Sunday, they all processed to mass; then in the afternoon they staged morality plays. The festival ended the following day with another procession.[29] Again we see in the festival of the Prince de Plaisance of Valenciennes the same pattern that we have discerned in other processional observances: the farces, morality plays, and the banquet with its entertainments were all stationary nodes of dramatic activity in a larger processional drama.

All of the processional genres that we have examined have at least three structural components in common. First, there is a physical, linear movement involving all participants in the procession. Second, there are stationary nodes of dramatic activity along the line of march, at which points the forward movement of the procession is interrupted for periods of varying duration. Third, there is a dual dramatic perspective in the sense that the participants in one spectacle are simultaneously the spectators of another spectacle. This is quite evident in the procession proper, but we also noted that the dual perspective was carried over to the fixed nodes of dramatic activity in the carnival banquet and in the mystery plays.

Thus, the surface variations that one sees in these processional dramas – tournament, royal entry, funeral cortège, carnival parade, mystery play – should not hide the fact that at a deeper structural level there is an identity of form that provides a basis for generic distinctions. Related genres, after all, are structurally similar entities that manifest superficial differences. The processional form, therefore, is far more than a convenient, but dispensable, setting for a group of plays. It has a semantics of its own that links the dramatic nodes into a meaningful whole. The meaning in its totality is undoubtedly difficult for us to grasp because there was in the late Middle Ages a 'unity of play and reality that is no longer accessible to our experience'.[30] Medieval people did not make our distinctions between life and art, between literal act and drama. But in order to understand their drama, it is imperative that we understand their distinctions and their perceptions of the world. This is what we have tried to do throughout the present study.

In this chapter we have posited the processional form as an over-genre, so to speak, of which the processional dramas examined above are generic variants. In the next chapter we shall once again change the scale of our mapping of medieval dramatic genres in order to examine closely a single genre – the typical farce. We shall even limit our consideration to a single thematic type of that genre in order to enter as fully as possible into the fictional world depicted there. This will enable us to experience a genre from within, as it were, and to compare the farce world revealed by sympathetic reading with that posited by generic theory. It is only by combining this kind of experience of the medieval genres with a knowledge of their formal and cultural contexts that we can ever come close to understanding the distant otherness of the medieval dramatic world.

Notes

[1]George R. Kernodle, *From Art to Theatre* (Chicago: University of Chicago Press, 1943), p. 17.

[2]Kernodle, p. 16.

[3]Konigson, *L'Espace théâtral*, p. 280.

[4]Glynne Wickham, *Early English Stages*, vol. I (London: Routledge & Kegan Paul, 1959), pp. 13–50.

[5]Achille Durieux, *Le Théâtre à Cambrai avant et depuis 1789* (Cambrai: J. Renaut, 1883), p. 145.

[6]Durieux, p. 150.

[7]Wickham, pp. 22–24.

[8]Konigson, *L'Espace théâtral*, p. 63.

[9]Bernard Guenée and Françoise Lehoux, *Les Entrées royales françaises de 1328 á 1515* (Paris: Centre National de la Recherche Scientifique, 1968), p. 12.

[10]Guenée and Lehoux, p. 75.

[11]Guenée and Lehoux, pp. 75–79.

[12]Guenée and Lehoux, p. 64.

[13]Guenée and Lehoux, p. 76.

[14]Guenée and Lehoux, p. 29.

[15]*L'Ordre tenu et gardé a l'entree de treshault et trespuissant prince Charles Empereur tousjours Auguste, en la ville de Paris*, (Paris: Gilles Corrozet & Jehan du Pré, 1539).

[16]Konigson, *L'Espace théâtral*, p. 200.

[17]Ralph E. Giesey, *The Royal Funeral Ceremony in Renaissance France* (Geneva: Droz, 1960), p. 14.

[18]Frances A. Yates, 'Dramatic religious processions in Paris in the late sixteenth century', *Annales Musicologiques*, 2 (1954), 215–70.

[19]Yates, 'Dramatic religious processions', p. 267.

[20]Yates, 'Dramatic religious processions', p. 249.

[21]Petit de Julleville, *Les Mystères*, II, 209.

[22]Gaignebet, p. 41.

[23]I have adopted Montifaud's reading of *vices* for *vites* in the original text: Marc de Montifaud, ed., *Les Triomphes de l'abbaye des Conards*, 2nd ed. (Paris: A. Lacroix, 1877), pp. 28–29.

[24]Rey-Flaud, pp. 79–82.

[25]Elie Konigson, *La Représentation d'un mystère de la passion à Valenciennes en 1547* (Paris: Centre National de la Recherche Scientifique, 1969), pp. 20–21.

[26]Konigson, *L'Espace théâtral*, p. 59.

[27]See Alan E. Knight, 'Drama and society in late medieval Flanders and Picardy', *The Chaucer Review*, 14 (1980), 379–89.

[28]Edouard Fleury, *Origines et développements de l'art théâtral dans la province ecclésiastique de Reims* (Reims: A. Cortilliot, 1880), p. 265.

[29]Lefebvre, I, 69–71.

[30]Rainer Warning, 'On the alterity of medieval religious drama', *New Literary History*, 10 (1979), 285.

CHAPTER VII

The conjugal farce

Of the many dramatic genres that flourished in late medieval France, the farce was decidedly one of the most popular. Du Verdier attests to this in his *Bibliothèque françoise* (1585): 'On ne sauroit dire les farces qui ont esté composées et imprimées, si grand en est leur nombre. Car au temps passé chascun se mesloit d'en faire.' Their brevity and ease of production contributed, no doubt, to a wide acceptance among both writers and players. Their dramatic simplicity and ease of comprehension contributed likewise to their popularity with audiences. Yet the same virtues of brevity and simplicity that gave the farce its tenacious hold on the popular imagination also excluded, for the most part, the subleties of character development and the complexities of personal relationships that are possible in longer dramatic forms. This is in no sense a deficiency, however, for in their place we find the quickly grasped character types that foster a mordant wit and the fixed character relationships that permit immediate satirical thrusts at social abuses. The latter traits in the medieval French farce are patterned on the established group relationships in the society contemporary to the plays. Thus a relationship between two farce characters or types is usually a dramatic mimesis of the interaction between two social roles. This is why so many farce characters have no other name than that of the social role they fulfill: Le Mari, La Femme, L'Amoureux, Le Juge, Le Savetier, and so on. Even when a character has a proper name, it usually designates a type rather than an individual: Tendrette is the young, seducible wife; Finette is the deceitful wife; Jenin is the deceived husband; and Frère Frappart is the lascivious monk.

Role relationships in the farce tend always to be simple in that one character usually fulfills only a single role in regard to another

character. In the case of a married couple, for example, the man and
woman will most often interact on the sole basis of their roles as
husband and wife. If, however, they should play the roles of mother
and father, as they do in *Maistre Mimin*, then their conjugal roles
become dramatically insignificant. Thus farces normally treat family
and social relationships analytically rather than synthetically.[1]
Because farce characters are so typed and because social roles are
systematized in this way, one can group the plays of the typical farce
genre into thematic categories such as conjugal farces, student farces,
braggart soldier farces, and the like. Such groupings will enable us to
recognize similar patterns of action among character types within each
category and will ultimately enhance our understanding of the genre
as a whole.

   We noted earlier that the fictional world in which farce characters
live and act is a world dominated by folly. One can easily see a
depiction of that world in Breugel's painting, *The Blue Cloak*. Breugel
has here portrayed a world turned upside down, in which each of the
many figures is acting out the literal meaning of a proverb – a comic
device found frequently in the farces. One person is swimming against
the stream; another is winnowing feathers in the wind. In the centre of
the painting a young, stylishly dressed woman is covering her old
husband with a vivid blue cloak. This is a literal depiction of the
proverb: 'The woman who gladly welcomes favours here and there
must hang the Blue Coat round her husband.'[2] The centrality of the
Blue Cloak theme in the painting parallels the central importance of
the conjugal theme in the farces. Its importance is both numerical, in
that more than half of the typical farces may be classed as conjugal
farces, and conceptual, in that the farce tends to be a domestic genre.
In the three sections that follow we will examine the conjugal farce
from the point of view of the major character types involved: the wife,
the husband, and the lover.

The Farce Wife

Medieval drama provides an extremely valuable body of material for
examining questions raised by the relationship of literature to society.
In approaching this material, however, we should take care to avoid
the simplistic notion that drama, even so-called realistic drama, gives
us in any sense a photographic image of the society that produced it.
We must also keep in mind the fact that drama, like literature and the

other arts, is first of all a product of the imagination. It may take its raw material from the society that gives it birth, but its character and direction are derived from the more general and abstract ideals of that society, as expressed through the medium of its own mythology.[3]

Let us consider some of the questions surrounding one of the points at which literature and society intersect – that is, the image of woman in the late medieval French farce – not with the idea of determining what it was like to be a woman in the late Middle Ages, but with the hope of seeing more clearly some of the complex literary relationships underlying that particular image. Once we see how the formal and structural elements of the farce are interrelated on the imaginative level, we will be in a better position to understand how a dramatic genre embodying such elements functions in society on the existential level.

As in most historical periods, society in the Middle Ages was thoroughly masculine in both structure and orientation. Its political, ethical, and theological models had been created by men and shaped to fit men's needs and desires. Such a social structure, even at its best, will put strain on the general relations between men and women; but if these relations are widely viewed with suspicion, especially in the basic institutions of marriage and the family, then harsh treatment of the sex designated as 'weaker' is bound to ensue. Medieval moral treatises are replete with formulas for testing the love of one's wife or children and with warnings against showing them too much affection lest they be spoiled or given occasions for pride. Collective attitudes of this kind are symptomatic of a profound mistrust of self that has been unconsciously and defensively transferred to others. In a male dominated society, women, of course, will constitute a large segment of such 'others'. Consequently, the ethical and social restraints devised to preserve moral 'law and order' will be far more stringently binding on women than on men.

The position of women in the Middle Ages gave rise to a number of conventional literary images that tended to cluster around the polarized categories of bad women and good women. These, in turn, were patterned on the archetypal figures of Eve, the mother of the fallen race, and Mary, the mother of the god-redeemer. Literary works based on these conventional images of women formed the nucleus of a continuing debate or *querelle des femmes*, the beginning of which antedated Rabelais' *Tiers Livre* by several hundred years. A brief glance at three of these conventional images of women as expressed in the satirical, moral, and courtly love traditions will provide a background for our discussion of the farce wife.

In the late thirteenth-century antifeminist satire, *Le Blastange des fames*, the anonymous author, speaking of the treachery and deviousness of women, asserts:

Ce sont unes choses bien certes
Que fames sevent par nature
Pou bien et trop mal aventure.
En eles est toz mauz repus.[4]

What is striking in this passage is not so much the medieval commonplace that women conceal every evil within themselves, but the contention that the evil is there by nature. The author is not speaking here of the second nature of acquired habit – the kind of mental habit, for example, that makes his assertion seem so natural – but of the first nature of inherent and essential qualities. It was widely accepted in the Middle Ages that the differences between man and woman were so great as to constitute two distinct natures. Mathéolus in his *Lamentations* reminds us that woman, after all, was made from bone, while man was made from the dust of the earth. And since bone is more clangorous than earth, women are naturally more vociferous and argumentative than men. From this he concludes: 'De nature leur vient a toutes/Qu'elles sont foles et estoutes'.[5]

Implicit in this general view, or this myth, is the conviction that, because of woman's inherently imperfect and evil nature, the world would quickly be plunged into moral chaos if female behaviour were not strictly controlled by rigid rules and constant policing. Woman's inferior social status, which was explained and justified by the literally accepted Hebrew myth of human genesis, was thus reinforced by a general belief in her defective nature. In a kind of self-confirming circularity, this attitude influenced the interpretation of the myth of the expulsion from an earthly paradise, where, it would seem, only Adam fell from a true state of original justice. Eve may have been *innocent* before the Fall, but the seeds of evil were already implanted in her nature, awaiting only the season of temptation to germinate. Adam, by his position and his nature, was solely responsible for the moral future of mankind, and, had he not been deceived and led astray by woman's wiles, Eve's flirtation with the serpent would have had no consequences for the human race.

Our concern here is with a literary sub-structure in the form of a social myth rather than with theological positions on the origin and nature of mankind. Yet it is worth noting that the theologians who wrestled with similar questions concerning woman generally fell into the same misogynist camp as the satirists. Thomas Aquinas, following Aristotle, held woman to be defective and misbegotten: 'Per respectum ad naturam particularem, femina est aliquid deficiens et occasionatum.'[6] Bonaventure insisted that the feminine sex was more inclined to evil than the masculine sex: 'Quantum est ex parte naturae, nisi adsit fortitudo maioris gratiae, facilius incurvatur ad malum sexus femineus.'[7]

From the numerous moral treatises written in the Middle Ages for the instruction and correction of women, a somewhat different image of woman emerges. It is true that the authors of these works impose severe limitations on women's behaviour and activities. It is likewise true that in these works women are regarded more as objects, ranging from courtly ornaments to chattel, than as persons. When Robert de Blois says in his *Chastoiement des dames*, for example: 'Famme n'est bele ne plaisanz/Quant ele est de tancier ardanz',[8] he implies, among other things, that any expression of strong feeling by a woman reduces her ornamental value. Or when Philippe de Novare says in his *Quatre ages de l'homme*: 'Mout sont fames avilenies, quant eles sont blamées, et plus quant eles mesfont',[9] his concern is prompted as much by a male aversion to accepting used merchandise in marriage as it is by Christian morality. But, in spite of all this, there is one characteristic of paramount importance that distinguishes these works from the antifeminist satires. Every moral treatise is an act of faith in the educability of woman and is therefore fundamentally optimistic. Think, for example, of the tender concern and sanguine hopes that moved the Chevalier de La Tour Landry to compose his book of instructions for his daughters. To expect that one's daughters will learn to live by such a book is to believe that woman is essentially capable of responsibility and that she is not naturally and ineluctably inclined to evil.

The image of woman that was created and elaborated in the love poetry of the Provençal troubadours stands in sharp contrast to the images we have seen in the satirical and moral traditions. Here, woman is sought after for her beauty and feminine graces; she is the beloved, who bestows her love on whom she will. Far from being defective by nature, she is a model of perfection and an occasion of virtue for her lover. Instead of being reviled, she is adored and given all the attentions and considerations that poetry can invent. Thus woman becomes the centre of a cult whose liturgy is the language of love. The sex object is metamorphosed into a goddess, and the energy of male desire is transformed into a ritual of poetic service. Rather than take the desired object by force, the lover allows himself to be awed by the power that the beloved holds over him. This respect of woman is the fundamental distinguishing characteristic of the courtly love tradition, separating it from the other literary traditions of satire and moral instruction. But it is a feeling that endures only so long as the quest game lasts.

Each of these three literary traditions gives expression to a different relationship between man and woman. Antifeminist satire describes woman from the point of view of the victim; moral treatises portray her from the guardian's point of view; and courtly love poetry views her through the eyes of the lover. The farce, when it treats of amorous or conjugal relationships, is always satirical in its portrayal of woman, and at least one male character – usually the husband – is presented as the victim of woman's malevolence. As we shall see, when the satirical farce absorbed certain elements of the other two traditions without also assuming their point of view, the result was parody and caricature.

Though farce wives are depicted according to the satirical stereotype, they are not all of a kind and the variations in their negative qualities are worth noting. The most common type is the deceitful wife. This fact points to a focus of anxiety in medieval society, where great importance was placed on external traits such as appearance, manners, reputation, and social insignia. The deception of the farce wife usually turns on an act of marital infidelity, which in turn presupposes an inclination to disobedience and an insatiable sexual desire. A good example of feminine deceit is found in *Martin de Cambray*, where the wife is kept under lock and key by a jealous husband. She has her lover, the parish priest, appear in devil's disguise and carry her off to 'hell' before her husband's eyes. On being returned home by the same 'devil', she tells Martin that jealous husbands suffer the worst torments in hell, whereupon he gives her the key to the house and her freedom to come and go as she pleases.

A considerable number of farce wives, in addition to being deceptive, are domineering to the point that their husbands cower in submission to their sharp tongues, never daring to talk back. Some of these Caspar Milquetoasts endure their subordinate position throughout a play, while others reassert their authority at the end by punishing the wife or by chasing the lover away. Because the ability to dominate is a talent with which these farce wives are richly endowed by nature, there would be an inherent absurdity in a university trying to confer such an ability with one of its degrees, even if it gave degrees to women. Yet, in *Les Femmes qui se font passer maistresses*, a certain Maistre Regnault arrives in Paris with papal letters empowering him to confer university degrees on women. Two young wives, each with two years experience in marriage, present themselves as candidates. After being examined on how well they have learned to dominate their husbands, they are officially given the degree of *Maistresse* in both the university and their own households.

A third basic type of farce wife is the malicious wife. Generally speaking, malice is not an isolated characteristic, but is found in combination with the other negative qualities described above. The wife of Jehan in the *Farce du pasté* is not only deceitful and domineering to a high degree, she is also malicious, spiteful, and cruel. She forces Jehan to heat wax to mend a water pot while she and her lover, the local priest, eat the pâté that the famished husband so desperately craves. During the meal, she drinks to his health while he is busy heating the wax. (*Chauffer la cire*, according to Cotgrave, means 'to attend long for a promised good turne'.) After the pâté has been devoured by the lovers, the wife asks Jehan with feigned concern and innocence, 'N'avez vous pas souppé?'

By contrast, there are farces where the wife is faithful to her husband and, moreover, makes no effort to deceive him. In plays of this kind, the action is focused on a relationship other than the conjugal one, and the satire is aimed at characters other than the wife. *Maistre Pierre Pathelin* is a good example. Guillemette is the true and faithful wife, who supports her husband, even in his petty thievery. While her role is essential to the action, her marital relationship to Pathelin is not. This farce turns on the relationships that exist among the three men: Pathelin, the draper, and the shepherd. Guillemette's role could be assigned to some other accomplice without disturbing the play's central point of 'à trompeur, trompeur et demi'. Plays of this sort are not conjugal farces because the wife claims no victims and because the conjugal relationship is accessory to the dramatic action. A conjugal farce, then, is a farce in which the conjugal relationship is central to the dramatic action. In most of these plays the husband is the victim of his wife's infidelity, or her usurpation of authority, or both.

There are also conugal farces from which the husband is absent – or at least he is not the victim – and in which the central relationship is that between the wife and her lover. Still, the conjugal relationship remains essential to the action, since an unmarried woman would completely alter the dramatic situation. In this kind of play, the lover replaces the husband as victim of the woman's machinations. We know that in the courtly love tradition one of the refinements inspired in the lover by the beloved is the ability to sing her praises in elegant verse. When, however, the high style of courtly love poetry is imitated in a satirical work where the lover is victim of the beloved, the content becomes laughable and the result is formal parody. In *Les Trois Amoureux de la croix*, three young gallants, Martin, Gaultier, and Guillaume, are all in love with a married woman who does not share their amorous feelings. Each of the lovers secretly approaches the lady and declares his fervid and undying love in swatches of florid verse. Martin is the first to greet his beloved:

Dame, de mon povre pover,
Je vous salue tres humblement,
Vous suppliant tres doulcement
Que je soye en vostre demaine,
Car vous estes la primeraine
Des dames, et plaisez a tous. (47–52)

When she expresses surprise at this sudden declaration of love, he continues:

Las! Je suis prins
Et si hardement lié
De vostre amour. Si n'en suis delié
Bref par vostre doulceur,
Certainement je suis asseur
De mourir sans aucun secours! (66–71)

Unfortunately for Martin, as his rhetoric becomes more extravagant, the woman's skepticism becomes more pronounced:

Entre vous, galans, scavés tours
Subtilz et faictes les semblans
D'estre malades et tremblans
Tousjours, mais ce n'est que faintise. (72–75)

When, finally, he offers her ten ducats for her love, she cynically accepts the money and sets a time and place for a tryst that she has no intention of keeping.

Gaultier next approaches, and the scene is repeated in much the same language:

Ha! Ma dame, je vous diray,
Nul n'y sauroit remede mettre
Que vous, car vous estes le maistre
Et l'euvre de ma maladie.
Que voulés vous que je vous die?
Je seuffre tel paine et douleur
Pour vous que, se vostre doulceur
Ne consent a moy secourir,
Force me sera de mourir
Du mal que j'ay et du martire. (146–55)

Again the woman accepts money and sets a tryst. The same action is then repeated with Guillaume, including the parody of courtly love poetry. The woman has told each suitor to come in a certain disguise in order to protect the secret of his love from her husband. The first is to be dressed as a priest, the second as a dead man, and the third as a devil. The scene of confusion and chaos that develops when the three disguised men meet at the cross in the square is one of the most comic in all the farces. When the gallants ultimately recognize one another, they swear never again to trust in women's promises.

If the declarations of love just quoted are parodies of the courtly love style, then the characters who make them are caricatures of courtly lovers. Their professions of love are too sudden and too awkward to be part of the serious tradition. Moreover, they show no consideration for the feelings of the lady. But the most serious breach of the courtly ethic is the payment of money for the lady's love. The woman in *Les Trois Amoureux* is likewise a caricature of the beloved. It is true that she never pretends to be what she is not, but the continual reference to her as *dame* places her in a position that is not common to the ordinary farce wife. It is the trick she plays on the lovers and, above all, her acceptance of money that characterize her as a petty bourgeois housewife and that create the caricature of the courtly ideal of woman as inspirer of brave deeds and manly virtues.

The caricature is much broader in scope, however, than just aiming at aristocratic love conventions. The farce wife is a concrete embodiment of all the traits and qualities that the books of manners and the moral treatises warn women to avoid. Consider, for example, a few of the lessons in the *Chastoiement des dames* of Robert de Blois, a work that was still current in the early sixteenth century, since it was

printed in the *Jardin de plaisance* in 1501. The most basic assumption
of this and all other moral works was the absolute and unalterable
necessity of a wife's faithfulness and obedience to her husband. But we
have already seen that the infraction of these cardinal requirements of
wifely conduct is a commonplace of the conjugal farce. Robert teaches
women never to lie, yet deceit is essential to the farce wife. He
admonishes women never to show anger, never to engage in disputes or
fights; yet the farce wife is typically a termagant or a shrew who resists
taming. Personal hygiene is an important lesson for Robert, who
devotes several sections of his work to the subject; yet such expletives
as *sale, orde,* and *puante* are among those most frequently hurled at
farce wives.

In some of the farce couples we see caricatures of the philosophical
and theological conceptions of the differences in authority and dignity
between man and woman. In the farce version of these distinctions,
woman is a creature of a different species from man. Her character is
so totally at odds with man's character that the two can only be in
conflict when they are brought together. Thus the enmity between the
sexes has its source in the order of nature. In the farce of *Tarabin et
Tarabas* a husband and wife are at war. Tarabin cannot stand her
husband's *teste* and declaims against it in a striking passage of verbal
fantasy:

O mauldite teste de fer,
Teste testue, teste verte,
Teste posee en faulx test,
Teste qui jamais ne se taist,
Teste hongnant, teste hargneuse,
Teste lunatique et fumeuse,
Teste a doze paire de tocques,
Teste plaine de friquenoques,
Teste cliquant a tous propos,
Me donneras tu jamais repos? (7–16)

Similarly, Tarabas, who has an antipathy for his wife's *cul,*
vituperates against the offending part in a passage redolent of
descriptive detail:

Bon gré en ait Dieu et mon ame
Du cul et de la culerie,
Du trou de la baculerie!
Et suis je en tel point baculé,
Parclus, infait, las, aculé?
Fendasse puante et punaise,

Cul rond a tres orde mesure,
Crevasse plaine d'ordure,
Trou breneux dont tant de bren sort,
Le cul de tous les culz plus ort,
Me donneras tu ja pacience? (23–33)

Their servant, Tribouille Mesnage, tries to stop the battle and unite the couple but to no avail. Just as *teste* and *cul* are irreconcilable opposites, so man and woman are forever separated by opposing natures.

Caricatures of types of women in the conjugal farces sometimes bear a resemblance to the *exempla* of bad women in moral works. They should, however, be read with a different emphasis because the primary orientation of the farce is aesthetic rather than ethical. Exaggerated depictions of wantons and harridans, even if they do function to some degree as cautionary *exempla*, mainly serve comic and dramatic purposes in these plays. As we saw in the case of parodies of courtly love poetry, a farce may incorporate the form of another genre without adopting its point of view or its conception of the world. The extent to which medieval farces were didactic – if one may say that all literature is to some extent didactic – is a question that makes sense only in terms of the social function of the farce, to which we now return.

We noted earlier that literature does not provide us with a direct picture of a society, but that it expresses collective wishes and anxieties through the medium of that society's own mythology. We have, so far, described the myth of woman that underlies anifeminist satire, and we have examined it in several of its literary manifestations, especially as it pertains to the farce wife. It is now appropriate for us to ask what wishes or anxieties of late medieval society this myth expressed and, conversely, how the myth functioned in that society through the dramatic medium of the conjugal farce to fulfill those wishes or to allay those anxieties.

Men in the Middle Ages were in general agreement that, in accordance with the divinely established order of nature, women were subject to their authority. And in a society where even men were so little their own masters, this authority was close to what we would call ownership. In the upper classes, for example, marital matches were made between fiefs or fortunes in the sense that a betrothal was important principally for the transfer of property involved. In the lower classes, where the dowry was small or non-existent, the same principle obtained, but the woman herself became the major property given in a marriage. Thus, medieval marriage was more a political and economic institution that it was an affective bond between a man and a woman, and the anxieties surrounding this kind of marriage are perhaps more easily understood expressed in political and economic terms. In this sense, adultery was fundamentally a matter of theft, and a wife's disobedience was tantamount to insurrection.

Since the social structure, with all its rigid categories, was held to have been established by God and was therefore immutable, a husband's clear obligation was to exercise his familial authority. If he failed, then not just his domestic tranquility, but the divine and social orders as well were threatened. This is why, in a society where wife-beating was accepted as normal, henpecked husbands and husbands who were beaten by their wives were frequently made objects of public derision. Petit de Julleville reports the following custom from the city of Lyon: 'L'exercise favori des suppôts de la Coquille consistait à promener assis à rebours sur un âne, les maris qu'on accusait de se laisser battre par leurs femmes; usage singulier qu'on rencontre au moyen âge dans beaucoup de provinces.'[10] In these comic processions, weak members of the community or their proxies were isolated and ridiculed as they were driven through the streets on asses. Whether or not these popular ceremonies had a direct influence on the behaviour of husbands in the community, the major function of such a ritual was not so much to punish the offender as to neutralize a threat to group solidarity by making the deviant person seem ludicrous. The heaping of ridicule on a real life scapegoat served to alleviate group tensions and anxieties in the area of marital relationships.

The farce, on the other hand, created a hypothetical or fictional world without power to impose sanctions directly on weak husbands. It therefore utilized a character type to hold up to ridicule the *idea* of a weak husband. The conjugal farces may have had a certain indirect influence on the behaviour of husbands in the audience by reinforcing some of the basic values of the community, but, just as in the comic processions of Lyon, the major social function of these plays was the neutralizing of a threat to group stability. In this case, the farce husband who allowed himself to be dominated and victimized by his wife became the vicarious scapegoat to which the audience transferred its fear and contempt through laughter.

There is another way in which the conjugal farce offered solace to the paterfamilias who bore the anxiety of total authority. It provided him with an easy explanation of whatever family or domestic difficulties he might have by dramatizing, and thus reinforcing, the myth of woman as the fountainhead of evil. By dint of constant repetition of the myth, it had become a kind of article of faith that each woman was a new Eve, capable of opening her Pandora's box of evils at any time. Like Eve, every woman supposedly bore within her the seeds of pride and rebellion, awaiting only the right moment to germinate.

We find this doctrine particularly well illustrated in the farce of *Resjouy d'Amours*. Tendrette, Gaultier's wife, is a young girl who gives the impression of being newly married. She has been well brought up and prepared for marriage, being able to quote numerous maxims concerning the beauty of the conjugal state, which she has probably learned from some moral treatise. She knows a wife's duties to her husband and endeavours to keep herself physically attractive to please him. She has been warned to beware of golden-tongued gallants and knows full well that their flatteries are intended only to deceive. Finally, she gives every appearance of being happy with her husband. Yet, when Resjouy comes along with his high-flown words of love, Tendrette, after first making a weak effort to resist, succumbs to his blandishments and asks him to return at an hour when Gaultier is certain to be at work. Gaultier, however, learns of the plan and comes home at the appointed hour in order to catch the lover. In a fraction of a second, this young wife is able to invent a ruse that saves her lover and baffles her husband. She tells Resjouy to hide in a sack, and when Gaultier sets fire to the house to smoke the gallant out, she saves the sack because it contains their 'worldly goods'. Thus Resjouy escapes, leaving Gaultier confounded by his own rashness.

What seems to be happening in the person of Tendrette is a kind of coming of age – a passage from innocence to experience – by which she comes into full possession of all her natural instincts. A similar progression is discernible in other farce wives. As Franc Arbitre expresses it in *Regnault qui se marie a Lavollee*: 'Tousjours est jallouse et rebelle/Quant elle vient ung peu a l'aage' (52–53). Tendrette is an apt name for a young farce wife, suggesting both tender years and a sensual nature, but also implying a susceptibility to seduction. Still, the name is rare in farce. Finette is a more common name for a farce wife and is more appropriate for a woman whose innate deceitfulness has already become manifest. There is a sense in which all wives in the conjugal farces begin as Tendrette and end as Finette, because they eventually call upon their natural cunning to perplex and confound their husbands. Lubine, the mother of Mymin, articulates an axiom of farce when she says in *Maistre Mymin qui va a la guerre*: 'Il n'est finesse que de femme' (331).[11] We see, then, that in the conjugal farce, disobedience, infidelity, and deceit are an integral part of woman's nature – innate vices that will appear in her conduct sooner or later, no matter how steeped in moral maxims or how well married she may be.

This, then, was the myth of woman that was embodied in the conjugal farces. It was one of the elements in medieval society that helped men to externalize and thus cope with certain of their fears and conflicts. Just as natural disasters were often explained as the work of malicious demons, so responsibility for personal or group conflicts was easily projected onto persons who were, by definition, sources of evil. One may add that women, who were villains in the plays, sometimes became scapegoats in real life, and the extent to which they were blamed for the ills of late medieval society is attested by the sharp rise in recorded witch trials in the fifteenth and sixteenth centuries.

The undeviating image of woman in the conjugal farces provided a certain continuity with the past and perhaps even an illusion of stability in a changing society. At a time when the crystalline structure of the earlier medieval culture was disintegrating and a new social order was emerging, bringing with it a somewhat more liberal view of woman, the farce maintained very strong ties to the past by adhering blindly to the old antifeminist tradition. There is a tenacity in verbal images and literary structures that, in combination with an outmoded myth, can turn a literary genre into a force for resisting change. On the surface, the parody of courtly love poetry that was absorbed by some of the farces may, indeed, have been the revolt of an uncomprehending popular audience against the seemingly unnecessary poetic constraints of aristocratic formalism. Likewise, the farce's caricature of the ideal woman as portrayed in moral and diactic works may, indeed, have been a kind of folk rebellion against the rigidity of official morality. But on the deeper structural level of its informing social myth, the conjugal farce functioned as a conservative force in the midst of social upheaval. On this level there was never a suggestion of rebellion or even of change. The farce wife and her scapegoat husband may have provided a momentary psychological release for individuals in the audience, but the long-held myths of human nature and social relationships embedded in the conjugal farce served only to maintain the image of woman as a new Eve.

The Farce Husband

The most prevalent characteristics of farce husbands are those that stand in opposition to the characteristics of farce wives. Since wives are usually depicted as having too much of a quality that they should not have, such as physical strength or domestic authority, then husbands are necessarily portrayed as having a deficiency of these same qualities. There are three major deficiencies that appear in the character of the farce husband, either singly or in combination. These may be categorized as mental, physical, and moral, with each category admitting of several degrees.

In the category of the mentally deficient husband, the degree of least deficiency is represented by the naive husband. He is by no means devoid of reason, but he is occasionally lacking in foresight and a certain healthy skepticism. The husband in the *Farce du Patinier* believes his wife to be unfaithful, but has no proof of her wayward conduct. His neighbour offers to help by luring the wife into a compromising situation, at which point he will signal the husband to enter. Only after a very long wait does the husband realize that he has been duped by his wife's secret lover. Reasserting the authority that he had naively surrendered, he gives them both a good drubbing.

Slightly more deficient in rational powers is the husband that we may term the simpleton. He is not greatly debilitated by the weakness of his intellect, but it is a permanent condition in contrast to the temporary nature of naiveté. Such a simpleton is Jolyet (*La Farce de Jolyet*), who learns that his wife is to give birth only a month after the wedding. When she assures him that the child is his, he proudly calculates that he can expect 72 children in the next six years. Then, because he could never feed so many mouths, he returns his wife to her father. In order to protect his daughter's honour, the father promises to support all the children born less than ten months apart. Jolyet, certain that he has the better of the bargain, agrees to take her back. We sense that the mental deficiency of this type of farce husband is such that whatever he learns in one situation will never be applied to another.

In some cases the simpleton is protected from human predators by an innate cleverness, giving us a character that parallels the oxymoronic figure of the wise fool. One such clever simpleton is Naudet (*La Farce du Gentilhomme*), whose wife, Lison, has caught the eye of the local Seigneur. When Naudet is asked to cool some wine in a pail of water, he carefully pours the wine into the water. But when he is confronted with an amorous poacher, he cleverly turns the tables on the philandering Seigneur. Naudet's cleverness extends even to a creative mastery of the language with which he chides the Gentilhomme for his ungentlemanly conduct:

Gardez donc vostre seigneurie,
Et Naudet sa naudeterie.
Se tenez Lison, ma fumelle,
Naudet tiendra ma damoyselle.
Ne venez plus naudetiser,
Je n'iray plus seigneuriser. (p. 269)

Finally, there is the husband who is a full-fledged fool. He is thematically related to the village idiot on the one hand and to the circus clown on the other. He was frequently played by the Badin, a traditional role or *emploi* of the medieval theatre. The Badin was a white-faced, humpbacked clown, who wore a *béguin* or child's bonnet.[12] He also played other farce characters, such as tricky servants, dull-witted schoolboys, and husbands of the clever simpleton type. In farces where the husband is a complete fool or buffoon, the marriage relationship is usually less vituperative than in the other conjugal farces. It is more on the order of a comic battle of wits or, to be more precise, a mock battle between Wit and Witless. The husband of the *Farce de l'arbalestre* is a 'sot de nature'. His major problem – and the basic comic device of the play – is that he understands all figurative expressions literally. When his wife tells him that in order to be wise he must 'parler a trait', he speaks, not only to the arrow, but to the whole shooting mechanism – lock, bow, and cord. For good measure, he insists that his wife speak to the crossbow too, but she ultimately rebels against him and his folly. At the end of the play the Badin steps out of his role as the foolish husband in the dramatic fiction in order to draw a moral lesson for the audience:

. . . l'homme fait la femme telle
Qu'il la veult, ou douce, ou rebelle,
Ou en luy n'a point de raison. (p. 29)

The husband in *La Femme et le Badin* undertakes to sell a bushel of peas at the market, but he is tricked out of his produce by a pair of crooks who send him for payment to Zorobabel, a name he cannot possibly remember. When he later hears the priest repeat the name in a text from the Bible, the befuddled husband promises him anything to

tell him where Zorobabel lives. Plays in which the husband is a
complete fool do not generally deal with questions of marital infidelity,
yet one suspects that even the buffoon is not immune from cuckoldry.
The husband tells his wife to reward the vicar generously when he
comes to reveal Zorobabel's address, to which she replies ambiguously:

Ses plaisirs seront recognus
Soyt en blé, en orge ou en boys,
Tandy qu'irés chercher vos poys.
Pieca sy grande joye je n'us. (p. 32)

The second type of deficiency found in the farce husband is physical.
It may occasionally be a matter of physical strength, though this is not
always easy to determine. The wives in *Le Cuvier* and *Le Pasté*, for
example, may be able to threaten and intimidate their husbands
because they (the wives) are physically stronger, but their dominance
could as well have a basis in a psychological or a social superiority.
More commonly the physical deficiencies of farce husbands are
translated into sexual deficiencies, which occur in a number of
different situations.

The husband in *Le Nouveau Marié* has yet to consummate his
marriage a month after pronouncing the vows. His mother-in-law
wonders if he is 'organisé de ses membres', but her daughter assures
her that he is. In the end, the young husband agrees to perform his
marital duty, justifying his behaviour only with the cryptic statement:
'Car j'avais autre empeschement'. Even less happy is the marital bed of
the couple in *Les Femmes qui demandent les arrerages*, where the wife
is asking sexual arrears of more than a year. Again, the husband has no
satisfactory explanation for his behaviour, and only the threat of a
lawsuit makes him capitulate to his wife's desires.

Sometimes the farce husband is not completely impotent, but is
nevertheless not vigorous enough to satisfy the sexual demands of his
wife. The other side of this coin is that the farce wife is frequently
portrayed as sexually insatiable. In *Le Cuvier*, for example, one of the
duties that Jaquinot is instructed to write on his *rollet* is to 'faire cela',
to which he readily agrees:

Vous en aurez une gouppee
En quinze jours ou en ung moys.
    LA FEMME
Mais tous les jours cinq ou six fois;
Je l'entens ainsi pour le moins. (p. 39)

The type of sexual deficiency most frequently encountered in the farce is the impotence attributable to old age. Occasionally this situation reflects the normal aging process in a long marriage, as when the wife in *Le Ramonneur de cheminees* wistfully complains:

> Je le scay par ma cheminee
> Qui souloit estre ramonnee
> Tous les jours bien cinq ou six fois,
> Mais il y a bien troys mois,
> Voisine, qu'il n'y voulut penser. (309–13)

Usually, however, we find an old man, financially comfortable, who has taken a young wife. The farce image of the old husband and young wife is an antitype of the image of Joseph and Mary that was prevalent in the Middle Ages. The latter union of old husband and young wife was made fruitful by the intervention of divine grace, but in the farce world there is no such fructifying grace. There is only the illicit, comic aping of the ideal marital union by the wife and her lover. One of the most comical of these situations is found in the *Farce de frere Guillebert*, where the lusty monk is long on words but short on courage. The husband in this play is old, but not entirely impotent. Once a week, however, is worse than nothing for his young wife, who is about to 'mourir de soif empres le puis'. The two husbands in *Les Femmes qui font refondre leurs maris* are old and sickly. Thibault explains simply: 'qui ne peult ne peult', while Collart counsels his wife to cultivate the virtues of patience and chastity. When the wives have their husbands recast in youthful form, they discover that their independence is severely curtailed because sexually vigorous husbands are also masters of their households.

In this sense the physical weaknesses that we have noted in farce husbands are closely related to the third major deficiency, which is a moral deficiency. I use this term in a broad sense to include deficiencies of will, courage, and authority. The husband in *Les Amoureux qui ont les botines Gaultier* is completely dominated by his wife. He stays home to do the cleaning and sewing while she is free to follow her pleasure. It is fairly clear, however, that the source of her authority is his sexual impotence. In a verbal exchange that has a particularly revealing erotic double meaning, Rousine, the wife, compares the cloth made in Reims to other fabrics and concludes:

> Il n'est ouvrage que de Rains.
> Paris, qu'est ville bien assise,

Est fourny d'ouvriers, sans faintise,
Qui sont tous seurs et bien certains
De faire l'ouvraige de Rains.
        GAULTIER
De cela j'en oste mes mains;
Je ne m'y congnois point, m'amye. (67–73)

The exercise of domestic authority in the farce is traditionally coupled with the ability to wield a stout stick or *bâton*. The phallic shape of the *bâton* makes the association between sexual virility and domestic authority all the more striking. The mother of Robin Mouton even refers to her son's phallus as a 'baston au bout rouge'. Thus when Gaultier disclaims knowledge of 'l'ouvraige de Rains' (i.e. reins), he is admitting, not only his sexual impotence, but also his inability to exercise authority in his own household.

The lack of authority that characterizes many farce husbands is treated in two distinct ways in these plays. In some, the loss of authority by the husband is only temporary; in others, it is a permanent condition. The husband's reassertion of authority in the first type of play is always accomplished by the vigorous use of a *bâton*. Perhaps the most straightforward example of the *bâton* used as an instrument of authority is found in *Le Pont aux asgnes*. Here a husband learns how to make his wife obey him by observing the manner in which a woodcutter makes his donkey cross a bridge. On returning home, his application of a 'gros baston de haistre' achieves the desired result immediately. The same lesson is applied in other farces such as *Une Femme a qui son voisin baille ung clistoire*, both versions of *Le Patinier*, and *Les Femmes qui font baster leur maris aux corneilles*. While the *bâton* is not specifically mentioned in the beating scenes that terminate these plays, we may assume that it was indeed the instrument of punishment. This is clear from a statement made by the husband in *Le Patinier* just before the final scene: 'Je doubte qu'il y ara feste/A baston' (423–24). Similarly, the husband in *Une Femme . . . clistoire* makes an ironic reference to the instrument of beating as a candle. Moreover, there is a clear association in this play between the *báton* and the *clistère*, which also has a sexual reference, in that both are used to dominate the woman. We may see this as further evidence that domestic authority and sexual virility are virtually inseparable in the world of the farce.

The moral deficiency responsible for a man's permanent subservience to his wife is a condition that is rather frequently

encountered in farce husbands. Here too we may distinguish degrees of
deficiency and corresponding degrees of servility. In *Martin de
Cambray*, as we have seen, a jealous husband is tricked into giving his
wife the keys to the house and permission to come and go as she
pleases. The deceit is accomplished with the aid of the parish priest,
who, dressed in a devil's costume, spirits the wife away to 'hell'. Upon
returning, she informs Martin that those who suffer the greatest
torments there are jealous husbands. At this point his will to maintain
domestic order is dissolved by the fear of damnation, and he
permanently relinquishes his authority over the household. The
images of hell that, in this play, suggest a kind of domestic damnation
for the husband without authority are transformed into infernal
reality in *Le Munyer*. Lucifer and his henchmen try to capture the soul
of the ailing miller, while the miller's wife entertains her lover before
his eyes. The devils fail in the end to take his soul, but the scenes of
infernal chaos, alternating with scenes of the miller's domestic
torment, bring into sharp relief the brutalizing bondage of a husband
who has no control over his wife's destructive drive for pleasure.

There is a final degree of moral deficiency for the farce husband in
cases where he is made a scapegoat or a sacrificial victim for the sins of
the other husbands of the community. In dealing with the concept of
farce victim, however, we must keep in mind that it is quite distinct
from the notion of tragic victim. Viewed from within the play, there is
no apparent purpose to be served by the suffering of the farce victim;
there is no fate, no catharsis, no purification at the end. All actions
relating to the 'suffering' of the victim are random and sterile. From
without, there is no identification of the audience with the farce victim.
Members of the farce audience identify with each other, forming a
community of peers to bring judgment on the dramatized social abuses
by laughing them to scorn. This creates a psychic distance from the
farce characters that preserves the comic nature of the plays. If the
spectators were to see the farce victim as identical with themselves
rather than as an object of ridicule, the play would no longer be a farce,
but another genre altogether.

The imagery of ritual sacrifice is found, for example, in *Les Femmes
qui se font passer maistresses*. Alison and her *commères*, two Parisian
wives, are awarded the academic degree of *Maîtresse*, which gives
them authority in both university and household. Maistre Regnault
has them swear the following oath at the commencement ceremony:

Vous jurez que tous les tourmens,
Tout le travail, toute la peine,
Nuyt et jour toute la sepmaine,
Que vous pourrés et que scaurés
A voz maris procurerés. (272–76)

Alison, on returning home, declares her husband, Martin, to be old, dessicated, and inflexible. We already know that he is sexually deficient, since Alison has long prepared for her degree by studying *under* members of various religious orders. Because Martin is now useless as a husband, Alison has decided to leave him. Here the figurative expression, 'planter là pour reverdir', which means to let someone shift for himself, is acted out literally on the stage. Martin is planted head down in the earth 'comme ung poureau' and is watered so that the green may appear by summer. The farce was no doubt written to enliven the annual Basoche festivities at the planting of the May tree. It also reflects the folk custom of giving wives rights over their husbands on May Day. There is, however, a deep ambiguity in the dramatic image. The joyful image of the planting of the May tree to bring about the return of fertility has, when applied to a person, the effect of exiling him from the community and abandoning him to the mercy of the elements, thus ridding the community of his sterility. In other words, the fertility ritual and the scapegoat ritual are, in this play, two sides of the same dramatic coin.

Finally, we come to a farce that is, as it were, a *summa* of all the characteristics so far discussed. The play is *George le veau*, in which George, the husband, exhibits a severe mental deficiency. He is, according to his wife, 'ung badault sans nulle science'. His efforts throughout the play are directed toward the simple matter of determining his own identity in terms of his ancestry. After much anguished deliberation, however, he is not even certain of being a son of Adam. In addition, there is the tell-tale sign of physical deficiency – the presence of a lover. In this case it is the parish priest, with whom his wife more or less openly consorts. Finally, he is morally deficient in that he lacks the strength and will to assert his rightful authority in his own household. At one point he is praying in the church for guidance in his quest for identity, when a voice instructs him to obey his wife in all things. This is, of course, a trick of the priest. Moreover, he is given a 'celestial' garment to wear that will reveal his identity. But when he returns home, his wife takes him for a devil. While this too is a trick, it provides us with the infernal imagery that is often associated with the

chaos that results from the dissolution of authority. After the priest
has exorcized the 'demon', ears are noticed on the hood of the garment
and all recognize George for what he is – a calf or *veau*. (Cotgrave
translates *veau* as 'hoydon, dunce, jobbernoll, or doddipole'). Simple
George is happy at last to have found his identity. The trick, however,
does not end there. His wife points out that calves walk on four feet,
and George obediently drops to his hands and knees, from where he
pleads:

Alyson, je vous crie mercy.
Plus n'aurez de scavoir soucy
Qui je suis; je suis filz de vache.
Et si n'ay mesfaict, que je sache,
Si ce n'est a ce cas de crime
Que je n'ay pas payé la disme
Des veaulx envers nostre curé. (p. 400)

In a scene reminiscent of the judgment of the ass in La Fontaine's fable,
Les Animaux malades de la peste, both wife and priest agree that the
tithe must be paid and that George will be the *veau de disme*.
(Cotgrave translates: 'a notable sot, a blockhead, a notorious
lobcock'.) Only the text itself can convey the full impact of this scene of
comic ritual sacrifice as George, the scapegoat, is led away to the
slaughter:

GEORGE LE VEAU
Plus George ne suis, mes amys;
J'ay pire nom que esperit d'abisme.
LE CURE
Or allons, sus! gros veau de disme,
A quatre piedz vous fault marcher.
LE CLERC
Je voys au devant du boucher,
Qu'il apporte son grant cousteau.
GEORGE LE VEAU
Helas! c'est faict du pouvre veau;
Voicy l'heure de son trespas.
Alyson, ne me oubliez pas.
Que je boyve avant que mourir.
LA FEMME
Je ne vous scauroye secourir,
Foy que doy a sainct Mathieu. (pp. 400–01)

We must not forget that this play is a farce and that the final scene
was without doubt hilariously funny to the medieval audience.
Technically, the scene is another instance of the common device of

translating a figurative locution into the literal, physical terms of the stage. Beneath the comic surface, however, the manifest sacrificial imagery of this final scene is startling. One has the impression that the fears and anxieties of all those in the audience who bear the burden of guarding the social order have been laid upon the back of this meek little clown. He wraps himself in the raucous ridicule of the spectators, as he had wrapped himself in the mock celestial robe, and obediently proceeds on hands and knees to his slaughter. Of the many scapegoat scenes in late medieval farces, none is so close to being a pure scapegoat ritual as the closing scene of *George le veau*.

There were real scapegoat rituals in the late Middle Ages – ceremonial occasions on which a member of the community was shamed and ridiculed in order to neutralize a threat to group solidarity. We have already noted the practice in Lyon of making husbands who had been beaten by their wives ride through the streets seated backwards on an ass. Conjugal farces in which husbands were ridiculed for their deficiencies were dramatic analogues of such rituals and functioned for their audiences in a similar, though less direct, manner. Weak husbands were not the only scapegoats of the farce world, however, for farce wives, in spite of their superiority and dominance, were scapegoat figures of another kind. The difference derives from the different myths underlying the images of man and woman in the Middle Ages. There was, on the one hand, the etiological myth of woman, which held her to be the cause of man's fall from original justice and the source of all evil in the world. On the other hand, there was the teleological myth of man, which held him to be the ruler and guardian of an ideal social order. Farce wives, then, were scapegoats for all the misfortunes attributable to the fallen condition of humankind, while farce husbands were scapegoats for all the deficiencies that prevented the realization of order and harmony in the world.

The Farce Lover

There have been,
Or I am much deceived, cuckolds ere now;
And many a man there is, even at this present,
Now, while I speak this, holds his wife by th'arm,
That little thinks she has been sluiced in's absence,
And his pond fisht by his next neighbor.

So speaks Leontes in *The Winter's Tale* (I, 2), who feels that the garden of connubial bliss is particularly vulnerable to the intrusions of crafty poachers. The farces of the late Middle Ages, themselves winter's tales of another sort, illustrate this conviction many times over in scenes of temptation and yielding, of illicit amorous delights, and of exposure and retribution. The lover is a constant presence in the conjugal farce, always ready to fill any emotional vacuum that might develop in a marriage relationship. Yet he is not portrayed as pure predator; his role in these plays is more that of tempter or catalyst and, like the serpent in Eden, he is powerless without the complicity of the other inhabitants of the garden.

There are three basic types of lovers in the farce. First there is what we might call the professional gallant, in the sense that he has no other occupation and no other identity. He is constantly on the prowl for new conquests. His type ranges from urban smooth-talkers to village Don Juans. The second type is the wayward cleric, belonging either to the secular or the regular clergy. He differs from the professional gallant in that he has another occupation, but even so, he seems to spend no less time than the gallant in pursuit of his quarry. He may be encountered as Messire Jehan, the parish priest, or as Frère Frappart, the legendary monk who was known to Rabelais. These first two types of lovers are popular analogues of the *chevalier* and the *clerc* in the courtly love debates of an earlier period. While the farce friar is by no means as refined as his courtly counterpart, the gallant not infrequently speaks a language that echoes and even parodies the courtly love style. Thirdly we have the type Leontes speaks of – the man next door. He is not the type to set out in quest of a paramour, but when he notices that the wife of his neighbour is in desperate need of attention, he does not refuse to be neighbourly.

An excellent example of the neighbour lover is found in the *Farce d'une femme a qui son voisin baille ung clistoire*. Doublet is a medicine man who hawks his herbs and potions at a stall before his house. Next to him live Trubert Chagrinas and his young wife, Frigalette, but all is not well with them. Trubert is a serious provider who thinks of nothing but work, while his wife's thoughts keep drifting to a certain other duty of the marriage state that he is apparently shirking. An argument ensues, which is overheard by Doublet. When Frigalette leaves the house in anger, he stops her and offers to fill the gap in her emotional life:

Se vous avés mestier de moy,
Je suis tout vostre, par ma foy,
Pour vous servir soir et matin. (153–55)

Frigalette gracefully replies: 'Et certes, c'est dit de voisin'. They hatch a plan whereby she pretends to be sick and Doublet convinces the husband to send her over for a good strong clister. Ultimately Trubert realizes what kind of clister he had in mind, and when Frigalette returns, he applies another kind of medicine with a good strong stick. Doublet, hearing her cries, comes to investigate and he too gets a dose of Trubert's remedy.

The farce lover is obviously a figure of ridicule. Because of this, it is important to note how the playwrights dispose of these characters in the plays. A few of the lovers, such as the one in *Pernet qui va au vin*, are completely successful in their endeavours because the husband is too timorous to interfere. A few others achieve their desired end, but, like Doublet, are punished for their transgression. Most of the lovers, however, are frustrated on the threshold of success by the return of the husband, by a stupid servant, or by some other contretemps. This situation creates an infinite variety of comic possibilities with the lover hiding under the bed, in a chest, or in the privy, with visions of castration dancing in his head. Often in such cases, a ruse of the wife enables the lover to escape unharmed. He may, at this point, forswear women forever, though we know that his determination will evaporate as soon as the next opportunity presents itself.

One of the most amusing plays of this last type is the *Farce de Frere Guillebert*, in which we also find a good example of the second type of lover. Frère Guillebert is a man of wit who conquers his world with words. He chances upon a young woman whose old and impotent husband has created within her a veritable desert of desire for the waters of physical affection. The friar, who lives in a kind of desert of his own, asks for some rather unusual alms:

M'amye, je vous pry qu'il vous plaise
Endurer tois coups de la lance;
C'est belle osmosne, sans doubtance,
Donner pour Dieu aux souffretteux. (pp. 309–10)

No sooner said than agreed to. The woman sends her husband to the market to insure his absence. Meanwhile the lovers have no more than undressed, when fate reminds the husband that he forgot his shopping bag. Fate also puts the bag in Frère Guillebert's hiding place when the husband returns, but the latter, mistaking the friar's breeches for the bag, leaves again for the market. The friar dashes back to the monastery unbreeched, while the wife runs to her friend next door for help. When the husband returns, having guessed the truth, the neighbour intercepts him to explain that his wife had borrowed 'les brayes de Saint Françoy' from the monastery to help her conceive. The naive husband believes her and seeing Frère Guillebert pass by, returns what the friar had colourfully called his 'sac a coilles' as though it were a precious relic. Quickly grasping the situation, Frère Guillebert has them all kneel and kiss the 'holy' garment, 'Car c'est un fort beau reliquere'.

In the conjugal farces a lover may appear at any stage of a marriage to threaten its tranquility or, if that has already departed, its *modus vivendi*. Clearly in an older marriage, where years of misunderstanding and conflict have generated a chronic discontent, the farce lover is likely to find his easiest conquest. But far more revealing of the nature of the farce lover are the plays in which he intrudes on a young or newly wed couple and therefore meets with more resistance. In some of these farces, where the couple have not yet become disillusioned, the young wife seems still to possess the strength that innocence often confers, making her less susceptible to temptation. Innocence is a rare quality in the farces; the closest one usually comes to it is a kind of benign naiveté. Robin Mouton, for example, on his wedding day is still possessed of a wide-eyed simplicity that might pass for innocence, but his bride, whose name is Peu Subtille, has already plucked the fruit of the tree of knowledge and is about to share it with her boyish husband. In several plays a state of innocence is wistfully evoked by a character describing his relationship with another person, but in each case it is either a trick to make a third person envious or a utopian dream that could never come true in a farce.

There is, however, one play whose opening scene has such a strong suggestion of newly-wed innocence that for a moment one has the impression of watching the end of a comedy rather than the beginning of a farce. The play is entitled *Resjouy d'Amours* and, incidentally, it provides us with an example, which we have not yet had, of the first type of lover. Resjouy d'Amours is a golden-tongued gallant in search of the ideal woman. In an opening epithalamion, his friend, Gaultier Guillaume, describes to him the perfections of his young wife, Tendrette, and the joys of married life:

A passer temps toute saison
Ne veuil qu'estre en ma maison,
Ma vie sera la finee.
C'est rouge feu.
      RESJOUY D'AMOURS
        Quel embrassee! (31–34)

Inspired to intensify his quest, Resjouy happens upon Tendrette, unrecognized as Gaultier's wife, whom he overhears reciting a series of maxims on the duties and qualities of a good wife. Here, at last, in one person, Resjouy beholds the sum of all feminine perfections. Invoking the name of Venus, the gallant introduces himself and declares his love in phrases strongly reminiscent of the courtly love tradition. Tendrette, like the daughters of the Chevalier de La Tour Landry, has been taught to beware of eloquent people. She flatly refuses his offer of love and orders him out of the house. Resjouy hastens back to Gaultier to inform him that he has found the most beautiful woman since Helen. Undaunted, he returns to Tendrette and again lays siege to her virtue. She continues to resist saying: 'Voz motz sont trop cours/A bouche venimeuse' (211–12). Finally his impassioned pleas reach an intensity sufficient to melt her resolve and she sets a time for their tryst. Overjoyed, Resjouy goes once more to tell Gaultier of his good fortune, this time mentioning the name of his beloved. (The reader has no doubt already recognized the comic device of the lover confiding in his rival that Molière exploited so brilliantly in *L'Ecole des femmes*.) Gaultier, who suddenly realizes that his domain has been invaded, plans a surprise attack on the two lovers. At the rendezvous, Resjouy has no more than claimed his first kiss when Gaultier pounds on the door. In the ensuing confusion Tendrette is quick to regain her composure and hides Resjouy in a sack. Gaultier becomes so enraged at not finding the lover that he sets fire to the house. The only thing Tendrette can save from the flames is the sack, from which Resjouy eventually emerges to slip away unnoticed. When no lover is seen to take flight from the burning house, Gaultier repents his rash and reckless act: 'Aussi le grant dyable d'enfer/M'a bien fait faire cest ouvrage' (373–74).

I have narrated the action of this play at some length because I feel that it has a particular importance in any effort to understand the structure and function of the farce as a dramatic genre. Virtually all other conjugal farces begin their action at a point where it is already apparent that something has gone awry in the human relationships portrayed. By contrast, *Resjouy d'Amours* begins on a lyrical note of innocence and good will among the characters. The mood does not last long, however, and soon there is as much amiss in this household as in that of any other conjugal farce.

From a structural point of view, the passage from innocence to experience in combination with a marital triangle is strongly suggestive of the Eden myth. The plot structure in both instances is almost identical, including the opening epithalamion, the remnants of which are found in the last verses of *Genesis* 2, beginning, 'This is now bone of my bones and flesh of my flesh'. The persuasion of the lover is formally related to the temptation of the serpent. Though the serpent is not intent on committing adultery, by persuading Eve to act, he becomes her master and thus commits a kind of adultery of authority. Tendrette, like Eve, yields to the tempter and breaks faith with her husband and with society's norms of behaviour – the analogue of God in the farce. As a consequence of burning the house, Gaultier and Tendrette are deprived of their garden of domestic bliss, just as Adam and Eve are evicted from their earthly paradise.

Even the imagery of the play, in comparison with that of the biblical narrative, betrays a resemblance that is more than superficial. The serpent of the Eden myth was early associated with Satan and therefore with the world of demonic imagery. Resjouy's relation to the serpent and the demonic world is brought into relief by Tendrette's reference to his 'bouche venimeuse' and by Gaultier's insistence that the devil in hell made him do what he did. Like the serpent, Resjouy is deprived of limbs as he crawls into the sack. At the end of the play, he escapes by slipping out of the sack like a serpent shedding his skin. The joyous fire of connubial bliss that we saw in the epithalamic refrain, 'C'est rouge feu. Quel embrassee!', is transformed at the end of the play into the consuming fire of the fallen world. This parallels the angel's fiery sword that guards the tree of life from the exiles, thereby insuring their death. Finally, in both the creation myth and the play, an abode of innocence is exchanged for the scorched wasteland of experience.

Here we return to the farce world as described earlier in our generic paradigm. For the world portrayed in these brief plays is the fallen world of confusion and error, of shortcomings and deficiencies, of deceit and fakery. It is a world in which the clever take advantage of the foolish, in which the strong exploit the weak, in which, as Plautus said, 'Lupus est homo homini'. But even the clever and strong are not immune to predators – for every Pathelin, there is an Aignelet waiting to turn the tables and cheat the cheater.

Marriage as a ceremonial structure is a ritual mimesis of the achievement of an ideal state. In drama this is the point to which comedy always brings us as the young hero and heroine, having triumphed over the obstructions of an older generation, unite to form the nucleus of a new society.[13] But because any such ideal state implies a kind of static perfection, it cannot, by definition, persist in a living social organism. It is at this point that the farce begins and from which it moves quickly through a fall from connubial grace – most farces do not even represent it – to the disenchanted world of imperfection and chaos. The opening of *Resjouy d'Amours* provides us with a brief glimpse of the marriage ideal, but we know that it cannot last. The lover–tempter appears, as indeed he must, to lure the young couple into change and time – for the fall from a paradise of static perfection is a fall into time – and time will devour their happiness. Time will also devour *them*, just as Kronos devoured his children. The farce is an ironic genre whose wasteland imagery is commensurate with existence in the belly of Kronos or, to keep our biblical metaphor, in the belly of the Leviathan. Time in the farce does not renew as in comedy; nor does it redeem as in tragedy. Nothing of fundamental importance ever happens in a farce. No heroes appear; no new societies arise; no one is saved; no one dies. It is a sterile and wounded world where husbands are impotent and where the attempts at the procreative act are made by lovers and are therefore illicit. In the final analysis, even the point of departure – the innocence before the fall – is an illusion, and Resjouy d'Amours makes his serpentine way through a false Eden. The myths of Eden and the Golden Age are myths of freedom and free choice, and the very last thing that a farce character is, is free. As befits an inhabitant of a sterile world, he is a slave to his own humour; he lives in subjection to a social mask; and he is compelled to interact with others on the basis of narrow and rigid relationships. A background of illusory innocence in a farce only brings the characters' bondage more into relief.

The farce is a mimesis of the fallen world where time neither expiates nor brings to fruition, where it has neither past nor future, and where the characters, as a consequence, are condemned to an endless repetition of the same errors. The farce is, therefore, an ironic genre that lies between the death of the hero on the one hand and the birth of a new society on the other. Or, to return to the speech of Leontes with which we began this section, the farce is a winter's tale told to beguile the barren days between the autumn of tragedy and the spring of comedy.

Notes

[1]Barbara C. Bowen, *Les Caractéristiques essentielles de la farce française et leur survivance dans les années 1550–1620* (Champaign: University of Illinois Press, 1964), p. 53.

[2]Robert L. Delevoy, *Breugel* (Geneva: Skira, 1959), p. 46.

[3]Jean Duvignaud, *Sociologie du théâtre* (Paris: Presses Universitaires de France, 1965), p. 42.

[4]In *Jongleurs et trouvères*, ed. Achille Jubinal (Paris: J. A. Merklein, 1835), p. 77.

[5]*Les Lamentations de Mathéolus*, ed. A. G. Van Hamel (Paris: Emile Bouillon, 1892), p. 53.

[6]Thomas Aquinas, *Summa Theologiae*, I, 1. 92, a. 1, ad 1.

[7]Bonaventure, *II Sententiarum*, dist 21, a. 1, q. 3.

[8]John Fox, ed., *Robert de Blois, son oeuvre didactique et narrative* (Paris: Nizet, 1950), p. 141.

[9]Philippe de Novare, *Les Quatre Ages de l'homme*, ed. Marcel de Fréville (Paris: Firmin Didot, 1888), p. 50.

[10]Petit de Julleville, *Les Comédiens*, p. 243.

[11]The same statement is found at the end of *Le Badin, la Femme et la Chambriere.*

[12]Rousse, pp. 302–3.

[13]Frye, *Anatomy*, p. 163.

Conclusion

The major guiding principle of this study has been that our understanding of the late medieval French drama is dependent on a proper conception of the various dramatic genres at all levels. That this proper conception has never been achieved is evident from the tentativeness with which critics, both past and present, have spoken of these genres. Indeed, since the sixteenth century, when the classical distinction between comedy and tragedy was first introduced into France, there has been a tendency among critics to make an analogous distinction among medieval plays. The category of religious plays has long been perceived as corresponding to ancient tragedy, while the analogue of comedy has been the medieval comic plays for some and the profane plays for others. But because such generic distinctions are alien to the culture in which these works were originally conceived, they falsify the true generic relationships among the plays and not infrequently distort our perception of their meaning.

In order to make meaningful distinctions among medieval dramatic genres one must begin with criteria that are compatible with the medieval perception of the world. Just as comedy and tragedy grew out of the conceptual contexts of Antiquity, so the medieval genres bear a special relationship to the society whose values they express. Thus the notion of context, both historical and cultural, is important in defining genres. It was on this basis that we made the first broad distinction in late medieval dramatic genres – the distinction, that is, between the historical and the fictional genres. Not only did these two kinds of plays incorporate different subject matters, but, more importantly, they also served clearly distinguishable social functions. In the group-oriented society of the Middle Ages the history plays served a memorial function, while the fictional plays served an exemplary function.

Obviously, the historical genres share many of the rhetorical techniques and formal characteristics of fictional genres, but, because medieval drama was so intimately involved in the life of the community, it has proved more fruitful to examine its genres in terms of their social functions.

One of the major stumbling blocks in previous attempts to classify late medieval French plays according to genre has been the morality play – a genre so varied in its style and content that it could not be wholly contained in categories such as religious, comic, or profane. In order to deal with this problem I adopted as another criterion of generic distinction the kind of world created by the playwright for his characters to inhabit. Accordingly, the second broad generic division in the preceding study was made on the basis of a fundamental opposition between the fictive world of the morality play and that of the farce. This may be termed a textual criterion of generic classification in contrast to the contextual criterion described above. From this point of view we examined all the sub-genres of the fictional drama, finally establishing a generic paradigm, by which virtually all late medieval French plays can be classified. The paradigm has the added merit of resolving several problems that have long been vexed questions of medieval dramatic criticism, such as the distinction between farce and *sottie* and the place of dramatic monologues in the scheme of medieval drama.

No classificatory system, however, is rigidly perfect, whether it pertains to the world of nature or the world of human culture. In both areas there are always hybrids that cross generic boundaries. In this study we have examined three types of hybrid plays (wedding plays, carnival plays, and *bergeries* played at royal entries), whose presence in medieval society was explained in terms of the social and institutional contexts in which they were produced. We saw in these three cases how easily the social context of medieval plays could impinge upon and modify their generic structure. This led us to examine more closely the processional form as a context of dramatic spectacle. In doing so we shifted our scale of perception to view medieval drama as a single generic entity to be set alongside and compared with other cultural forms such as the tournament, the funeral cortège, and the carnival parade. In all such spectacles, including the drama, we found the common traits of processional structure and dual dramatic perspective. We also noted that because of the processional context of medieval drama, it is sometimes difficult to draw a clear line of demarcation between literal act and dramatic representation.

Finally, an attempt was made to bring together the concepts of social function and fictional world as they apply to genre definition by examining a single genre in detail. In another shift of scale from the macroscopic level of large processional spectacles to the microscopic level of the conjugal farce we saw how medieval myths about the nature of man and woman and about their roles as husband and wife form a social context for this genre. At the same time we were able to corroborate from a different point of view the characteristics of the farce world that had previously served to distinguish the farce from the morality play. Specifically, we found the farce to be an ironic genre without heroes, portraying a sterile world where, contrary to the morality play, time has the power neither to renew nor to redeem.

Throughout this study I have referred to the dramatic works and genres under consideration as medieval or late medieval despite the fact that many of them were written, played, and printed in the sixteenth century when the French Renaissance was in full flower. The Renaissance, however, brought with it a shift in cultural perspective that enabled writers to create quite different fictional worlds. It should be clear at this point that such changes of perspective in literary and dramatic works, even where subject matter or techniques remain the same, often result in new genres. There was no such change in the dramatic genres we have been considering. The medieval plays of the mid-sixteenth century represented the same historical and fictional worlds that their counterparts of a century earlier had represented. Auerbach points out that 'late medieval works are confined within a definite frame, socially, geographically, cosmologically, religiously, and ethically'.[1] Cultures that place clear limitations on their visions of the world foster generic stability. Indeed, it is only the consistency of this cultural frame, of this conceptual mould in which the plays were formed, that makes it possible for us to know and to describe the late medieval dramatic genres.

When the dramatic perspectives of Antiquity were absorbed by sixteenth-century playwrights, new, non-medieval genres began to appear. The old mystery plays, banned in Paris in 1548, continued for a while in the provinces. The farce, despite the introduction of comedy, was more tenacious and had a longer history. Virtually unchanged, it could still influence Molière in the seventeenth century. The morality play, however, underwent a gradual transformation. Its protagonist began to absorb some of the individuating characteristics of the protagonists of the saint's life and the miracle play. By the end of the sixteenth century he became a figure closely resembling the tragic hero. All that a play with such a character needed to become a genuine tragedy was a slight shift of perspective to make us sympathize with the hero's flaws as well as his virtues. But that is the subject of another study.

Notes

[1]Erich Auerbach, *Mimesis* (Garden City; N.Y.: Doubleday, 1957), p. 241.

Bibliography

I Collections of plays and abbreviations

The four major collections of short plays were compiled in the sixteenth century. They have been reproduced in the following modern editions:

1. *The British Museum Collection*

   BM Fac. – *Le Recueil du British Museum*. Facsimile edition. Introduction by Halina Lewicka. Geneva: Slatkine Reprints, 1970.

   ATF – *Ancien théâtre français*. Gen. ed. Viollet le Duc. Vols. 1–3 ed. by Anatole de Montaiglon. Paris: P. Jannet, 1854.

2. *The Trepperel Collection*

   Trep. Fac. – *Le Recueil Trepperel*. Facsimile edition. Introduction by Eugénie Droz. Geneva: Slatkine Reprints, n.d. (1966).

   Trep. I – *Le Recueil Trepperel: les sotties*. Ed. Eugénie Droz. Paris: Droz, 1935.

   Trep. II – *Le Recueil Trepperel: les farces*. Ed. Eugénie Droz and Halina Lewicka. Geneva: Droz, 1961.

3. *The Florence Collection*

   RFF – *Recueil de farces françaises inédites du XVe siècle*. Ed. Gustave Cohen. Cambridge, Mass.: The Medieval Academy of America, 1949.

4. *The La Vallière Collection*

   La Val. Fac. – *Manuscript La Vallière*. Facsimile edition of BN MS. 24341. Introduction by Werner Helmich. Geneva: Slatkine Reprints, 1972.

   La Val. – *Recueil de farces, moralités et sermons joyeux*. Ed. A. Leroux de Lincy and Francisque Michel. 4 vols. Paris: Techener, 1837.

5. *Other Collections*

   Aubailly – *Deux jeux de carnaval*. Ed. Jean-Claude Aubailly. TLF 245. Geneva: Droz, 1978.

   Fournier – *Le Théâtre français avant la Renaissance*. Ed. Edouard Fournier. Paris: Laplace & Sanchez, 1872.

   Philipot – *Trois farces du recueil de Londres*. Ed. Emmanuel Philipot. 1931; rpt. Geneva: Slatkine Reprints, 1975.

   Picot – *Recueil Général des sotties*. Ed. Emile Picot. 3 vols. SATF. Paris: Firmin Didot, 1902–12.

   Pic. & Nyrop – *Nouveau recueil de farces françaises*. Ed. Emile Picot and

Christophe Nyrop. 1880; rpt. Geneva: Slatkine Reprints, 1968.
6. *Other Abbreviations*
   BN – Bibliothèque Nationale (Paris)
   CFMA – Classiques Français du Moyen Age
   EETS – Early English Text Society
   SATF – Société des Anciens Textes Français
   TLF – Textes Littéraires Français

II *Plays cited in the text*

The genre designations in parentheses are those found in the original titles. Where appropriate, both the original source and a modern edition of each play are listed. Manuscripts and early imprints are listed with their catalogue numbers in the Bibliothèque Nationale.

Abraham sacrifiant. By Théodore de Bèze. Ed. Keith Cameron, *et al.* TLF 135. Geneva: Droz, 1967.

L'Agneau de France (Bergerie). Trep. Fac., No. 35. Ed. Halina Lewicka. TLF 96. Geneva: Droz, 1961.

L'Alliance de Foi et Loyauté. In *Nativités et moralités liègeoises du Moyen Age.* Ed. Gustave Cohen. Brussels: Palais des Académies, 1953, pp. 251–59.

L'Amour d'un serviteur envers sa maistresse (Tragedie françoise). By Jean Bretog. Lyon: Noel Grandon, 1571. BN Rés. Yf. 3988.

Les Amoureux qui ont les botines Gaultier (Farce nouvelle). RFF, pp. 67–77.

L'Arbalestre (Farce nouvelle). La Val. Fac., fol. 28v; La Val., Vol. I, No. 5.

L'Astrologue (Sottie nouvelle). Picot, I, 195–231.

L'Aveugle et le Boiteux. By André de La Vigne. BN MS. Fr. 24332, fols. 234–40; Fournier, pp. 155–61.

Le Badin, la Femme et la Chambriere (Farce nouvelle). BM Fac., No. 16; ATF, I, 271–88.

La Bataille de Sainct Pensard a l'encontre de Caresme. Aubailly, pp. 1–70.

Beaucop Veoir et Joyeulx Soudain (Dialogue fort joyeulx). Trep. Fac., No. 24; Trep. II, 11–24.

Les Béguins (Sottie). Picot, II, 265–97.

Bien Advisé et Mal Advisé (Mistere). Paris: Pierre le Caron for Anthoine Verard, n.d. (late 15th c.). BN Rés. Vélins 602.

Bien Mondain (Farce morale). BM Fac., No. 55; ATF, III, 187–98.

Les Blasphemateurs du nom de Dieu (Moralité tressinguliere). Paris: Pierre Sergent, n.d. (early 16th c.). BN Rés. Yf. 30.

Le Brigant et le Curé (Farce nouvelle). RFF, pp. 79–82.

Le Capitaine Mal en Point (Farce nouvelle). RFF, pp. 391–404.

The Castle of Perseverence. In *The Macro Plays.* Ed. Mark Eccles. EETS 262. Oxford: Oxford University Press, 1969.

Cautelleux, Barat et le Villain (Farce nouvelle). RFF, pp. 87–93.

La Cene des dieux. Trep. Fac., No. 17; Trep. II, 97–144.

Les Chamberieres (Farce nouvelle). RFF, pp 413–20.

Charité (Moralité nouvelle). BM Fac., No. 64; ATF, III, 337–424.

Chascun et Plusieurs (Moralité). La Val. Fac., fol. 239r; La Val., Vol. III, No. 42.

Les Cinq sens de l'Homme (Farce moralisee). BM Fac., No. 61; ATF, III, 300–24.

Le Coeur et les cinq sens. By Jean Gerson. Ed. Robert Bossuat. In *Mélanges . . . offerts à Ernest Hoepffner*. Paris: Les Belles Lettres, 1949, pp. 356–60.

Colin qui loue et despite Dieu. BM Fac., No. 14; ATF, I, 224–49.

La Condamnacion de Bancquet. By Nicolas de La Chesnaye. In *La Nef de santé et Condampnation des banquetz avec le Traicté des passions de l'ame*. Paris: Anthoine Verard, 1507. BN Rés. Tc^{10}. 51A; Fournier, pp. 216–71.

La Confession du Brigant. See *Le Brigant et le Curé*.

La Confession Margot. BM Fac., No. 21; ATF, I, 372–79.

La Confession Rifflart. Trep. Fac., No. 27; Trep. II, 55–62.

Les Coppieurs et lardeurs (Sottie nouvelle). Trep. Fac., No. 8; Trep. I, 147–83.

Courtois d'Arras. Ed. Edmond Faral. CFMA 3. Paris: H. Champion, 1967.

Le Cuvier (Farce nouvelle). BM Fac., No. 4; ATF, I, 32–49; Philipot, pp. 121–40.

Le Cycle de mystères des premiers martyrs du manuscrit 1131 de la Bibliothèque Sainte-Geneviève. Ed. Graham A. Runnalls. TLF 223. Geneva: Droz, 1976.

La Destruction de Troye la grant (Istoire). By Jacques Milet. Ed. E. Stengel. Marburg and Leipzig, 1883.

Deulx Gallans et Sancté (Farce). La Val. Fac., fol. 53v; La Val., Vol. I, No. 11; Picot, I, 177–99.

Deux hommes et leur deux femmes (Farce moralisee). BM Fac., No. 10; ATF, I, 145–78; Picot & Nyrop, pp. 115–61.

Le Dict des jardiniers. Ed. François Mugnier. Paris: H. Champion, 1896.

L'Eglise et le Commun (Moralité). La Val. Fac., fol. 60v; La Val., Vol. I, No. 14.

Eglise, Noblesse et Povreté qui font la lessive (Moralité nouvelle). La Val. Fac., fol. 109v; La Val., Vol. I, No. 23.

Ung Empereur qui tua son nepveu (Moralité). Trep. Fac., No. 16; BM Fac., No. 53; ATF, III, 127–70.

Les Enfans de Maintenant (Moralité nouvelle). BM Fac., No. 51; ATF, III, 5–86.

L'Enfant de perdition (Moralité nouvelle). Lyon: Pierre Rigaud, 1608. BN Rés. Yf. 2918.

L'Enfant ingrat (Histoire). Lyon: Benoist Rigaud, 1589. BN Rés. Yf. 2929.

L'Enfant prodigue. Paris, n.d. (16th c.). BN Rés. Yf. 1596.

L'Envie des freres (Moralité). BM Fac., No. 52; ATF, III, 87–126.

Envye, Estat et Simplesse (Moralité). La Val. Fac., fol. 50r; La Val., Vol. I, No. 10.

Estourdi et Coquillart (Sotie et farce nouvelle). Trep. Fac., No. 2; Trep. I, 17–28.

Everyman. In *Everyman and Medieval Miracle Plays*. Ed. A. C. Cawley. 2nd ed. London: Dent, 1960.

Faulte d'Argent et Bon Temps (Farce nouvelle). RFF, pp. 379–83.

Une Femme a qui son voisin baille ung clistoire (Farce nouvelle). RFF, pp. 219–26.

La Femme et le Badin (Farce nouvelle). La Val. Fac., fol. 289r; La Val., Vol. III, No. 50.

Une Femme qui avoit voulu trahir le cité de Romme (Moralité ou histoire rommaine). BM Fac., No. 54; ATF, III, 171–86.

Les Femmes qui demandent les arrerages (Farce nouvelle). BM Fac., No. 8; ATF, I, 111–27.

Les Femmes qui font baster leur maris aux corneilles (Farce nouvelle). RFF, pp. 227–34.

Les Femmes qui font refondre leurs maris (Farce nouvelle). BM Fac., No. 6; ATF, I, 63–93.

Les Femmes qui font renbourer leur bas (Farce nouvelle). RFF, pp. 283–86.

Les Femmes qui se font passer maistresses (Farce nouvelle). RFF, pp. 113–22.

La Folie des Gorriers (Farce nouvelle). Picot, I, 137–75.

Folle Bobance (Farce nouvelle). BM Fac., No. 40; ATF, II, 264–91; Picot, I, 235–70.

Les Foulx (Sermon joyeux). BM Fac., No. 37; ATF, II, 207–22.

Le Franc Archier de Bagnolet (Monologue). Ed. L. Polak. TLF 129. Geneva: Droz, 1966.

Frere Guillebert (Farce nouvelle). BM Fac., No. 18; ATF, I, 305–27.

Genre Humain (Moralité nouvelle). Trep. Fac., No. 18.

Les Gens nouvealux (Farce moralisee). BM Fac., No. 58; ATF, III, 232–48; Picot, I, 113–36.

Le Gentilhomme et Naudet (Farce nouvelle). BM Fac., No. 15; ATF, I, 250–70.

George le veau (Farce nouvelle). BM Fac., No. 22; ATF, I, 380–401.

Le Gouvert d'Humanité. By Jean d'Abundance. Ed. Paul Aebischer. *Bibliothèque d'Humanisme et Renaissance*, 24 (1962), 282–338.

Le Grant voiage et pelerinage de saincte Caquette. Trep, Fac., No. 23; Trep. II, 81–96.

L'Homme Juste et l'Homme Mondain. By Simon Bougouin. Paris: Anthoine Verard, 1508. BN Rés. Yf. 125.

L'Homme justifié par Foy (Tragique comedie francoise). By Henry de Barran. N.p., 1554. BN Rés. Yf. 4064.

L'Homme Pecheur. Paris: Le Petit Laurens for Guillaume Eustace, n.d. (early 16th c.). BN Rés. Yf. 27.

Jeninot qui fist un roy de son chat (Farce nouvelle). BM Fac., No. 17; ATF, I, 289–304.

Le Jeu d'Adam (Ordo representacionis Ade). Ed. Willem Noomen. CFMA 99. Paris: H. Champion, 1971.

Le Jeu de Saint Nicolas. By Jean Bodel. Ed. Alfred Jeanroy. CFMA 48. Paris: Champion, 1925.

Jolyet (Farce nouvelle) BM Fac., No. 5; ATF, I, 50–62.

Langue Envenimee (Moralité nouvelle). Trep. Fac., No. 34.

Le Lazare (Moral). La Val. Fac., fol. 231r; La Val., Vol. III, No. 41.

Le Lymon et la Terre (Moralité). Trep. Fac., No. 19.

Maistre Mimin (Farce joyeuse). BM Fac., No. 44; ATF, II, 338–59; Philipot, pp. 141–63.

Maistre Mymin qui va a la guerre (Farce nouvelle). RFF, pp. 27–33.

Maistre Pierre Pathelin (Farce). Ed. Richard T. Holbrook. 2nd ed. CFMA 35. Paris: H. Champion, 1962. There is a recent edition of the BN MS. Fr. 25467: *La Farce de Maistre Pathelin*. Ed. Jean-Claude Aubailly. Paris: Société d'Edition d'Enseignement Supérieur, 1979.

La Maladie de Chrestienté (Moralité). By Mathieu Malingre. Paris: Pierre de Vignolle, 1533. BN Rés. Yf. 2917.

Les Maraux enchesnez (Farce nouvelle). RFF, pp. 327–32.

Marchandise et Mestier (Farce nouvelle). BM Fac., No. 59; ATF, III, 249–66.

Marche Beau (Farce morale). La Val. Fac., fol. 376v; La Val., Vol. IV, No. 67; Fournier, pp. 36–43.

Le Mariage Robin Mouton (Farce nouvelle). RFF, pp. 253–57.

Martin de Cambray (Farce nouvelle). RFF, pp. 317–26.

Le Mauvais Riche et le Ladre (Moralité nouvelle). N.p., n.d. (16th c.). BN Rés. Yf. 1594.

Memoyre (Monologue). La Val. Fac., fol. 26v; La Val., Vol. I, No. 4.

La Mere de ville (Farce nouvelle). La Val. Fac., fol. 144v; La Val., Vol. II, No. 28; Picot, III, 99–120.

Le Mesnage et la charge de mariage (Joyeux sermon). Picot & Nyrop, pp. 191–98.

Mestier, Marchandise et le Berger (Farce moralle). La Val. Fac., fol. 401v; La Val., Vol. IV, No. 72; Fournier, pp. 44–53.

Mieulx Que Devant (Bergerie morale). BM Fac., No. 57; ATF, III, 213–31.

Le Mistere du Vieil Testament. Ed. James de Rothschild. 6 vols. SATF. Paris: Firmin Didot, 1878–91.

Le Monde (Sottie). Picot, II, 323–46.

Le Monde et Abuz (Sotise). By André de La Vigne. Picot, II, 1–104.

La Moralité du jour Saint Antoine. In *Deux moralités inédites*. Ed. André and Robert Bossuat. Paris: Librairie d'Argences, 1955, pp. 29–88.

Moralité, mystere et figure de la passion de nostre seigneur Jesus Christ. By Jean d'Abundance. Lyon: Benoist Rigaud, n.d. (late 16th c.). BN Rés. Yf. 14. Also in *Jean d'Abundance: A Study of his Life and Three of his Works*. Ed. David H. Carnahan. University of Illinois Studies, Vol. III, No. 5, 1909, pp. 49–123.

Le Munyer de qui le deable emporte l'ame en enffer (Farce). By André de La Vigne. BN MS. Fr. 24332, fols. 241–54; Fournier, pp. 162–71.

Le Mystère de la passion. By Arnoul Gréban. Ed. Omer Jodogne. Brussels: Palais des Académies, 1965.

J. Duculot, 1959.

Le Mystère de la passion. By Jean Michel. Ed. Omer Jodogne. Gembloux:

Le Mystère de la passion nostre Seigneur: du manuscrit 1131 de la Bibliothèque Sainte-Geneviève. Ed. Graham A. Runnalls. TLF 206. Geneva: Droz, 1974.

Le Mystère du roy Advenir. By Jean Du Prier. Ed. A. Meiller. TLF 157. Geneva: Droz, 1970.

Nature (Moralité). La Val. Fac., fol. 256r; La Val., Vol. III, No. 45.

La Nourisse et la Chamberiere (Debat). BM Fac., No. 49; ATF, II, 417–34.

Le Nouveau Marié (Farce nouvelle). BM Fac., No. 2; ATF, I, 11–20.

L'Omme Pecheur. See *L'Homme Pecheur*.

L'Ordre de mariage et de prebstrise (Farce nouvelle). RFF, pp. 243–51.

L'Orgueil et presumption de l'Empereur Jovinien (Histoire). Ed. Emile Picot. Paris: Henri Leclerc, 1912.

La Pacience de Job. Ed. Albert Meiller. Paris: Klincksieck, 1971.

Paix et Guerre (Moralité). By Hanry du Tour. Ghent: Henry van de Keere, 1558. BN Rés. Yf. 2927.

Le Pape malde (Comedie). Rouen, 1561. BN Rés. Yf. 4120.

La Passion d'Autun. Ed. Grace Frank. Paris: SATF, 1934.

La Passion de Semur. Ed. Emile Roy. In *Le Mystère de la passion en France du XIVe au XVIe siècle*. 1903; rpt. Geneva: Slatkine Reprints, 1974.

La Passion du Palatinus. Ed. Grace Frank. CFMA 30. Paris: H. Champion, 1970.

Le Pasté (Farce nouvelle). RFF, pp. 145–58.

Pathelin. See *Maistre Pierre Pathelin*.

Le Patinier (Farce nouvelle). RFF, pp. 273–82.

Une Pauvre Fille villageoise (Moralité). Paris: Simon Calvarin, n.d. (16th c.). BN Rés. Yf. 2933.

Pernet qui va au vin (Farce nouvelle). BM Fac., No. 12; ATF, I, 195–211.

Le Petit et le Grand (Moralité). BN MS. Fr. 25467, fols, 1–47.

Le Pont aux asgnes (Farce nouvelle). BM Fac., No. 25; ATF, II, 35–49.

Le Pouvre Jouhan (Farce nouvelle). Trep. Fac., No. 30; Trep. I, 117–45. Ed. Eugénie Droz and Mario Roques. TLF 84. Geneva: Droz, 1959.

Pyramus et Tisbee (Moralité nouvelle). Ed. Emile Picot. Paris: Henri Leclerc, 1901.

Les Quatre ages (Moralité). La Val. Fac., fol. 74v; La Val., Vol. I, No. 16.

Les Quatre elemens (Moralité nouvelle). Trep. Fac., No. 22.

Les Queues troussees (Farce nouvelle). RFF, pp. 43–49.

Le Ramonneur de cheminees (Farce nouvelle). RFF, pp. 235–41.

Le Raporteur (Farce). La Val. Fac., fol. 157r; La Val., Vol. II, No. 30.

Les Rapporteurs (Sotie nouvelle). Trep. Fac., No. 6; Trep. I, 53–72.

La Reformeresse (Farce). La Val. Fac., fol. 68v; La Val., Vol. I, No. 17; Picot, III, 149–68.

Regnault qui se marie a Lavollee (Farce). RFF, pp. 51–56.

Resjouy d'Amours (Farce nouvelle). RFF, pp. 135–43.

Le Sacrifice de Abraham (Moralité nouvelle). Trep. Fac., No. 1.

Le Savetier et le Moyne (Farce nouvelle). RFF, pp. 259–68.

Science et Asnerye (Farce nouvelle). La Val. Fac., fol. 279v; La Val., Vol. III, No. 49; Fournier, pp. 334–39.

The Second Shepherds' Play (Secunda Pastorum). In *The Wakefield Pageants*. Ed. A. C. Cawley. Manchester: The University Press, 1958.

Sermon pour une nopce. By Roger de Collerye. In *Oeuvres de Roger de Collerye*. Ed. Charles d'Héricault. Paris: P. Jannet, 1855, pp. 111–22.

Les Sobres Sots (Farce moralle). La Val. Fac., fol. 357r; La Val., Vol. IV, No. 63; Picot, III, 45–77.

Tarabin et Tarabas (Farce nouvelle). RFF, pp. 95–101.
Le Testament de Carmentrant. By Jean d'Abundance. Aubailly, pp. 71–87.
Les Theologastres (Farce). N.p., n.d. (16th c.). BN Rés. Yf. 63.
Tout le Monde (Moral). La Val. Fac., fol. 273r; La Val., Vol. III, No. 48; Picot, III, 25–44.
Les Trois Amoureux de la croix (Farce nouvelle). RFF, pp. 57–66.
Les Trois Estatz (moralité nouvelle). Trep. Fac., No. 20.
Les Trois nouveaulx martirs (Farce nouvelle). RFF, pp. 309–15.
Les Troys Brus (Farce nouvelle). La Val. Fac., fol. 199r; La Val., Vol. II, No. 36; Picot, III, 79–97.
Troys Galans et le Monde (Farce joyeuse). La Val. Fac., fol. 123v; La Val., Vol. II, No. 26; Picot, I, 11–46.
Troys Gallans et un Badin (Farce nouvelle). La Val. Fac., fol. 219r; La Val., Vol. II, No. 39; Picot, III, 321–44.
Troys Pelerins et Malice (Farce morale). La Val. Fac., fol. 373r; La Val., Vol. IV, No. 66; Picot, II, 299–321.
Les Veaulx (Farce). La Val. Fac., fol. 179r; La Val., Vol. II, No. 33.
Le Vendeur de livres (Farce joyeuse). La Val. Fac., fol. 64r; La Val., Vol. II, No. 40. Ed. Emmanuel Philipot. In *Six farces normandes*. Rennes: Plihon, 1939, pp. 22–34.
La Vendition de Joseph (Moralité). Cf. *Le Mistère du Vieil Testament*, I, xxxi.
Le Ventre (Moral joyeulx). La Val. Fac., fol. 172v; La Val., Vol. II, No. 32.
La Verité cachée. N.p. (Geneva): Antoine Cercia, 1559. BN Rés. Yf. 4684.
La Vie de Saint Martin. By André de La Vigne. BN MS. Fr. 24332, fols. 1–233. Ed. André Duplat. TLF 277. Geneva: Droz, 1979.
La Vie et hystoire de madame saincte Barbe. Paris: Veuve Trepperel & Jehan Jehannot, n.d. (early 16th c.).
Les Vigilles Triboullet (Farce ou sotie). Trep. Fac., No. 11; Trep. I, 217–38.

III Processions

Following are the complete titles of the two printed processions cited in the text, together with the locations of the copies consulted.

L'Ordre tenu et gardé a l'entree de treshault et trespuissant prince Charles Empereur tousjours August, en la ville de Paris, capitalle du Royaulme de France. Paris: Gilles Corrozet & Jehan du Pré, 1539. BN Rés. Lb[30]. 84.
Les Triomphes de l'abbaye des Conards sous le resveur en decimes Fagot, Abbé des Conards, contenant les criees et proclamations faites depuis son advenement jusques à l'an present. Plus l'ingenieuse Lessive qu'ils ont conardement monstree aux jours gras en l'an M.D.XL. Rouen: Loys Petit, 1587. Bibliothèque Municipale de Rouen, Fonds Leber, No. 2612.

IV Critical works and editions

Arden, Heather. *Fools' Plays*. Cambridge: Cambridge University Press, 1980.
Aubailly, Jean-Claude. *Le Monologue, le dialogue et la sottie*. Paris: H. Champion, 1976.

———. *Le Théâtre médiéval profane et comique*. Paris: Larousse, 1975.

Auerbach, Erich. 'Figura'. In *Scenes from the Drama of European Literature*. New York, Meridian Books, pp. 11–76.

———. *Mimesis*. Garden City, N.Y.: Doubleday, 1957.

Bevington, David M. *From Mankind to Marlowe*. Cambridge, Mass.: Harvard University Press, 1962.

Bossaut, Robert. 'Jean Gerson et la moralité "du coeur et des cinq sens" '. In *Mélanges de philologie romance et de littérature médiévale offerts à Ernest Hoepffner*. Paris: Les Belles Lettres, 1949, pp. 347–60.

Bouchet, Jean. *Epistres morales et familières du Traverseur*. Introd. Jennifer Beard. 1545; rpt. New York: Johnson Reprint Corp., 1969.

Bowen, Barbara C. *Les Caractéristiques essentielles de la farce française et leur survivance dans les années 1550–1620*. Illinois Studies in Language and Literature, 53. Champaign: University of Illinois Press, 1964.

Bozon, Nicole. *Les Contes moralisés de Nicole Bozon*. Ed. Lucy Toulmin Smith and Paul Meyer. SATF. Paris: Firmin Didot, 1889.

Brown, Howard Mayer. *Music in the French Secular Theatre, 1400–1550*. Cambridge, Mass.: Harvard University Press, 1963.

Carnahan, David H. *The Prologue in the Old French and Provençal Mystery*. New Haven: Tuttle, Morehouse & Taylor, 1905.

Christine de Pisan. *Lavision-Christine*. Ed. Sr Mary Louis Towner. Washington: The Catholic University of America, 1932.

Clouzot, Henri. *L'Ancien théâtre en Poitou*. Niort: L. Clouzot, 1901.

Cohen, Gustave. *Le Théâtre en France au Moyen Age*. 2 vols. I, *Le Théâtre religieux*. II, *Le Théâtre profane*. Paris: Rieder, 1928–31.

Coquillart, Guillaume. *Oeuvres*. Ed. Michael J. Freeman. Geneva: Droz, 1975.

Cotgrave, Randle. *A Dictionarie of the French and English Tongues*. 1611; rpt. Columbia: University of South Carolina Press, 1968.

Culler, Jonathan. *Structuralist Poetics*. Ithaca: Cornell University Press, 1975.

Curtius, Ernst Robert. *European Literature and the Latin Middle Ages*. Bollingen Series, 36. Princeton: Princeton University Press, 1967.

Delevoy, Robert L. *Breugel*. Geneva: Skira, 1959.

Des Autels, Guillaume. *Replique de Guillaume Des Autelz aux furieuses defenses de Louis Meigret*. Lyon: Jean de Tournes, 1551.

Droz, Eugénie, ed. *Le Recueil Trepperel: les sotties*. Paris: Droz, 1935.

——— and Halina Lewicka, eds. *Le Recueil Trepperel: les farces*. Geneva: Droz, 1961.

——— and A. Piaget, eds. *Le Jardin de plaisance et fleur de rethoricque*. Vol. I, Reproduction en fac-similé. Paris: Firmin Didot, 1910.

———, eds. *Le Jardin de plaisance et fleur de rhétorique*. Vol. II, Introduction et notes. Paris: E. Champion, 1925.

Du Bellay, Joachim. *La Deffense et illustration de la langue françoyse*. Ed. Henri Chamard. Paris: M. Didier, 1948.

Dubois, Alexis. *Récréations de nos pères aux XVe et XVIe siècles*. Amiens: L. Challier, 1860.

Durieux, Achille. *Le Théâtre à Cambrai avant et depuis 1789*. Cambrai: J.

Renaut, 1883.

Duvignaud, Jean. *Sociologie du théâtre*. Paris: Presses Universitaires de France, 1965.

Empson, William. *The Structure of Complex Words*. Norfolk, Conn.: New Directions, n.d.

Fabri, Pierre. *Le grand et vrai art de pleine rhétorique*. Ed. A. Héron. 3 vols. Rouen: E. Cagniard, 1889–90.

Fleury, Edouard. *Origines et développements de l'art théâtral dans la province ecclésiastique de Reims*. Laon: A. Cortilliot, 1880.

Fox, John H., ed. *Robert de Blois, son oeuvre didactique et narrative*. Paris: Nizet, 1950.

Frank, Robert Worth, Jr. 'The art of reading medieval personification allegory'. *English Literary History*, 20 (1953), 237–50.

Frappier, Jean. *Le Théâtre profane en France au Moyen Age*. Paris: Centre de Documentation Universitaire, 1960.

Frye, Northrop. *Anatony of Criticism*. Princeton: Princeton University Press, 1957.

——. 'Old and New Comedy'. *Shakespeare Survey*, 22 (1969), 1–5.

Gaignebet, Claude. *Le Carnaval*. Paris: Payot, 1974.

Giesey, Ralph E. *The Royal Funeral Ceremony in Renaissance France*. Geneva: Droz, 1960.

Guenée, Bernard and Françoise Lehoux. *Les Entrées royales françaises de 1328 à 1515*. Paris: Centre National de la Recherche Scientifique, 1968.

Guillaume de Deguilleville. *Le Pelerinage de l'ame*. Ed. J. J. Stürzinger. Roxburghe Club, 127. London: Nichols & Sons, 1895.

——. *Le Pelerinage de la vie humaine*. Ed. J. J. Stürzinger. Roxburghe Club, 124. London: Nichols & Sons, 1893.

Harvey, Howard G. *The Theatre of the Basoche*. Cambridge, Mass.: Harvard University Press, 1941.

Hirsch, E. D. *Validity in Interpretation*. New Haven: Yale University Press, 1967.

Jauss, Hans Robert. 'Littérature médévale et théorie des genres'. *Poétique*, 1 (1970), 79–101.

Jubinal, Achille, ed. *Jongleurs et trouvères*. Paris: J. A. Merklein, 1835.

Kernodle, George R. *From Art to Theatre*. Chicago: University of Chicago Press, 1943.

Knight, Alan E. 'Drama and society in late medieval Flanders and Picardy'. *The Chaucer Review*, 14 (1980), 379–89.

——. 'Fragments de trois farces du Recueil de Florence'. *Romania*, 94 (1973), 542–48.

——. 'From the sacred to the profane'. *Tréteaux*, 1 (1978), 41–49.

——. 'The medieval theater of the absurd'. *PMLA*, 86 (1971), 183–89.

Konigson, Elie. *L'Espace théâtral médiéval*. Paris: Centre National de la Recherche Scientifique, 1975.

——. *La Représentation d'un mystère de la passion à Valenciennes en 1547*. Paris: Centre National de la Recherche Scientifique, 1969.

Kris, Ernst. *Psychoanalytic Explorations in Art*. New York: International Universities Press, 1952.

Lacy, Norris J., ed. *A Medieval French Miscellany*. Lawrence: University of Kansas Press, 1972.

Langlois, Ernest, ed. *Recueil d'arts de seconde Rhétorique*. Paris: Imprimerie Nationale, 1902.

Lebègue, Raymond. 'Tableau de la comédie française de la Renaisance'. *Bibliothèque d'Humanisme et Renaissance*, 8 (1946), 278–344.

——. *La Tragédie religieuse en France*. Paris: Champion, 1929.

——. 'La Vie dramatique à Rouen de François Ier à Louis XIII'. *Bulletin Philologique et Historique du Comité des Travaux Historiques et Scientifiques* (1955–56), pp. 399–422.

Lecocq, Georges. *Histoire du théâtre en Picardie depuis son origine jusqu'à la fin du XVIe siècle*. Paris: H. Menu, 1880.

Lefebvre, Léon. *Histoire du théâtre de Lille de ses origines à nos jours*. 5 vols. Lille: Lefebvre-Ducrocq, 1901–7 [vol. 1, '07].

Lewicka, Halina, ed. *Bergerie de l'Agneau de France*. TLF 96. Geneva: Droz, 1961.

——. *Etudes sur l'ancienne farce française*. Paris: Klincksieck, 1974.

——. *La Langue et le style du théâtre comique français des XVe et XVIe siècles: la dérivation*. Paris: Klincksieck, 1960.

Lewis, C. S. *The Discarded Image*. Cambridge University Press, 1964.

Lintilhac, Eugène. *Histoire générale du théâtre en France*. 5 vols. Paris: Flammarion, 1904–11.

Monmerqué, L. J. N., ed. *Le Dialogue du Fol et du Sage*. Paris: Firmin Didot, 1829.

Montifaud, Marc de, ed. *Les Triomphes de l'abbaye des Conards*. 2nd ed. Paris: A. Lacroix, 1877.

Noomen, Willem. 'Passages narratifs dans les drames médiévaux français'. *Revue Belge de Philologie et d'Histoire*, 36 (1958), 761–85.

Parfaict, François and Claude. *Histoire du théâtre françois*. 15 vols. 1735–49; rpt. Geneva: Slatkine Reprints, 1967.

Payen, Jean-Charles. 'Le "cuvier": farce allégorique?'. *Revue d'Histoire du Théâtre*, 25 (1973), 257–61.

Petit de Julleville, Louis. *La Comédie et les moeurs en France au Moyen Age*. Paris: Cerf, 1886.

——. *Les Comédiens en France au Moyen Age*. Paris: Cerf, 1885.

——. *Les Mystères*. 2 vols. Paris: Hachette, 1880.

——. *Répertoire du Théâtre comique en France au Moyen Age*. 1886; rpt. Geneva: Slatkine Reprints, 1967.

Philipot, Emmanuel, ed. *Six farces normandes du recueil La Vallière*. Rennes: Plihon, 1939.

——, ed. *Trois farces du recueil de Londres*. 1931; rpt. Geneva: Slatkine Reprints, 1975.

Philippe de Novarre. *Les Quatre Ages de l'homme*. Ed. Marcel de Fréville. SATF. Paris: Firmin Didot, 1888.

Picot, Emile. *Les Moralités polémiques*. 1887; rpt. Geneva: Slatkine Reprints, 1970.

——. *Pierre Gringore et les comédiens italiens*. Paris: Morgan et Fatout, 1878.

——, ed. *Recueil général des sotties*. 3 vols. SATF. Paris: Firmin Didot, 1902–12.

——. *Répertoire historique et bibliographique de l'ancien théâtre français*. BN MS. Fr. Nouv. Acq. 12633.

—— and Christophe Nyrop, eds. *Nouveau recueil de farces françaises*. 1880; rpt. Geneva: Slatkine Reprints, 1968.

Rey-Flaud, Henri. *Le Cercle magique*. Paris: Gallimard, 1973.

Robert de Blois. See Fox, John H.

Rousse, Michel. 'Discussions' following 'La Farce jusqu'à Molière'. *Cahiers de l'Association Internationale des Etudes Françaises*, 26 (1974), 302–04.

Roy, Emile. *Le Mystère de la passion en France du XIVe au XVIe siècle*. 1903; rpt. Geneva: Slatkine Reprints, 1974.

Schell, Edgar T. 'On the imitation of life's pilgrimage in *The Castle of Perseverance*'. *Journal of English and German Philology*, 67, (1968), 235–48.

Schoell, Konrad. *Das komische Theater des französischen Mittelalters*. Munich, Wilhelm Fink, 1975.

Sebillet, Thomas. *Art poetique françoys*. Ed. Félix Gaiffe. Paris: Droz, 1932.

Seznec, Jean. *The Survival of the Pagan Gods*. New York: Pantheon, 1953.

Spivac, Bernard. *Shakespeare and the Allegory of Evil*. New York: Columbia University Press, 1958.

Stierle, Karlheinz. 'L'Histoire comme Exemple, l'Exemple comme Histoire'. *Poétique*, 3, (1972), 176–98.

Van Hamel, A. G., ed. *Les Lamentations de Mathéolus*. Paris: Emile Bouillon, 1892.

Warning, Rainer. 'On the alterity of medieval religious drama'. *New Literary History*, 10, (1979), 265–92.

Wartburg, Walter von. *Französisches Etymologisches Wörterbuch (FEW)*. Tübingen: Mohr; Basel: Zbinden, 1948 .

Weinberg, Bernard. *Critical Prefaces of the French Renaissance*. Evanston: Northwestern University Press, 1950.

Wickham, Glynne. *Early English Stages*. Vol. I. London: Routledge and Kegan Paul, 1959.

Yates, Frances A. *The Art of Memory*. Chicago: University of Chicago Press, 1966.

——. 'Dramatic religious processions in Paris in the late sixteenth century'. *Annales Musicologiques*, 2, (1954), 215–70.

Zumthor, Paul. *Essai de poétique médiéval*. Paris: Seuil, 1972.

——. *Langue, texte, énigme*. Paris: Seuil, 1975.

Index

The index contains titles and authors mentioned in the text, but not those appearing only in the notes. The topics have been limited mainly to those relating to considerations of genre.